CU00734874

PAINTING THE DAY:
THOMAS CHURCHYARD OF WOODBRIDGE

Painting the Day
Thomas Churchyard of Woodbridge

WALLACE MORFEY

THE BOYDELL PRESS

© Wallace Morfey 1986

First published 1986 by The Boydell Press
an imprint of Boydell & Brewer Ltd
PO Box 9, Woodbridge, Suffolk IP12 3DF

ISBN 0 85115 426 3

British Library Cataloguing in Publication Data

Morfey, Wallace
   Painting the Day: Thomas Churchyard of
   Woodbridge
   1. Churchyard, Thomas 2. Suffolk —
   Biography
   I. Title
   942.081'092'4   CT788.C47/
   ISBN 0-85115-426-3

Library of Congress Cataloging-in-Publication Data

Morfey, W. M. (Wallace Mortimer)
   Painting the day

   Bibliography: p.
   Includes index.
   1. Churchyard, Thomas, 1798 – 1865. 2.
Painters — England — Biography. 3. Lawyers
— England — Biography. 4. Woodbridge
(Suffolk) — Biography. I. Title.
ND497.C552M67 1986   759.2 [B]   86-24441
ISBN 0-85115-426-3

Typeset by MS Typesetting, Castle Camps, Cambridge
Printed in Great Britain by St Edmundsbury Press,
Bury St Edmunds, Suffolk

Contents

List of Illustrations

COLOUR PLATES

Kyson Point, Woodbridge. Oil on board, 56 x 23cm. The Rev. E. C. Charlesworth

Lawyer's Lane, Melton. Watercolour, 24.7 x 17.1cm. Christchurch Mansion, Ipswich

Portrait, at 29 Well Street. Watercolour, 31.5 x 26.8cm. Christchurch Mansion, Ipswich

Trees in the Wind. Watercolour, 26.8 x 38.2cm. The Rev E. C. Charlesworth

A touch of Autumn, Wilford Hollows, Melton. Watercolour, 22.3 x 33cm

Haugh Lane, Woodbridge. Watercolour, 20.4 x 29.3cm. The Rev E. C. Charlesworth

Spring Morning, Woodbridge. Watercolour, 20.5 x 29cm

The Down. Watercolour, 20.2 x 30cm.

Landscape with trees and stream. Watercolour, 26.8 x 39.5cm. Norwich Castle Museum

April Day, Old Melton. Oil on board, 18.5 x 26.5cm

BLACK AND WHITE

Storm passing down the Deben. Watercolour, 22.7 x 33cm. Christchurch Mansion, Ipswich

Trees by the River Deben. Watercolour, 27.4 x 39.5cm. British Museum

Preface

It is nearly forty years since I bought my first Churchyard watercolour drawings in Woodbridge. With the works came strange stories, preserved there in verbal tradition since early Victorian days. It was apparent from them that his life in the place had been an unusual one — highly unusual for a country-town attorney. Out of consideration for the feelings of his seven spinster daughters virtually nothing of all this had been put into writing, but bright glimpses of him could be sighted, in court, in painting in the countryside, in bohemian evenings with distinguished literary friends and days with his fellow sportsmen.

Following up these lines has led to the discovery of ever stranger aspects of professional and family affairs and the final sad fall from prosperity to ruin. When, some twenty or thirty years ago, his paintings became regularly collected and people wanted to know about him, it was apparent that the legends that had survived were hazy, often contradictory and with gaps that suggested good stories missing.

For the last twenty years I have delved into his past and made unlikely discoveries in unlikely places. To many individuals and institutions I am indebted for help without which the research would never have come to fruition. Initially it was my friend the Reverend Eric Charlesworth, sometime curate of St Mary's Woodbridge, who encouraged my undertaking this book and has spurred me on throughout the years of its composition.

Among many who have helped me with information have been George Arnott, great in his lifelong knowledge of Woodbridge, who lent me the Book Club minutes and Ben Moulton's diary: the late Mr L. R. Christie who inherited and allowed me to transcribe the surviving Churchyard papers and lent me Girling's commonplace book: James Nohl Churchyard for the loan of letters from Woodbridge to his great-grandfather in Wisconsin: Mrs Gilbert Davis and John Baskett

ix

who enabled me to trace the Davis collection of Churchyards to the Huntington: Derek and Timothy Clifford for discovery of an invaluable batch of unpublished letters of Bernard Barton: Miss Jane Evans Curator of Woodspring Museum who helped in dating Churchyard's visit to Weston-super-Mare: Mrs Dalrymple-Hay for the papers dealing with Churchyard's troubles with Alexanders Bank: Philip Goodman for introducing me to some dramatic late Churchyards: my friend from schooldays, Irvine Gray FSA and his wife Margaret not only for finding answers to some research problems but for providing me with an hospitable base of operations in London: Miss Norah Henshilwood the writer, for sending me from South Africa the "Thos. Churchyard 1820" sketch: Tony Martin for loan of Parson Golty's Tithe Book: Adrian Parry for tracing the Miss Churchyards' showings in the Ipswich Art Club Exhibitions: Mrs Janice Pomp who has brought to light Churchyard's drawings of his wife and Young Tom: Norman Scarfe FSA for sight of the Elsie Redstone papers: another schoolfriend Hugh Spalding for the FitzGerald transcripts from his grandfather's diary, now lost to sight: Denis Thomas, who has written the authoritative work on Churchyard's painting for introducing me to his own many-sided collection of T. C.'s achievements in various media: Dr Robert Wark, for help over the Churchyard *At Gillingham, Dorset* in the Huntington: my New Zealand cousin, the painter Margaret Waters for information about some Churchyard paintings now in that country.

I am grateful to the Suffolk Records Society for permission to quote from their volumes of John Constable's Correspondence and to Mrs Annabelle Terhune similarly in the case of a FitzGerald letter to Marietta Nursey.

Many private collectors have delighted me with sights of their Churchyards and I am grateful for their willingness to allow several to be reproduced as illustrations.

Archives, Public Libraries and Galleries have naturally been vital sources of exact information. All have been helpful and several have gone beyond answering my enquiries by bringing to my notice fresh matter quite unexpected. The list of these is below but I must first, in particular, express my thanks to Miss Chloe Bennett, Senior Assistant Curator (Humanities) Ipswich Museums and Galleries, whose enthusiasm in restoring the Borough's fine collection of Churchyards has been of tremendous help.

The Alexander Turnbull Library, Wellington N.Z.
The Ashmolean, Oxford
Barclays Bank Archives
The British Library, Department of Manuscripts, London

The British Museum Print Room
City of Westminster Record Office
Dunedin Art Gallery, N.Z.
Greater London Record Office
The Fitzwilliam, Cambridge
The Guildhall Library, London
The Huntington Art Gallery, San Merino, California
The India Office Library
Ipswich Museum and Christchurch Mansion
Ironbridge Gorge Museum
The Law Society Library
The National Maritime Library
Norwich Castle Museum
The Public Record Office
The Putnam Museum, Davenport, Iowa
Suffolk Coastal District Council Records
The Suffolk Record Office
The Tate Gallery, London
The Victoria and Albert Museum Library

Abbreviations

Add. Mss.	Additional Manuscripts, British Museum.
BM	British Museum.
DNB	Dictionary of National Biography.
JCC	John Constable's Correspondence.
PRO	Public Record Office.
SRO	Suffolk Record Office.
SRS	Suffolk Records Society.
VCH	Victoria County History.

FOR ERIC

I acknowledge with thanks the courtesy of the Trustees of the British Museum for permission to reproduce copyright material, similarly of the Fitzwilliam Museum, the Huntington Gallery, the Ipswich Museums and Galleries, the Norfolk Museums Service, the Tate Gallery and the Victoria & Albert Museum.

Bringing Churchyard to Light

THIS ACCOUNT, set in early and mid-Victorian times, is of Tom Churchyard — the sparkling country-town attorney who might have become a famous painter, the enthusiastic local artist who might have risen to the loftiest peaks of the legal profession. More talked about than almost anyone in his corner of Suffolk, people saw him as a true original — talented, enigmatic, flourishing; heir to a comfortable fortune, yet dying overwhelmed by disaster.

Across the Woodbridge skies he had wheeled like some strange comet, unheralded, and for a full century afterwards lost to sight, together with the best of his achievements and the more diverting happenings in his career; likewise the more grievous. All these had been well remembered throughout the neighbourhood at his death in 1865. Obituaries referred to his skill as an attorney whose professional advice was sought by everyone from the poachers to the nobility: to his knowledge as a connoisseur who "might almost be said to be the man who first brought Crome's pictures into the high esteem they are now held". An obsessive painter himself, he was one of the earliest of whom it was said "he understands Constable".* At evenings with acknowledged writers and scholars he had shone "with conversation full of wit and anecdote to overflow". No small achievements for one whom the older people remembered as being son and grandson of nearby village butchers.

Not to be mentioned in the obituaries were occasions when he had astonished the locals with impulsive actions no ordinary small-town solicitor would have taken. What they were faded from memory, but there has always remained in Woodbridge the certainty that a great deal worth telling about him has never been put into writing.

---

* *The Letters of Edward Fitzgerald* (London 1901).

Consideration for the feelings of his seven spinster daughters, living on there so strangely and for so long, had confined everything to verbal tradition. For more than a century he remained a local legend. People were on firm ground, though, in believing there were skeletons in the Churchyard cupboard.

After the auction in 1866 when the London dealers came down and secured most of his Wilsons, Gainsboroughs, Morlands, Cromes and Constables, there was no general mention of Churchyard in print for nearly twenty five years. When Edward FitzGerald died and it was revealed that he was the author of the *Rubaiyat of Omar Khayyam*, it was remembered that Churchyard had been his cultured, closest friend in Woodbridge. The publication in 1889 of E. F. G's *Letters* showed a good number of them written to Bernard Barton the local bank clerk, in earlier years celebrated throughout the land as 'The Quaker Poet'. They contained a dozen or so mentions of the lawyer and one sentence that has become well remembered, in which he designated Barton, Churchyard and himself as the 'three chief wits of Woodbridge'; enjoying evenings of hilarity and good conversation over toasted cheese and porter: a strange trio envied by less fortunate littérateurs in the town.

Probably not many people read the slim volume published a few years later, *Bernard Barton and his Friends*, by a Quaker writer, the young E. V. Lucas. Those who did would have learnt of his call on Ellen Churchyard, eldest of the daughters, who showed him some of her father's paintings. Lucas immediately saw the affinity between his work and that of Constable and declared that the East Bergholt master was his 'great examplar'. Churchyard's idolatory of Constable was a thread running through all his life.

Although hardly mentioned in print during the sixty years following his death, the name remained in everyday Woodbridge conversation. The ne'er-do-well youngest son Charley was a constant scandal. The singular life of the daughters was much remarked upon. Brought up with governesses, boarding school at Bury St Edmunds and elegance at home with Mamma, they had suddenly found themselves penniless. To the one household, the Redstones, on whom they leaned in times of bereavement they disclosed, years afterwards, things revealed to no others. They told them how their father, shortly before his end, had said 'my dears there won't be any money for you but I will leave you my paintings which will one day be worth more than any money I could ever have hoped to make'. The ruin was indeed complete. An appeal was launched in Woodbridge to raise funds for his widow and seven daughters left destitute. Listed among those who responded were some of the highest Law Lords in the land.

For the next fourteen years the girls were badly off: looked upon with some misfavour for the way they held themselves aloof from the rest of the town. But in 1879 Woodbridge relented, came to regard the talented sisterhood as something not only unusual but special and eased their lot by giving them the care of the Seckford Library and the comfortable old Schoolhouse in which it was kept. It was 1927 before the last of them departed, just short of ninety one.

Whatever the Miss Churchyards may have told their particular friends about family affairs, they kept back far more. The Redstones, answering enquirers, said they believed that Thomas had married Harriet, daughter of General and Susan Hailes at St Nicholas Ipswich. No such soldier is to be traced and not till I came across a graveyard inscription there "Sacred to the memory of Susannah relict of Captain Hailes R.N." did it become evident that it was a naval officer's daughter he had wed. The family Bible contains the baptisms of their children and records which of them had had the measles and the whooping cough, but the marriage is left blank.

The sailor's Service Sheet reveals perilous excitements on the Atlantic in the Napoleonic Wars and an unusual command at the mouth of the Woodbridge river but the ladies never mentioned the existence of their grandfather the Captain; they never spoke of their elder brother; nor of the domestic unheavel wrought by Papa when they were children.

They believed implicitly their father's prophecy that his paintings would eventually come to be recognised as having a special place in the English Landscape School, and agreed to keep his *oeuvre* intact and out of general view till that day should come. It had not arrived by the time the last of them died. At the subsequent auction, any chance that his work might then have had a splendid emergence was ruined by the deliberate lotting up many of his paintings and sketches with an even greater heap of his daughters', some good, some bad. Connoisseurs taking home a watercolour that might pass for a Constable, were puzzled by others with it that they could only suppose to be "Churchyard at his worst".

A generation passed before the wheat was sifted from the chaff and his hand became recognised. The *Introduction* to an Arts Council exhibition in 1955*, referring to his admiration of Constable, declared that he "on occasions came very close to the master". Nearly twenty years later he was hung in the Tate. Surprise is often expressed that an untrained amateur should have come to such excellence. It has entirely escaped notice that at one time he set up in London as a professional artist; an enterprise that ended with a dire misunderstanding at Christies.

When, after the last war, he became regularly collected, it began to

* See p. 185.

3

be asked what was known about him. With Woodbridge having confined his memory to gossip, not writing, there was added a further potent cause for uncertainty. He himself kept virtually no papers. In consequence facts, hazy traditions and plain mistakes appeared mixed together in mentions of him in exhibition catalogues and paragraphs in volumes on Victorian painters. It is not surprising therefore that the author of the first proper assessment of him as a painter, had as a man to "leave him a shadowy and elusive figure".

There are later finds that help fill earlier voids and bring back into sight forgotten exploits. The most continuous source lies in the local press. One of the liveliest provincial newspapermen of the day reported Churchyard week by week in court and sometimes outside it. In hundreds of cases he is to be heard conducting pleas weighty or comic, from accusations of poisoning to drunken driving of a horse and cart or neighbours at loggerheads. There are many accounts of his propounding obscure technicalities that rescued clients from what seemed certain conviction. He would wax indignant in defence of the purity of English Law if he thought it was being misused against poor people unskilled in rebutting an accusation. His unsurpassed acquaintance with the intricacies of the laws against poaching, sheds light on that vast, black economy of the Suffolk countryside of his time.

The papers tell of spectators crowding Sessions in the locality, prepared to give up a day to hear Lawyer Churchyard conducting an exciting case. They crowded, too, the public gallery at County Courts, willing to listen for five hours to an otherwise dull dispute made entertaining by his handling of it. His part in the defence of the Suffolk arsonists in the worst years of the Hungry Forties brings to view the nightly glare of burning ricks and buildings. The newspaper covering the Assize gives in full the chilling speech he listened to by Baron Alderson, as "in a voice quivering with emotion", he addressed the guilty before sentencing them to transportation for life.

Unexpected paragraphs detail facts quite forgotten. The Ipswich Journal of 15th January 1825 carries a discreet announcement of the "marriage in London, a few days since, of Thos. Churchyard, Solicitor, Woodbridge". It has enabled one to trace the lawyer's visit to Lambeth Palace and his securing an Archbishop's Licence to marry the next day. A few lines in 1863 report the wreck of a ship carrying emigrants to Canada. Churchyard's grandchildren were among the passengers. Its drama has passed into Newfoundland folk-song, though only in recent years has the full story been brought together.

Letters are a fruitful source. An unpublished twenty written by the voluble Barton contain colourful accounts of the Wits, by then joined by the impulsive Parson Crabbe, son and biographer of "The Poet of Aldeburgh". Beyond the evenings of good talk, good liquor and

4

furious smoking, they relate twelve months of Churchyard's exploits in art-dealing; some of his purchases now hanging in the world's galleries.

A few Woodbridge letters by different hands to a Churchyard cousin in Wisconsin pass on the news of Uncle Isaac's ruin of the family fortune. They tell of the lawyer's behaviour in the resulting financial calamity and open the page on to a very strange family relationship. There are single letters associated with the daughters in old age concerning rich relatives in distant Gloucestershire and poor ones in nearby Wickham Market.

Beyond the newspapers and the letters there are the documents kept by Church and State from which a number of sightings of him emerge. His grandfather Jonathan, butcher and churchwarden of Melton, is seen in 1784 establishing the family's prosperity by boldly embarking upon the drovering trade: the great enterprise of taking London's meat each week eighty miles up to Smithfield on the hoof. The ledgers of Alexanders Bank in Woodbridge show Tom's father settling year by year with the headmaster of Dedham Grammar School for the boy's boarding fees: his parents' only child. It is engaging that Churchyard, one of the earliest to see landscape painting through the eyes of Constable, should have learned his Latin on the hard oak benches his great exemplar had known there fifteen years before.

Serving after school his articles at Halesworth, the young man was to find how virtually impossible it was to break into the tightly drawn network of country solicitors, except through matrimony. The Law Lists show every attorney there, and at Woodbridge, to be either son, son-in-law, brother-in-law or nephew of some other local practitioner. A close neighbour during his four articled years, however, may have given him other thoughts. Young William Hooker, future Director of Kew, but then a partner in the Halesworth Brewery, was already acknowledged as a splendid botanical draughtsman. Churchyard tried his hand at being the same. A dozen years later the will of a rich uncle in the City enabled him to change his career entirely.

In more than forty years at Woodbridge he touched its small-town life at many points and can be glimpsed through many different eyes. Of three lifelong friends with the same interests as him, two kept diaries: one a devoted field-sportsman, the other a magpie collector. The third was a professional painter with whom he sketched when they were young men urging one another on to getting hung at the Academy.

From elsewhere amusing incidents are recorded, some in script, some in small bright drawings: a night at the Woodbridge Theatre; a Boxing Day meet on the ice; his children on holiday at Aldeburgh; his being accidentally carried beyond Woodbridge by the Lowestoft train.

5

There were graver occasions when he narrowly escaped death on his first day of the partridge season, or when he suffered the blue devils as his debts began to overwhelm him.

Minutes of the Woodbridge Book Club record him every Thursday of the full moon, with eleven companions, discussing the latest London publications and deciding which should be bought that month. With "Our Artist" at "all times amusing and delightful", one could never have foreseen that he would be driven by a literary catastrophe of Fitz-Gerald's to forsake their genial gatherings for the last ten years of his life.

One great discovery was made by his daughters going through his things after his death. There were three scraps of paper relating to his idol. Two were brief notes written to friends by Constable and begged off them later by Churchyard. The third is more remarkable. It is a record he made of a visit paid him by John Charles Constable very soon after his father's death. The young man, present at the fatal seizure, had been so prostrated that he was unable to attend the funeral. Yet a few days later he called on Churchyard and described to him in detail the great painter's last hour. The lawyer hastened to get it written down the moment the caller had left. It supersedes the account given by Leslie in the *Life*, obtained later from one who had not been there.

An inventory of the Churchyard home in 1854 takes one through every room of a cultured Victorian household and shows it as particularly Thomas's by detailing the many books and the many fine paintings on its walls. One way and another, there can hardly be a country solicitor or a local painter in mid-Victorian England about whom so much is to be known.

Enigmatic, however, he remains. The roles of lawyer and painter were not the only instance of his having a foot in two camps. From circumstances of family and friends, of work and leisure he could find himself a member of circles hard put to it to understand one another. His life was beset with great contradictions.

II

The London Road

THOMAS was born on 22nd January 1798 at the family shop fronting the street at Melton, the village before Woodbridge on the way from Yarmouth. His grandfather Jonathan had opened there as a butcher a little over thirty years earlier when it was virtually a new settlement. Old Melton, lying placidly in the low meadows by the church and the watermill, was by then becoming deserted and soon to be quite erased, its inhabitants attracted to the bustle and business of the highroad half a mile off, as the heyday of the coaching age drew on.

By the turn of the century, the turnpike running from Southtown to the prodigious capital city had taken a firm hold on the imagination of those living in the countryside through which it passed. The parson of Wherstead on a glittering starlight night talking with a villager and saying something about the Milky Way, was met with "We don't call it by that name. We call it the London Road. Its name is the London Road because it is the light of the lamps of the carriages and wagons that are travelling to and from London"*.

Like most boom places, the street of the utilitarian second Melton was nothing much to look at. The village was the more utilitarian in that at the same time as Jonathan set up in business there, the local Guardians of the Poor built the Melton House of Industry. In bad times it doubled the parish's population by accommodating two hundred and fifty paupers. Payers of the Poor Rate called it the Melton House of Idleness.

Thomas's father, Jonathan the Younger, when twenty-seven had married, on 27th September 1796, Anne, twenty-three-year-old daughter of Thomas White, grocer and draper of Peasenhall. Anne's boy was their parents' only child and they christened him with the

* F. B. Zincke, *Wherstead: some materials for its history*, 2nd edn. 1893, 257.

White's favourite name. His earliest recollections were coloured by the excitements of Napoleon's threatened invasion. At Melton these were no less keenly felt than they were along the Channel Coast for there was always the possibility that Boney's attempt might be made across the North Sea from the ports of the Low Countries. Nelson had given his opinion that if such a landing were contemplated, Shingle Street at the mouth of the Alde would be the place most likely to be chosen.

The Melton butcher's shop stood at the eastern entry to the village, opposite the Horse and Groom at the junction with the roads from Orford, Shingle Street and Bawdsey. The corner became in consequence the hinge on which preparations against any such French attempts turned. Five thousand troops were hastily put into camp on Bromeswell Heath a mile down the coast road. In the July of 1803 carpenters arrived from London to build permanent wooden hutments for them at Woodbridge, where two gazebos were erected above Dry Bridge Hill, one carrying the signal apparatus to connect with the stations on the coast at Felixstowe and Bawdsey a good eight miles away; an invasion beacon was kept ready for firing on the top of St Mary's Church tower.

To be able to clear Melton street of everything that might hamper the movements of the military was a prime necessity. A detailed scheme was drawn up for the evacuation of the civilian population should the French have landed. Kept ready on the Churchyard mantelshelf was the ticket instructing them as to whom they all, including small Thomas, were to report. Every wagon in the village had its load of refugees specified, together with the route it was to take inland to Earl Soham, a village well known to earlier generations of the family. A trial alarm and invasion-repelling exercise by the troops threw the neighbourhood into great confusion.

Thomas had been too young to remember being held in his mother's arms at the shop door in the November of 1800 to witness the passing by of the Norfolk Hero, landed at Yarmouth and travelling in company with the Hamiltons on his way to London. At a change of horses the people draw his carriage to the end of the village: elsewhere they stood outside their cottages and sang Rule Britannia as he passed. That within a decade of this the butcher's son should be being bred on the classics, as a boarder at a notable grammar school, would have surprised the earlier Churchyards.

From the time of the first of them to be seen in the county, John of Ilketshall, married in 1567, the family had all been small yeoman farmers in High Suffolk, the great land of cheese and butter. "The cow district", and "the seat of the dairies", Arthur Young called it in his *General View of the Agriculture of Suffolk* 1797. On the flat, heavy pastures of the boulder clay, never broken up since the early enclosures, their livings were made by the red, brindled and dun Suffolk polled cows, admired for a snake head, thin legs and springing ribs. For their size and keep they were the best milkers in the kingdom.

John of Ilketshall was almost certainly grandfather of the Charles from whom the lawyer was descended. At Rendham under its extreme Puritan minister in the days of the Civil War, Charles had become a determined Independent. When in 1645 he came to Pitmans, a little farm in north-west Framlingham, he readily joined with the other Roundhead farmers in the township in refusing to pay his tithes to the loyalist parson Golty, soon to be "outed"*.

After the Restoration, by which time he had moved to a larger farm in the opposite corner of the parish, screened by woods and half a mile from the high road, he opened his house as a secret meeting-place for the Framlingham Congregationalists when their worshipping together was accounted a seditious conventicle, punishable by fines and imprisonment. A sense of being bound closely together, outside the usual run, was reflected two hundred years later in lawyer Churchyard's family itself.

Of Charles's sons, John at Wilby begat a family of ten, Isaac at Dennington, fifty years wedded to Abigail Canope was childless. She had brought him lands at their marriage; they had prospered and bought more, becoming thought of as the well-to-do uncle and aunt in this yeoman family. The new-fangled puritan name of Isaac became thereafter a kind of talisman among them, bestowed on more than a score of Churchyard boys during the next century and a half.

John set store by his eldest son John but quarrelled with his younger boy Isaac. "Five shillings, Item, I give him to cut him off coming in for any share of my goods". But the fortunes of Young John's descendants sunk lower, generation by generation, till they became near-paupers, while the sun rose steadily on his brother's line that led down to lawyer Thomas.

Isaac, the disinherited, married Hannah Buck of Earl Soham in 1701 and begat a family of ten that they brought up at Paradise Farm, Worlingworth. One of his sons, Charles, married Mary Turner of Monewden and went to farm at Charsfield, the "Akenfield folded away in one of the shallow valleys". Another son, Henry, apprenticed to a butcher at Brandeston, brought a new line of business into the family, to be followed not only by his two sons, but also by three nephews and four great-nephews who opened shop as butchers in nearby places. The small tribe of Churchyards usually acted closely together.

Old Jonathan, the lawyer's grandfather, was born in 1742, one of

---

* Golty's tithe book (in private ownership).

the ten children of Charles and Mary. Their second son Charles stayed at home on the farm but the rest of the six boys left the quiet valley of the Potsford Brook, served apprenticeships and shrewdly set up for themselves in adjoining villages along the bustling London Road. They were Henry, quickly succeeding as a butcher at Ufford; Isaac, farrier of Wickham Market; Jonathan, butcher at Melton; Benjamin, shoemaker at Wickham Market and Edward, yet another butcher in Woodbridge. When both their parents died in 1785 after a married life of fifty years, the boys and their sisters raised to their memory a headstone in the sun before the south wall of Charsfield church. They composed a simple epitaph, six words only but of uncommon grace. ''Persons of exemplary Piety and Charity''.

Jonathan, in 1768 married Hannah Waspe at Ufford, the pleasant village hidden away among the willows and alders in the lush Deben meadows a mile upstream from Melton. Thirteen children were born to them, seven of whom did not live to grow up. Hannah was related to the Waspes of Gusford Hall in Stoke-by-Ipswich, tenants on four hundred acres. The Melton butcher's commencement was altogether humbler, his house and ''Holme's Shop'' being of only £4 annual rent. But he quickly advanced to taking the old shoemaker's place and hiring lands to fatten his own beasts for slaughter, so that within eight years his holdings had gone up to the annual value of £53. By 1784 he had so prospered that he could buy his own small farm, Blocks Barn at the top of the hill, a few minutes walk from the shop.

But he was not content to remain a mere butcher of Melton. That September he advertised in the Ipswich Journal, directing his remarks to the Gentlemen, Farmers and Graziers. ''Jonathan Churchyard, Drover and Salesman in Melton, near Woodbridge in Suffolk, gives notice, That he intends drawing in Pigs for London, on Monday the 26th inst; and that day fortnight for Two months''.

The drovering trade that brought the meat for London on the hoof to Smithfield Cattle Market twice a week, was one of the wonders of the age. It called for great organising ability, the courage to take heavy risks, immense stamina and shrewd knowledge of human nature no less than expert judgement of cattle. There were bargains to be struck at the drawing in; reliable drivers taken on; food and lodging arranged for man and beast for each night of their week and a half on the London Road. At its end, as morning broke on market day, there was that ''stunning and bewildering scene'' that Oliver and Bill Sykes passed through as they set out for the burglary at Chertsey — ''the whistling of the drovers, the barking of dogs, the bellowing and plunging of oxen, the bleating of sheep, the grunting and squeaking of pigs; the cries of hawkers, the shouts, oaths and quarrelling on all sides; the ringing of bells and roar of voices, that issued from every public house

. . . the hideous and discordant din that resounded from every corner of the market''.

Starting with pigs, Jonathan had taken on the least tractable side of the drovering trade. Eight miles a day was the average that the mixed and perverse herd could be counted upon to cover. Friday was selling day for his droves at Smithfield, so there was little time to spare for the 78 miles from Melton to London by nightfall on the Thursday week. Acting also as salesman, he had still the bargaining to do with the London Carcas Butchers, and credit to give till that day fortnight when notes, drafts and purses of sovereigns would be handed over for bringing safe home from any highwayman.

In 1792 Young Jonathan was taken into partnership at twenty-three. He had inherited his father's energy, adding sheep to the droves, extending their hinterland up-country to include drawing in at Snape Crown and catering also for Romford Market. Jonathan senior could now devote himself wholly to the Melton end of the business. He had, ever since his marriage, taken a full part in parish affairs: nominating People's Warden, serving as Assessor of the Poor Rate, an Overseer of the Poor, adding his bold signature as one of the Principal Inhabitants to the allowing and settlement of accounts, for such items as washing of surplices, oil for the bells, 5/7½ paid the Boys for killing 22½ doz. of Sparrows and breaking 201 eggs. At Easter 1793 he was elected to serve a twelvemonth as Churchwarden with Richard Wood, attorney of Woodbridge.

It was at about this time that Old Jonathan's second son Charles set out along the London Road to seek his fortune. For him the end in view was different from that of dealing in Smithfield Market. He hoped to make his way in the city, under the shadow of the Royal Exchange itself.

In 1795 the Jonathans announced that ''Beasts'' would be drawn in. Henceforward cattle quickly became the Churchyards' foremost interest in the drovering. Finally in 1804 the Senior, 62, leaving the business to Young Jonathan retired to take up fresh activity. From Lord Rendlesham he leased Byng Hall in Pettistree, the parish beyond Ufford: its small village, just off the highroad, centred around the church and the Greyhound, within shouting distance of Wickham Market. The 112 acres of Byng lay a mile to the south, the farm with its noble set of buildings standing on its own down by the swift-running Byng Brook, hidden away among the alders.

Old Jonathan's wife had died just as the move took place and thereafter the housekeeping was in the hands of her daughters Ann and Hannah. Helping in the work of husbandry were James, twenty-six and Isaac, just twenty. Their father continued with Blocks Barn and shortly thereafter bought Floreys Farm Clopton, three miles to the

west. These were the lands on which he reckoned to make another fortune by bringing them into the great Suffolk agricultural revolution of
the Napoleonic Wars — a fortune that was to come to a sad end.

III

Mr Boneyparte, the Farmer's Grandfather

IN 1806 Thomas was eight and it must have been clear to his parents that this only child of theirs promised to be a remarkably clever boy. Young Jonathan determined that he should have an education that would fit him to be called to a higher state of life than his yeoman and tradesmen ancestors had heretofore enjoyed. The means were not lacking. Beyond the peacetime butchering and drovering there was the extra business generated by the war. The five thousand troops at Woodbridge had to be fed, many with their families, for up to forty percent of wives might be accepted as being on the strength.

Unlike the Navy, with victualling organised nationally, "almost all the Troops in this country are supplied under contracts made locally either by the General of the District or the Commanding Officer of a regiment". So wrote young Palmerston, newly in the Secretaryship-at-War, urging the Commander-in-Chief that this was a highly uneconomic system. The contracts that caused him most concern were those for meat from "a Butcher in a Country Town". They were, he reckoned, putting an unnecessary £80,000 a year into the pockets of these tradesmen. Young Jonathan was well placed to take his share of what was going. Tendering successfully for the requirements of official bodies was something with which the family was well conversant. In the dozen years before the war they had secured all the contracts for meat for the Melton House of Idleness.

Thomas's father wishing to send his son to an ancient grammar school just far enough away from home pastures, the choice lay between Ipswich and Dedham. "When Dedham is down Ipswich is up: when Dedham is up Ipswich is down" people used to say of the two schools in Georgian days. There was, at this time, a decided "up" for Dedham that stemmed from a sixty-six year family dynasty of forceful Cambridge wranglers — the Reverend Thomas Grimwood appointed

13

in 1732, followed by his son, the Reverend Dr Thomas Letchmere Grimwood, born and bred in the schoolhouse*.

Dedicated pedagogues with a keen eye to business, outside their obligation to give free education to twenty deserving poor boys of the town, they robustly asserted their freedom to take private paying pupils both as dayboys and as boarders in their own house. They divided the sheep from the goats by teaching the free scholars in a separate room and by renting the original grammar school playground from the trustees for the exclusive use of the fee-payers. An engraving shows the rest left free to bowl their hoops and whip their tops in the wide street between the school and the church. So on entering the Head's house as a boarder Thomas took a step that advanced him with one foot into the circle of the lesser country gentry, while the other remained among the tenant farmers and village tradesmen of his own family back at home. It was one of the earlier of the contradictions that studded Church-yard's life.

Upon his appointment the Reverend Mr Grimwood had persuaded the trustees to add to the old buildings two stately houses of lovely silver brick with their red dressings, one for the school the other for the Master. The segmented pediments, arched niche and great pilasters testify to a high feeling for style in those who planned their erection. When success brought more boys to the school a mansard roof was built over the Head's house as an extra dormitory to crowd in sixty boarders.

John Constable's thanksgiving for the Vale of Dedham — "these scenes made me a painter" — is probably the best remembered of his sayings. In the letterpress to David Lucas's engravings of his *English Landscape* he expanded it to declare that they "impart to this particular spot an amenity and elegance hardly anywhere else to be found; and which has always caused it to be admired by all persons of taste". The sense of Dedham's distinction extended beyond Constable's "lovers of Painting", to those concerned in the other arts. In architecture there was the lovely main street with so many fine houses, not least the English School, "Sherman's", rebuilt by the same masons who erected Grimwood's houses. It has perhaps the most sophisticated small Baroque facade in England. There was a long tradition, too, in music at a distinguished level. The celebrated Gibbs family of organists all sprang from Dedham, while when the New Concert Room was opened the stewards engaged for the vocal part of the evening Mr John Beard from Covent Garden, friend of Handel and darling of London in his favourite role of Macheath in *The Beggar's Opera*.

Dedham's small urbane society in Georgian days was regularly

* *Victoria County History: Essex*, II, 540.

enlarged by summer visits by "persons of taste", among them Dr John Fisher, tutor at Windsor Castle, later Bishop of Salisbury, and Sir George Beaumont "both well known admirers and patrons of painting". The latter made the acquaintance of young Constable and became his lifelong friend and guide.

By the time Thomas came to the school the Doctor had retired and been succeeded by the Reverend John Haggit, eleventh wrangler and Fellow of Sidney. The ledgers of Alexanders Bank at Woodbridge record the payments made to him by Young Jonathan for his son's education and board: £28.16s for the Michaelmas "Half" 1813.

There are brief sightings of some of the boys of his time. Harcourt and Robert Firmin, sons of the mercurial Peter, attorney of Dedham, provide more than one link in the story. When Harcourt left school a couple of years before Churchyard he served articles and became a solicitor in Woodbridge. Robert went up to Cambridge and entered Clare in 1818, as did also John Haggit the Head's son. Billy Clarke, son of the blind schoolmaster at East Bergholt, was Tom's exact contemporary and they went through the school together. He entered Jesus in 1817 and after becoming ordained served for three years at Ramsholt, half an hour's sail down the river from Woodbridge. He lived to be awarded a Fellowship of the Royal Society and to win fame in New South Wales: a devoted cleric who was a brilliant geologist, discoverer of the gold, coal, tin and diamonds of Australia. Such were the clever youths who were Tom Churchyard's contemporaries.

It was not only the school's more notable pupils who were remembered in the place of their upbringing. On the principle that there are no friends like old friends and no old friends like schoolfriends, past members, undistinguished and now forgotten, kept a yearly occasion to meet and exchange reminiscences. The *Ipswich Journal* announced: "The gentlemen educated by the late Reverend Mr Grimwood will hold their Annual Meeting at Bamford's Coffee House in Ipswich on Monday the 25th of this instant August.

Stewards R. Ingham Esq

Mr Andrew Edge

Dinner at One o'clock"

Among the recollections over which the youngest alumni present made merry, were those concerning Mr Dyer the unfortunate Usher who had come to them straight from strenuous and serious reading at Cambridge — the last person who should have been a schoolmaster. In later years Charles Lamb's friend and butt, he was the *G. D.* of the essay *Oxford in the Vacation*: a noted drudging scholar who once, in a fit of absent mindedness walked, in broad daylight, straight into the New River beside Elia's cottage at Islington. Rescued, his resuscitation had been completed by draughts of brandy and water prescribed (and liberally tested) by a one-eyed drunken quack doctor. So effective had this proved that when Lamb returned home he found his quiet friend put to bed and in a splendidly songful and reminiscent state of tipsiness. Of childlike ingenuousness, "Gall-less and simple minded", he had even swallowed Lamb's report that he was to be made a peer. It is not surprising that he lasted only one year as mentor to young barbarians on the lower forms of a Georgian grammar school.

In 1808 news to Thomas from home told of Uncle James at Byng having wed Margaret Moore of Wickham Market. Forthwith he had taken over his father-in-law's lease of another of Lord Rendlesham's farms in Pettistree — Stone Hall of 87 acres whose fields began only a hundred yards from those of Old Jonathan.

At Melton Tom's father was advancing himself too. In January 1809, with cattle now the main interest in his drovering, he respectfully informed his friends and the public that he would draw in Beasts, Sheep and Pigs, not once a fortnight but every week during the after-Christmas season. Furthermore, the droves, assembled on Mondays at Snape and Melton, were henceforward open to accept further drafts on Tuesday at the Running Buck at Ipswich and at Washbrook Swan: on Wednesdays at Bentley Tankard and Stratford Black Horse. Jonathan had thereafter the hazard of two large droves on the London Road at the same time, with only a week between them, and had them through the worst months of the year. Great difficulties could arise as in the bitter January of 1811 with its "very severe frost accompanied by an east wind extraordinary cold. The consequence was that the turnip crop suffered so very materially" that food for the sheep was unobtainable*.

Meanwhile Old Jonathan was boldly advancing the family's prospects by his style of farming at Pettistree and Clopton. Great rewards, he saw, were to be reaped by farmers who could make up the shortages of grain now that the war denied the millers their imports from the Continent. The most profitable results in all the land would come from breaking up the centuries-enriched old pastures of the cow country and sowing them down to corn. It spelled the end of the older Churchyards' High Suffolk as the seat of the dairies. Jonathan's shrewd reckoning on how things would go, turned out to his great advantage. Wheat that had fetched £3.10s. a quarter when he went to Byng rose to £6.8s. in 1812.

A commonplace book kept by William Girling who went into partnership with the Whites at Peasenhall in their expanding interests as maltsters, farmers, cart-grease manufacturers and auctioneers, gives several sightings of the local cousins. "My harvest supper was on the

---

* William Girling's commonplace book (present whereabouts not known)

19th Sept. and we had a jovial party and all got drunky''. For the following April 23rd, 1812, he wrote down in serious frame of mind: ''This week the Corn Market felt a great depression owing to the great News rec'd from France''. The great News was the signing in Paris of the Convention for the Cessation of Hostilities and the banishment of Napoleon to Elba. Although the farmers had anxieties they joined with the rest of the country in forwarding preparations for the ''general peace festivals in commemoration of the late splendid events that produced peace''. Girling recorded ''the Festival at Peasenhall was on the 25th July; dined about 600 in the open air at ten tables in Mr White's Malt Office Meadow''.

The Pettistree Dinner, five weeks earlier, was ''a sumptuous entertainment to a very large and promiscuous party, in celebration of the return of Peace — The rich and poor were placed upon a level and the day was closed with the utmost conviviality''. The finale everywhere was the burning of the effigy of The Tyrant, in many places preceded by sports with comic country events. Framlingham enjoyed such contests as grinning through a horse collar and the rumbustious humour of the chemise race in which, in addition to the prizes, ''each fair lass to be given a blue garter embroidered with the Trafalgar motto 'England expects every man to do his duty' ''.

The anxieties of the farmers proved well founded. Girling records in January 1815 wheat down to £2.4s. a quarter, ''These low prices created great distress in many places and particularly among the Farmers for they are prices no common foresight could guard against!!! From the recent changes in prices the old saying was verified, that the *Jackdaws* would beat the *Rooks* — or in other words the small farmers would save most money''.

The depression was only temporary, for in March, Girling could enter up with elation

> ''Boney Triumphant
> This month Mr Boneyparte entered France and in about fourteen days marched into Paris and was declared Emperor of France having been at the Isle of Elba about 9 months, he was always called the Farmer's Grandfather.

> Corn
> Upon receipt of this news prices advanced directly Wheat 7s. Barley 5s. Beans etc. in proportion''.

Thomas away at Dedham had Sunday by Sunday for the last half dozen years listened with the other boarders to the sermons of the brilliant Reverend Thomas Grimwood Taylor, in the great church which Constable considered ''perhaps unequalled in the beauty of its proportions and details.'' The incumbent of this fat living, himself an

17

old boy of the school, was nephew of the late Doctor. His sister kept Miss Taylor's Boarding School for Young Ladies a mile away at East Bergholt. In the May of 1815 she gave a ball for her pupils to which John Constable's brother Abram took a party that kept it up till half-past three in the morning. Perhaps Churchyard and other young gentlemen at the top of Dedham Grammar School were invited over as suitable partners for the bemuslined girls.

The troubles of the farmers, after the short-lived buying scramble of the Hundred Days, became chronic. Eighteen months after Waterloo "this county, heretofore so wealthy and happy" was a land where "if farmers of Suffolk had, for the last year, had their farms rent free they would not have made any money of them*". Within a few miles of Woodbridge there were tenants of farms of 400 acres gone bankrupt; yeomen with 60 acres working as labourers. The arable that had been old pasture was now in competition with cheap imports of grain. The foreign arrivals of wheat Girling declared to be "immense". He gives a glimpse of the Churchyards at Pettistree at this time of crisis: "1816. My Lord Rendlesham from the low price of corn abated his tenants 20 per cent". Perhaps it was at this time that Thomas White at Peasenhall named one of his fields "Labour in vain".

At midsummer that year Tom left school. His time there had, as his library a few years later bears witness, bred him up to an appreciation of the Classics, of French, of the English poets: to an interest in philosophical and religious speculation and in natural history. As to how far his love and his practice of art may have been given scope, there is the circumstantial evidence of a bill for a boy at the school in 1800 showing that a drawing master's services could be had as an extra.

It is unlikely that Thomas, a boy in his teens, became acquainted with Constable the bachelor in his late thirties, coming down to Bergholt from London each summer to wander sketching in the Vale. Nonetheless he had left Dedham knowing well the scenes out of which the great painter's masterpieces were fashioned and had taken back with him to the butcher's shop that appreciation of "an elegance admired by all persons of taste".

At home it was to be seen that however badly things had gone for the many, the Churchyards were now well enough moneyed not to be minished and brought low by the post-war slump. Jonathan the Elder, farming till 76, had plenty to bestow when he retired to Ufford and made his will. In May 1818 Susan Minter, daughter of his brother

---

* *Suffolk Farming in the nineteenth century*, ed. Joan Thirsk (Suffolk Records Society, Ipswich 1958) 92.

Isaac the farrier, came over from Wickham Market with her school-master husband to witness.

The coming of peace had not the same catastrophic effect on the meat trade as on the grain. There was profitable business for the younger Jonathan, drover and Smithfield salesman. London was scintilating and prosperous with "the splendid and useful metropolitan improvements" of the last years of the Regency and the early ones of the Monarch which, it was prophesied, would "render the name of GEORGE THE FOURTH as illustrious in the British annals as that of AUGUSTUS in those of Rome". The capital city was, in the elegant and self-assured couple of decades that followed, the setting for several decisive events in the Churchyard narrative.

IV

Qualified Persons

IT WAS decided that the youth's abilities should, upon leaving school, be directed to making his way in the Law. Jonathan was well mulcted in putting him into his legal training, for in addition to the customary premium of £100 there was a wartime tax of £80 that the government had clapped on to articles for clerks in the provinces. By the Michaelmas Law Term of 1816 it had still not been removed.

Most of what have been said to be recollections of Churchyard in Woodbridge, come from a newspaper character sketch written thirty years after his death by someone who probably never knew him. It is a final chapter of the unlikely sounding *Autobiography of a Suffolk Farm Labourer, 1816 – 1876*. This came out in weekly instalments in the *Suffolk Chronicle* of 1894 but was by no means what it claimed to be. Its author was in truth a John Glyde born in Ipswich in 1823, son of a barber and apprenticed to that calling. In his thirties he had, in the words of his obituary, "relinquished the shaving brush for the pen" to become a bookseller in the town and an energetic scribbler.

The *Autobiography*, brazenly announced as genuine, is set in the Churchyard country. The fictitious character of the Labourer is the peg on which the radically minded Glyde hung a series of pictures of the hard lives of the farm workers, dramatic happenings around Woodbridge and sketches of local celebrities and quaint customers. Much of his material for the early years he gathered by sending correspondents a searching questionnaire to be filled in and returned.

The *Autobiography*'s statement on Churchyard's entry into the legal profession is that he was "articled to a well-known firm of solicitors, Messrs. Crabtree and Cross of Halesworth" and it goes on to say that at Woodbridge "very soon after he settled down as a lawyer he acquired an uncommonly good share of Petty Sessions and County Court practice". The firm of Crabtree and Cross did not exist till 1844.

When Jonathan bought his boy his articles the practice was in the hands of Robert Crabtree alone, till in 1818 he took into partnership John Allcock. Nor could Churchyard have acquired in his early days a good share of work in the County Courts for they were not instituted till 1850.

With Glyde's accuracy on details so much in doubt, the question arises, seeing that Thomas's mother was a White, as to whether he may have served his articles at Halesworth in the office of Robert Gostling White. Consanguinity between the two families, living half a dozen miles apart, would explain the choice of profession. The lawyer Whites sprang from a seventeenth century Norwich grocer. Their line is clear: not so the grocers of Peasenhall who have been traced back no further than Anne Churchyard's father.

Robert White's will that might have contained a clue as to kinship is silent on any such matter. Drawn up in 1813 it names his beloved wife Elizabeth, sole beneficiary. "But in making this bequest I am apprehensive from the many debts I may leave behind me it will be of little value to her in a pecuniary view. It will, however, I am confident be endeared to her as a testimonial of my love and most affectionate esteem and of the sense I have ever entertained of her goodness of heart and in regard for me. Amongst my numerous children the division of so small a property would have been too minute to be useful. . . . To all of them I bequeath my blessing with a prayer to heaven for their prosperity and an injunction to them to preserve ever sacred and inviolate the bond of affectionate union amongst themselves".

Its reading after his funeral in 1828 sounded strangely for he had left behind not only a widow and ten of his fourteen children, but a splendid fortune as well. For four years an unsuccessful search was made for a later will that would have fitted in with the greatly altered circumstances but the old adage held, that a lawyer who deals with his own affairs has a fool for a client. At whichever of the two Halesworth offices it was that Churchyard served his articles, his mentor set him a bad example on so important a matter; Robert Crabtree having made a comfortable fortune died in 1840 leaving no will at all.

Beside the firms of Crabtree and of White there was in 1816 one other attorney's practice in the Halesworth of 2,000 population, that of John Cufaude. The Cufaudes kept very much to themselves, in contrast to the other lawyers, who, by shrewd alliances drew themselves into an unbelievably tight circle. Several members of the Jermyn family had practised in Halesworth in the seventeen hundreds. Peter Jermyn's sister Sarah was secured in marriage by John Tuthill, attorney, shortly after his coming from Norwich to be a junior partner. When in the next generation Peter Jermyn II died young, his place in the firm was taken by a recently qualified lawyer from London, Robert

21

Crabtree. In next to no time the newcomer had won as wife, Elizabeth daughter of John Tuthill aforesaid. His brother, Captain John Crabtree of the Honourable East India Company's Service, married Elizabeth Tuthill's sister Sarah. Robert Crabtree's two sons died in infancy leaving him with no heir to succeed; which may account for three of his daughters being snapped up by smart young attorneys with an eye to the main chance. Ann was carried off by John Meadows White of Great St Helens, Bishopsgate, son of lawyer Robert Gostling White who left the strange will. Mary was wed by her cousin Young John Crabtree of London, attorney, the East India Captain's son, and he it was, who, when his uncle died, secured the Halesworth practice. Four years later he took into partnership Frederick Cross, son of a previous rector. Cross thought it prudent to get himself tied into the Halesworth legal family network as soon as might be and forthwith married his principal's sister-in-law-cum-cousin, the late Robert Crabtree's youngest daughter Maria now nearly thirty-nine, eight years his senior. For good measure Laura Tuthill grand-daughter of lawyer John Tuthill had in the meantime wed Thomas Borrett attorney, of St Mary-le-Bone, London, junior partner of John Meadows White. Just how effectively the attorneys in the devil's little country town managed to keep the law business all within the family, young Churchyard may have been abashed to discover.

Lodging in the lawyer's house he was for four years a close neighbour of the Hookers at the Brewery House of Turner, Paget and Hooker. Young William Hooker, the future Director of Kew, had been anchored there by his father-in-law Dawson Turner the rich Yarmouth banker, partner in the Gurneys, antiquary and botanist. Ostensibly a partner of the brewery, Hooker was, in fact, kept hard at work providing the illustrations for the Turner magnum opus, *Historia Fucorum*, the natural history of the seaweeds.

Admitted a Fellow of the Linnean Society before he was twenty-one, Hooker was a supreme botanical draughtsman. Between 1816 and 1820 he published four works with his own splendid illustrations and was also busy on two hundred drawings for a new edition of Curtis's *Flora Londinensis*. It is not unreasonable to think that young Churchyard must have become acquainted with him, for flower illustration was, from the first, one of his own loves. "Botany also, was a favourite pursuit, and in his early time he made numerous drawings for a work on that subject of some note". So wrote John Loder the Woodbridge bookseller composing the obituary notice in 1865. It is frustrating that he, who of all people in the town was best placed to know the book's title, should have left it unmentioned.

The notable publication remains unidentified. Neither Kew nor the Hunt Institute for Botanical Documentation can find Churchyard's name anywhere in their multitudinous archives. It was a time when many botanical books were appearing and in most the illustrators remain anonymous. The Churchyard daughters could not have been ignorant of the book's existence, but with the reticence habitually maintained by the family they kept the knowledge to themselves. An item held back from the disposal of 1866 and treasured for sixty years was lot 366 in the 1927 sale: "Three old books of *Flower Painting* beautifully illustrated in colours". Examples remain of Churchyard's skill in this field. When late in his life he began sharing out his pictures between the girls, he allotted to Emma a little oil painting of flowers. In the opposite corner to that of her name are the initials *T. C.* in cursive style with his characteristic short top to the first letter that could lead to the initials being taken for *J. C.* It has been hung in the Mellon Collection in America as a John Constable.

Perhaps it was already in his articled years that he came to believe he could only fulfil himself by excelling in that genre of art practised by the Norwich School of painters. To have become captivated by the landscapes of John Crome its founder he would have to have journeyed to the Norfolk capital, since at that time the paintings were hardly to be found outside the homes of local collectors who had bought them at annual exhibitions of the Norwich Society of Artists. At Halesworth he was well placed to take a day's leave, rise early and at six o'clock on a Saturday morning travel up three hours into Norfolk by the Eclipse Coach and view the master's showings of 1817 and of the next three years.

As to what early instruction he may have had beyond lessons with a Dedham drawing-master, a guess can be made at one possibility. When in 1766 Old Jonathan's brother Isaac the farrier at Wickham Market married Widow Smart she had an eldest son John then thirteen. It was several years before his artistic gift was noticed whereupon he "went up to London at the age of twenty-nine and in the following year 1783 became a student in the Academy. He immediately turned his attention to portrait painting in which he excelled. He settled in Ipswich about the year 1787* and has painted the likeness of a great many persons in this town and neighbourhood". When he returned from London one of his first portraits was of his half-sister at Wickham Market, Susan Churchyard, then seventeen — "a beautiful painting somewhat in the style of Romney . . . It represents a girl with auburn hair. She is netting. The colouring is very pretty". It is pleasing to imagine that this was the "Portrait of a Young Lady" in the Academy exhibition of 1786, Smart's first work to be hung. Thereafter he practised at Ipswich till his death at the age of 85, when his obituary

---

* Redgrave confuses him at this date with John Smart the miniaturist, 1740 – 1811.

described him as "a most respectable teacher of drawing".

Susan married Robert Minter, schoolmaster at Wickham Market and christened her son Charles Churchyard Minter, at a date when such middle names were a considerable rarity; thereby declaring herself decidedly part of the family circle. So decidedly that between 1812 and 1829 Susan and Robert were asked to come over to witness wills and codicils of her uncles Charles the Younger at the Charsfield farm, of Jonathan the Elder and of her cousin Ann, both at Byng. This close association may have prompted Jonathan the Younger, finding that his boy had artistic as well as intellectual ability, to arrange for him to be given lessons by cousin Minter's half-brother, that most respectable teacher of drawing at Ipswich. Lessons with him suggest the likelihood of his having been taught also by Smart's fellow townsman and boon companion George Frost whose hand seems traceable in the strangely elongated human figures sometimes seen in Churchyard's backgrounds.

The owner of the portrait of the beautiful auburn-headed girl with the pretty colouring was in 1914 a Miss Susan Harriet Churchyard, granddaughter of Old Jonathan's brother Benjamin the Wickham Market shoemaker. Ben in his day had brought some discredit to the name of Churchyard. In 1792 after seventeen years of married life his wife died childless. Two years later Ann Beart, a village girl of twenty named her illegitimate child Ben Churchyard Beart and in 1797 bore a son Henry who resolutely called himself Henry Churchyard to the day of his death in Wickham Market at the age of 93. Ben, just short of fifty, let a further year pass before marrying Ann and commencing a legally begotten family of nine.

Susan Harriet has left some small lunettes on the kinsfolk at the time Thomas was removing from Dedham to Halesworth. She recalled the day when her father, Edward, Librarian of the Congregational Union in Finsbury, had brought her down to Pettistree after the last of the kinsmen at the Hall had gone hence. He wanted her to see Byng — "At that time unoccupied. I remember a nightingale was singing in a bush near the house. He told me that when a boy — about 1816 — he used to go to the Hall Farm for milk — for his aunts and uncles* lived there and that the aunties were very kind to him — also that his uncle used to ride into Wickham with his dogs to visit his father — also that his uncle's name was Isaac Churchyard".

In the summer of 1820 both the flower delineators left Halesworth. The brewery did badly and there was talk of selling up so Hooker could at last escape to take the chair of Botany at Glasgow University. Churchyard was due to go and serve the last year of his articles in Town.

---

* Actually first cousins, but thirty years his elders.

He had first a brief spell at Melton, and spent some of it painting landscape. A short while ago, there came to light in South Africa, the last remains of an album of watercolour drawings, many by then lost, but with one of the surviving pieces titled "Thos. Churchyard 1820". Others have attached to them the names Laura, Anna, Kate, three of his daughters. It must originally have been typical of the family albums that the girls used to put together, several of which are known. This one had been begged of her grandfather by a small girl from the Cape on holiday in England in 1914. The grandfather had bought it at the turn of the century as part of a lot in an auction sale near Cheltenham. Almost certainly it had been given by the Churchyards to their Hailes cousins, who after army service in India had gravitated to that traditional town of military retirement.

Throughout life Thomas seldom dated a painting. This was memorable for the time of its execution. Not only did that early autumn signal his forthcoming removal to London, it was filled also with the excitements and violent popular opposition to the trial of Queen Caroline. Many Woodbridgians were sitting up far into the night in the public houses, awaiting the arrival of the previous day's London papers with their latest reports of fresh bedroom scandal.

It is unlikely that the painter or his subjects had been late retiring. They had had to rise early, for the watercolour was drawn not long after sunrise. He had come to Woodbridge and seated himself half way along Fen Walk, from which point looking across the Abbey Field, reapers are seen at work cutting corn with sickles, binding the sheaves and setting them up in stooks. St Mary's Church and the roofs of The Abbey are in the background. It is an adventurous attempt, for the painter is looking almost straight into the sun that is about to dispel the mist and bring in a fine harvest day. Churchyard boldly scored the paper with a circle and radials to give the impression of the sun within the luminous haze that is about to evaporate and disclose all things bright and clear.

Of Churchyard's year in London nothing is known. It is difficult to imagine he did not seek artistic instruction in some of the numerous studios. It would be impossible to believe that he did not visit the Academy Exhibition in May 1821 where he would have seen perhaps his first Constable, the *Hay Wain* above all. Late that month, after the commencement of Trinity Term he qualified and was admitted on to the roll. His thus being able to describe himself "Attorney" — almost a gentleman — was a source of pride to his grandfather. The will of three years earlier was brought out and a codicil added "To Thomas Churchyard the only son of my son Jonathan Churchyard, £100." On 5 June the auburn headed Susan Minter and her husband were called upon once again, and came down to Ufford to witness.

Young Jonathan, too, must have treated his son lavishly at this time and there seems to have been no hurry for him to start earning his living. The Law Society has him recorded as commencing practice in 1822. He may have stayed on in London, or returned to Melton or gone on his travels. In the first mention of his own paintings there is *Copy of a Landscape by Ruysdael in the Louvre*. Among his books listed at an early time was Cuvier's four volume work *La Règle Animal* perhaps brought home from a visit across the Channel*.

In the last days of 1821 Old Jonathan died and his dispositions came into effect: to Jonathan, the house at Melton that had long been in his occupation; to Thomas the £100; his daughters Ann and Hannah, old maids of nearly fifty, to take what plate and furniture they chose for two rooms each. It is the first time the idea of Churchyard family silver came to be thought of. All else including his lands in Melton and Clopton to be sold and the proceeds divided equally between his six surviving children. The beneficiaries, however, in true Churchyard fashion and with faith in the value of land, preferred to keep their father's farms in the family. It was arranged that Young Jonathan's wife Anne should purchase from the executors Blocks Barn Melton, that her sister-in-law Ann at the Hall should buy Floreys at Clopton. Isaac continued tenant of the former; he and James together worked the latter. The rented Byng Hall continued to be thought of as the family seat.

The Woodbridge of four thousand souls in which Churchyard commenced practice was the most considerable place between Ipswich and Yarmouth, its port on the tidal Deben then a natural outlet for the produce of the local countryside, grain above all. Three dozen master mariners had here their homes and families, as likewise had the substantial proprietors of eleven maltings and breweries. The place supported two dozen inns and a further twelve beerhouses.

Those who had known the townscape in 1822 would not be much surprised by the appearance of its streets today. The narrow Thoroughfare — *Throughfare* to all good Woodbridgians then as now — ran from end to end of the town, never for long without some slight twist to one side or another, nor for long without some gentle rise or fall in its course. At the extremities are the best of the Georgian-fronted houses and a few regency villas and simple cottages. In the middle are the shops, whose proprietors in 1822 lived over them. Almost all the buildings flank directly the strip of pavement, holding themselves together in virtually unbroken line, very urban to the passer-by but often concealing fine gardens running unbelievably far back behind them.

The cross road from the Quay climbs up to the Market Hill, half filled with the Dutch-looking Shire Hall, and having to the south side

* Sale catalogue 1832.

the great airy church with its splendid tower aloof. Running out from the corners of the market-place are streets that led to the Theatre, the House of Correction, the Seckford Almshouses and to nearby villages. On its north side are sudden valleys and green slopes, quickly climbing again to the surrounding heights, enlivened in Churchyard's day with the sails of four windmills.

When he commenced practice, Woodbridge had not a super-abundance of attorneys — only four in a place twice the size of Halesworth. Although there was not the tight family circle as at the other place, nonetheless here all four lawyers were related, by descent or by marriage, to others who were also attorneys. There were Charles Moor from nearby Alderton whose sister was married to a lawyer in Ipswich; John Wood senior and John Wood junior with whose forebear, lawyer Richard Wood, Jonathan Churchyard the Elder had served as churchwarden thirty years earlier. At about that time Richard had built Melton Hall, standing back from the turnpike at the corner of the Hasketon Road*: a four-square, mid-sized, porticoed Georgian house of solid importance without, its rooms completed with architectural elegancies within. The Woods had become the most respected family of lawyers practising in Woodbridge at Tom's arrival.

An altogether different individual was James Pulham, attorney, a year older than John Wood senior. In ways unlooked for some of his actions came to fit strangely with what the fates had in store for Churchyard. Born in Sudbury he had, upon qualifying, married Frances Amys whose sister was wife of an attorney at Saxmundham. After a few years at Hadleigh he had come to Woodbridge in 1797 and opened his office at the eastern end of Thoroughfare. Concerning him David Elisha Davy of Ufford, the celebrated antiquary who must have known him well, made one of the few comments on character that he permitted himself among the hundreds of thousands of names in his *Suffolk Pedigrees*†. "He was an Attorney not in the highest repute".

Early in the century Pulham, for services rendered, had benefitted to the tune of a handsome £600 by the will of the easygoing bachelor Lord Chedworth, disposing of not much short of half a million of money. The fact that the beneficiaries were almost entirely his lady friends at the Theatre Royal Norwich, little milliners of Ipswich and the whist-playing daughters of Ipswich inn-keepers, moved his excluded relatives to contest the will on grounds of insanity. His Lordship's unpublished *Notes upon some of the Obscure Passages in Shakespeares Plays* were produced in court to help rebut the allegation and Pulham and the ladies were left to the quiet enjoyment of their legacies.

Mrs Pulham had some skill with the pencil and drew portraits of a

---

* Thereafter known as Lawyer's Lane or Wood's Lane.
† British Library, MS Additional 19146.

number of friends and acquaintances. Her likeness of Henry Jermyn of the Halesworth family, Suffolk antiquary and collaborator with Davy, was engraved for a London genealogical magazine a few months after his death.

Besides these four attorneys there had been a Robert Jackson who stayed for half a dozen years before leaving in 1820. He was succeeded in his practice by Churchyard's school-fellow Harcourt Firmin. In a little over a year after arriving, Harcourt made a typical young attorney's capture by securing the hand of Pulham's daughter Frances. He and his father-in-law were birds of a feather. Concerning him Abram Constable wrote to his brother the painter "he is a man I have a very bad opinion of both in word and deed. I look upon him as a Son of Belial, a child of the D---l, with such people I never *fall out*, nor *never mix*."* Within three years of his marriage he was on such bad terms with his brother-in-law, Young Pulham living in London, that the latter's wife refused to receive him when he and Frances were up in Town. "The wretch . . . wrote her a very rude letter in consequence".

Hardly had Firmin become established in Woodbridge than his volatile father Peter, decided to retire from being an attorney in Dedham and spend the remainder of his days in London. His going would leave vacant a practice that included the lucrative stewardships of several manors belonging to important personages in the Vale. These were too good to be let go out of the family and accordingly after putting in a locum tenens at Dedham, Harcourt took steps to dispose of his recently acquired practice in Suffolk so as to return to his native Essex.

Late in January 1821 he made a visit to London taking with him a letter from his future father-in-law to be delivered to John Constable at No. 1 Keppel Street. The artist was by now well known to the lawyer, having painted a portrait of Mrs Pulham three years earlier. On this later occasion it was that lady's likeness of the late Henry Jermyn that was the subject-matter of the letter.† It was being sent to Constable with a request that he would discuss with "the intended engraver" its reproduction for the *Herald and Genealogist Magazine*.

Seeing that all this could well have been dealt with through the post, there was likely to have been some weightier matter that brought Harcourt to travel to Town in person. Churchyard was within four months of qualifying and it may have been Firmin's purpose to discuss with him the possibility of his taking over the Woodbridge practice as soon

---

* *John Constable's Correspondence*, ed. R. B. Beckett (Suffolk Records Society, Ipswich 1962) I, 303.

† Not her miniature of the "venerable clergyman" (see p. 40 below), suggested as a possibility in *John Constable: Further Documents and Correspondence* ed. L. Parris, C. Shields and I. Fleming-Williams (Suffolk Records Society, Ipswich 1975), 124.

as the agreement with the locum at Dedham had run out. Some time in the next year the transfer was completed.

With the incubi of Harcourt and Pulham haunting Churchyard's early days in the law at the little country town, it was a start not under the best auspices. There were no other changes among the attorneys until 1828, when Thomas Carthew the Fifth qualified and re-established the family practice that had been in abeyance for several years following the early death of his lawyer-uncle. His father the Reverend Thomas, patron and incumbent of the living, four times married, begat thirteen children by his first wife and nine by his third, most of whom survived to fill their splendid house, ''The Abbey'', at the heart of the town. Nothing has come to light as to what lesser establishment Churchyard maintained on his return from London.

The local press in the 1820s recorded nothing in its weekly paragraphs on the Woodbridge Session beyond charges, verdicts and sentences: magistrates and miscreants only, no sight or sound of defending solicitors. The Labourer's account of Churchyard ''very soon after he settled down'' is imagined from what Glyde may have known of him nearly forty years later. He was on good ground, though, when he wrote that ''Churchyard so frequently defended in poaching cases that he became known as the Poacher's Lawyer. He was so well acquainted with the law relating to game offences that he was dangerous in a bad case and irresistible in a good one''.

The game laws had come to be described as ''the richest treasure a country attorney possesses''; When Churchyard commenced in practice the acts were still largely unaltered from the form in which they had been drawn up by the squirearchical parliament of the Restoration. They revolved around the conception of the Qualified Person: qualified persons being peers, knights, esquires owning land worth £100 a year, their eldest sons and their keepers. They alone might kill hares, pheasants and partridges, and they might kill them on anyone's land. No one else might take game, even on his own property, be he freeholder or tenant. No one, not even a qualified person, might sell game, although it was no offence to buy it.

This last safe let-out and the fiction of presents from some country squire enabled city merchants, bankers, parliament men, canons residentiary and indeed anyone who could afford the price, to serve throughout the season at their hospitable tables, game ''shot by the silver gun'', once it had safely reached them by the underground route of poacher, packer, inn-keeper, coachman and poulterer. The black market was vast and vastly lucrative. While Churchyard was serving his articles at Halesworth, William Smith, common carrier of that town, was in 1819 convicted and fined £100 by Sir Charles Blois, magistrate and not disinterested game preserver, for having in his van twenty hares. The fine was promptly paid, the equivalent of four years wages of a farm labourer.

Around Woodbridge there was an abundance of estates where the game was intensively preserved. Two that out-topped all others gave occasion for many a poaching case to come into Woodbridge Petty Sessions. There was Rendlesham where the Swiss merchant family of the Thellussons, recently raised to an Irish peerage, were visited "not only by many of the first nobility, but also by several branches of the Royal Family at *White House*, a princely residence surpassed by few in the kingdom."

Surpassed it was by neighbouring Sudbourne. There the house, "a plain regular mansion by Wyatt . . . in extensive grounds" was "used as a sporting residence; the park and neighbourhood abounding in game". A description some years later of the absurd lengths to which preservation went on this estate tells that "Stover stacks close by the premises were undermined by the hares till they had to be hurdled round to save the remnant from burying up the swarms that would come for a meal on a frosty night. Not a turnip could be left unclamped after October, and boys had to keep the pheasants off the peastacks. Once three thousand hares were killed on the estate between Monday morning and Saturday night, and on one of the days two hundred and forty more, alive and hungry, were counted on a field close by where the slaughter had just taken place. They were coursed by greyhounds till at last the dogs would wag their tails, turn their heads, and refuse to run after another hare."

The owner of Sudbourne, inheriting in June 1822, was the most Honourable Francis Charles Seymour-Conway, third Marquis of Hertford, Earl of Yarmouth, Viscount Beauchamp, Baron Conway of Ragley, Warwickshire, and of Killultagh, Ireland, Knight of the Most Noble Order of the Garter; in his life-time envied as vice-chamberlain to the Regent over whom he had great influence and remembered today as Lord Steyne in *Vanity Fair* and Lord Monmouth in *Coningsby*. Woodbridge remarked his coming to Sudbourne, sometimes not more than once a year, driving down in coach and four with two postillions; changing horses every ten or twelve miles and carrying his butler and his valet in the rumble. With the final team put in, "my Lord's carriage blazing with heraldic devices came whirling along . . . borne by the almost priceless horses" as Thackeray had visualised them in fiction on the Pincian Hill; and in reality swinging right-handed at Melton *Horse and Groom* for the last four miles to the mansion.

This was the so noble estate to which Young Jonathan's son, Lawyer Churchyard, small and of no reputation, was to become a thorn in the flesh for many a year.

V

Man and wife together

THERE HAD been at Halesworth, a wide circle open to Churchyard for lovemaking, that might advance his professional prospects. When he left at the age of twenty-two there was a bevy of eligible attorneys' daughters then unwed — Ann, Elizabeth, Fanny, Mary and Maria Crabtree; Elizabeth, Sarah, Eleanor, Emily, Ann and Harriet White; Laura Tuthill; Ellen Cufaude; Ann and Sarah Allcock. Odd man out as he so often was, his marriage when it took place had the opposite of the calculating caution indulged in by all his young learned friends.

The family of Harriet Hailes whom he wed had close associations with the Stour valley. Her father, Lieutenant George R.N., mentioned in his will a brother John, surgeon at East Bergholt, and father-in-law John Harris of Ramsey, Gentleman. All a little more elevated within the family than in the official world, where Hailes is described as apothecary and Harris as farmer.

It cannot be said that the Lieutenant's naval career entered upon in 1776 when he was thirteen, turned out to be a brilliant one. But as Youngster and later as Junior Officer, he had, in his early years afloat, his fill of dangers and disappointments far from home in the service of his country. Going to sea in the traditional way as Captain's Servant, his sea daddy Capt John Macartney of *H.M.S. Ambuscade* sailed away with him to eight years of war with the American Colonies and with France, patrolling off the coasts of New England and Nova Scotia and in the Channel and with spells on the Jamaica Station. It was from one of these last that he had his closest shave.

In July 1782 Rear-Admiral Thomas Graves was under orders to bring home from the West Indies the prizes taken in Rodney's action that shattered de Grasse off Dominique. Graves hoisted his flag in *Ramilles* of 74 guns and on 25 July set sail for England, Midshipman Hailes aboard. With most of the men-of-war in urgent need of refit after years of active service, the convoy has been described* as "the craziest squadron perhaps that ever put to sea. Some of them parted company at a very early stage and returned to Port Royal or bore up for Halifax; the rest got into a violent storm in mid-ocean on 16 September, when several of them went down, some with all hands. Of nine ships of the line that left Jamaica, two only got to England . . . *Ramilles* was one of those that were lost. She was laying-to on the wrong tack, and was taken aback in a violent and sudden shift of wind". Providentially her masts went by the board, otherwise she must have capsized and foundered. The equinoctial gale briefly abated, the ship's company got safely aboard the *Belle* merchant ship and *Ramilles* was abandoned and blown up in the forenoon of the 21st.

On 10 October the merchantman arrived at Cork and Hailes was transferred to *H.M.S. Grampus* for Liverpool. Three weeks later he was able to present himself to the Board of Examiners of their Lordships of the Admiralty. His records and recommendations were in order and having survived the viva-voce quizzing by the old sea-dogs he was duly promoted Lieutenant. A few months in the *Asia* patrolling the Channel; a few weeks shore leave and then a posting once again to Jamaica. The autumn of 1783 saw peace proclaimed and early next year Lieutenant Hailes entered upon the Passage Home in the captured *Duc de Chartres*. Reaching England on 5 May he found awaiting him a communication from the Navy Board informing him that he was placed on half-pay. It was signed by three Commissioners "We are your Affectionate Friends".

Within a few months his own affections were engaged and he had formed a romantic attachment with Susan Harris, a girl of eighteen, daughter of a substantial farmer at Ramsey, Essex. Ramsey Hill looks down the Stour to the distant sea and over to Shotley Gate, Orwell Haven and Harwich Harbour, a great stretch of safe, salt water, then crowded with the tall sticks of men-of-war and merchantmen. There was a great glamour of the Navy thereabouts; the gallant young officer of twenty-two, freshly home from the dangers of the sea and from the violence of the enemy, proved irresistible. Some time in the summer of 1785 there was a Young George born outside the bonds of matrimony.

Susan had perhaps eloped, for neither the birth nor the subsequent marriage has been traced locally. Whatever upset in the family her slip may have caused, it was not of lasting duration. The girl forfeited no part of her father's good will and the child grew up to be a favoured grandson to whom the farmer, in after years, advanced £600 for establishing him as a grocer at Bury St Edmunds.

The two settled down to wedded life ashore, mostly at Henley near

---

* See *Dictionary of National Biography* sv. Thomas Lord Graves.

Ipswich, and the arrivals of Susan, Sophia, John, Augustus, Henry, James, Harriet on 8 September 1797 and lastly Mary Elizabeth. For nine of those dozen years the Lieutenant was "on the beach" on half-pay. Only the temporary scare of the French Revolution gave him employment from 1790 to 1793, patrolling the North Sea in *Daphne* of twenty guns. Four years later the threat of invasion by Napoleon brought preparations for his return to active service in May 1798. He moved his family briefly to Snape and then settled them in Ipswich for the next seventeen years. In 1801 the Borough Assembly marked its appreciation of his being on active service by presenting his son, John, with a Foundation Scholarship at the Grammar School. With his fellow form-mate Harry Jones*, he joined others in filching gunpowder stored by the military in a hundred barrels under the Schoolroom, making fireworks that they let off before the open doors, in imminent danger of blowing up the whole place. †

The war gave the Lieutenant his first command. It was a stone frigate one, the Felixstowe Signal Station. As a berth it was snug enough. The stations around the south and east coasts were fitted with comfortable quarters for a Lieutenant, who had with him a Midshipman and two seamen. ‡ It was hardly the ladder to fame for an officer now thirty-six. Perhaps his several stays in "that infernal Bakehouse, Port Royal, Jamaica" and the unwholesome cruises that saw the bodies of so many of his shipmates committed to the deep, victims of the dread Yellow Jack fever, had incapacitated him for further service afloat. Appointments to these Napoleonic signal stations were often made upon application by partially disabled officers, such as the one who explained that he was unfitted for active service in consequence of a stroke that had affected an arm and one of his eyes. "An officer of a signal station ought to have two eyes, and damned good eyes they should be" commented the First Lord, the great St Vincent.

Until Trafalgar there was plenty of work for the four pairs of damned good eyes at Felixstowe, scanning the sea for signs of invasion and on the look-out for signals from our patrolling vessels, from adjacent stations and from the Woodbridge gazebo. In 1803 Hailes's command was shifted across the mouth of the Deben to the next station up the coast at Bawdsey. After Trafalgar and Napoleon's Army of England being marched off to do battle with the Austrians, it was a long dull war for the Lieutenant and his crew. Their main source of interest was now watching the building of the Suffolk Martello Towers, fifteen of them within sight together between Shotley and Hollesley Bay; but that not

---

* Later Commanding RE before Sebastopol.
† Purland MS., *A Pilgrimage to Ipswich*, Suffolk Record Office.
‡ *The Mariner's Mirror*, July 1911.

begun till 1809, only after long official argument and delay and when the danger of invasion had quite passed.

Finally, with Napoleon banished to Elba, employment on the stations came to an end and George Hailes made the final entry on his Service Sheet 11 January 1815. On half-pay once more he rejoined his family and set up house at Melton. In 1819 he was put on the retired list in the rank of Superannuated Commander, having remained in that of Lieutenant for thirty-seven years. From the end of schooldays at Dedham the Churchyards and the Hailes were neighbours. Thomas and Harriet may have seen one another at church, if nowhere else, for nearly ten years before their marriage.

The Family Bible showed that their firstborn, Thomas, was delivered 16 March 1825 and baptised at St Mary's Woodbridge five days later. It omitted mention of the wedding but the locals had seen the news two months earlier, in a discreet announcement carried by the *Ipswich Journal*: "A few days since was married in London, Thos. Churchyard Esq., solicitor, Woodbridge, to Harriet, third daughter of Captain Hailes R.N.". The neighbourhood had, as a mark of respect, promoted the Superannuated Commander to a courtesy rank. A wedding so overdue could hardly have improved the young attorney's standing with the solid, respectable people of Woodbridge. His continuing in the town where he was well known, rather than seeking a practice far removed, suggests that he did not much mind what people thought.

Nothing has come to light to provide the explanation as to why the wedding came to be performed in so oblique a manner. Threats of horsewhipping by indignant brothers; the machinations of a clever spinster already in sight of thirty; mutual romantic passion — Byron was Thomas's favourite modern poet — all can be imagined. There could be more solid ground for surmise were it known whether Harriet was then living with a sister in London, with her father at Melton or with her mother at St Nicholas, Ipswich. Since 1820 the sailor and his wife had been living apart.

The licence under which the marriage could take place forthwith without publication of banns, was granted on 8 January. It was for a wedding to be performed in the parish church of St John the Evangelist, Westminster. Harriet was married from the house of her sister Susan, wife of Charles Henry Obbard, proprietor of a Fancy Dress and Masquerade Warehouse at 16 Tavistock Street, Covent Garden. Their home still stands in Horseferry Road, the only private house now left in that great canyon of modern buildings. It is in a short terrace of small two-storey, stock brick, narrow-fronted villas; with railings, an area, and steps up to the front door. A pair of tall Georgian windows light the front parlour that opens out of the hall; upstairs the

windows above it are balconied. A quaint double circle leaded into the
fanlight above the front door carries the number in the road, 90.

No doubt it was Charles Henry who made the arrangements with
the officiating minister, for the bridegroom did not present himself at
Lambeth Palace to secure the licence till the day before the marriage. It
was only a few minutes walk from the Obbards' villa to the great
baroque temple of St John's, Smith Square, outstanding among the
brick built streets of Westminster. Chance could hardly have hit upon a
consecrated building more unlike their own small parish church at
Melton, down in the meadows, deserted by its village.

Fitted in at some hour between the regular services on the First Sunday after Epiphany, Charles Henry gave away his sister-in-law and
Thomas and Harriet gave and pledged their troth either to other. The
curate, the Reverend D'Arcy Haggit, a relative of the bridegroom's
Headmaster, pronounced them man and wife together, having earlier
reminded them in stiff, puritan, Tudor English that one of the causes
for which Matrimony was ordained was to avoid fornication, that such
persons as have not the gift of continency might marry and keep themselves undefiled.

Although the union did not take Churchyard into the ring of legal
families that almost all aspiring solicitors managed to enter via
matrimony, it did bring him into a circle unlike any in which his
forebears had moved. There was a decidedly Services aura about the
Hailes. Besides the courtesy Captain R.N. there were two of Harriet's
brothers who were officer gentlemen. John had left Ipswich Grammar
School in 1807 and joined the Honourable East India Company Service as a Cadet and gone out to the east two years later. By 1825 he was
a Captain in the Fourth Native Infantry, having fought in the Nepal
and Mahratta Wars. There was, too, Augustus who had been commissioned in 1811 as a Second Lieutenant of the Royal Marines and with
the coming of peace had been placed on half-pay which he continued to
enjoy at three shillings a day for the succeeding forty-three years. Her
brother Henry had gone to tropical climes as a planter.

With the firm line at that time drawn between gentility and trade,
any Emma Woodhouse would have been puzzled as to how to take the
Hailes family. In contradistinction to the sailor, the soldiers and the
planter there was Susan married to a masquerade warehouse proprietor and George a grocer at Bury St Edmunds. He, though, had
already been dead four years by the time of Harriet's marriage, having
returned to spend the last months of a painful illness with his mother.

Among the Churchyards there was a like diversity, where within the
immediate kinship there were substantial farmers, cattle salesmen, successful and unsuccessful butchers, men of business in the city, farriers,
property owners, small shopkeepers and great uncle Ben still sewing

shoes at Wickham Market. Rich and poor relations were one of the pairs of contrasting elements that the attorney had to endeavour to keep in balance throughout his days.

At Young Tom's christening all three sponsors were decidedly of the riper years — great-uncles Thomas White of Peasenhall and Charles Churchyard of Cornhill, London; great-aunt Hannah of Pettistree. The lawyer had taken a tenancy in Woodbridge of 29 Well Street, a small red brick Georgian house, semi-detached but fronting the pavement with a fine air of distinction. It was a residence of like importance to those which other young Woodbridge attorneys took at the start of their careers. With his appreciation of the "elegance admired by all persons of taste" and enabled by his father's lavish generosity in setting him up, he is likely to have surpassed them in the manner of the house's furnishing and embellishments; its fine library of books, Old Master paintings and excellently chosen examples of the English Landscape School.

A glance at the setting to which he brought back his bride is provided in the pair of portraits that he commissioned in early married days. The rose Harriet holds in her lap betokens summer, probably 1825. Their withdrawing room is papered with a broad regency stripe and on the long wall hangs an important oil — a high heathland, lit by a bright streak low in the sky and with the houses of a village in the background. Harriet is seated before it in the corner of a red scroll-ended sofa. On the side wall can be seen a large, handsome, concave glass with golden ball ornamentation round the cavetto. It is flanked by an elegant wall lustre, no doubt one of a pair.

In the office where quill in hand, Thomas in flowing house-coat and red slippers sits in a wing armchair at one end of his knee-hole desk, there hangs over the fireplace a large oil that must be a *Moonlight* by Old Crome. The paintings in both rooms (the other may well be by the Norwich master also) are set off in sumptuous frames.

The artist has caught the look of Churchyard's seemingly perpetual youth. Already into his twenty-eighth year at least, he is as boyish as though still on the top form at Dedham. Fair curly hair, round face with straight nose, full sensuous mouth; a smile of assured satisfaction and high future hopes. Harriet's dark curls cluster above an unusually broad forehead, gloriously arched eyebrows and intensely bright blue eyes; her face narrows daintily to a little chin, below a small mouth set in a pretty bow. She inclines her head slightly forward and to one side: poised, enigmatic and desirable. One can think that the painter saw in them a well-matched, well-pleased pair of lovers.

Eighteen months after young Tom, the first of the daughters was christened Ellen. On this occasion the parents invited the child's great-uncle Isaac of Byng Hall as godfather: for godmothers her grandmother, Anne Churchyard of Melton and Mary Elizabeth Hailes, the young aunt from St Nicholas, Ipswich. Captain George R.N. is not named as having a part in either ceremony although living so near Woodbridge. It suggests that Harriet favoured her mother rather than him.

In October 1825 Jonathan II died in the family house at Melton. He was 56, young for a Churchyard whose five immediate progenitors in the male line had averaged twenty years longer. He left his house to his wife, together with the acre of meadow behind it that had been the first, small grazing where Old Jonathan had started to draw in animals for Smithfield. His widow was to have also the whole of the "plate, linen, wearing appearel, books and all furniture of what nature or kind soever which shall be in my dwelling house at the time of my decease". All his other personal estate was to be converted into money and given to his wife and son, to be equally divided between them share and share alike. It is the first time in the family that, in addition to silver, books had become sufficiently important to be mentioned. To all this Thomas knew himself to be sole heir.

That same October there arrived in the town an engaging young man of nineteen, who was to become Churchyard's staunchest friend in workaday Woodbridge. Benjamin Moulton from Worlingworth had tried his hand as assistant to the master of Laxfield Charity School, and afterwards endured a few months as a timber merchant's clerk before seeking a life of greater variety in the office of Mr Cana the auctioneer. Sales, valuations, affidavits, insurances, writs, laying Exchequer informations, writing bills, collecting them — every day a different day — are recorded in the diary that he kept in Simpson's Gentleman's Almanack and Pocket Journal for the year of our Lord 1827. Almost the first action of his new employment was to fee Churchyard in the sum of £3 "to sopenia (sic) Clarke of Brandeston".

His own time is recorded as being passed very agreeably, nor did he hesitate to add to it by taking a couple of days off to go shooting or attending Tannington Races: away to Ipswich also, to the more fashionable races there and to the uproarious chairing of the Tory-members who had unseated the Yellows on a parliamentary election petition. In Woodbridge he attended half-price performances at the theatre; "skaiting" on the Canal in the Abbey grounds, fishing, ten-pin bowling. He was for ever buying a new dog and sometimes losing him. He was confirmed by the Bishop of Chichester; sat to have his likeness taken; went to balls at the Volunteer and the White Horse, frequently winning and losing at cards; spent any number of "very comfortable" evenings at a variety of hostelries, or with young ladies whose names are entered in cipher; beat a friend in shooting for a bottle of wine.

Dog and gun were indeed his ruling passion and when he bought a new piece for £7 from Oxborrow the gunsmith on Market Hill, he celebrated by dining off chops with his friend Josselyn and getting very drunk. Shooting entries out-top all others in the diary — every bird and beast is found in the bag; the walking them up is recorded in a dozen different parishes. All Saints Day being noted in the Pocket Book as "Holiday at the Bank, Exchequer and South Sea House" Moulton excused himself from the office to go "Shooting all day". On others it was "up in the morning early after rabbits" or "to Orford Shooting Beach Birds home 3 o'clock morning" or "fell into the mud, shot 1 Brace Snipes". The entry for 14th September records "Shooting with T. Churchyard." The previous week he had won five pence off him: at Brag probably, the game most frequently mentioned. It had not taken the two devoted field sportsmen long to discover that, despite the disparity of ten years in their ages, they enjoyed one-another's company as bright kindred spirits.

The Ipswich *Journal* of that 1st September carried the announcement "Sunday last died at Melton, after a painful affliction, aged 65, Captain Hailes, R.N." By this time a numerous family had been arriving at the Well Street house. Thomas and Ellen were followed by Emma in May 1828, Laura in the March of 1830 and Anna in January 1832. This was to be the year of destiny in the lawyer-artist's career. A chain of circumstances had linked itself together during the first decade of his practising in Woodbridge that was to draw him away into a more hazardous field.

VI

Artistic acquaintances

AT FIRST sight it seems strange that a considerable number of London artists with no obvious connection with Woodbridge should have become closely acquainted with the town in the first third of the century. The originator of all this was a practising connoisseur, Perry Nursey, who through his easy friendships with nationally recognised painters, had become regarded as the oracle on matters artistic in this corner of Suffolk. Shortly after qualifying as a surgeon, he had secured the hand and fortune of a ward in Chancery that enabled him to lay aside the scapula, and practise as an amateur with the pencil and palette. From The Grove, the largest house in Little Bealings, three miles from Woodbridge, he first sent up his works to the Academy in 1799. A few years later, an ever growing circle of painters in the metropolis began being invited to enjoy his hospitality and life passed very stylishly as he set himself up as a devotee of the Picturesque. A fourth son was christened Poussin Hazard while from 1806 there were girls, Corinthea, Mariette Syrani, Fontance Lavinia and Rosalba Violante. It had grown to be an obsession with their father that at least one son should become a great painter and in 1816 there came a boy to be christened Claude Lorrain Richard Wilson Nursey.

Meanwhile Perry had engrossed himself in landscaping and early "began to improve his estate and laid out his grounds in the best style of ornamental planting"*. In January 1814 he had written to the short-lived *East Anglian Magazine* "A letter on Picturesque Gardening, Painting and Rural Improvements of Established Residences, addressed to the Nobility and Gentry . . . with a few recommendatory Hints" (five thousand words) offering his services "by no means on extravagant terms". It was indeed an advertising puff. He attacked the "tame

---

* A. Page, *Topographical and Genealogical history of Suffolk* (Ipswich 1847) p. 43.

insipidity'' of such celebrated Improvers as William Kent, Capability
Brown and Humphry Repton whose fault lay in not themselves being
practical painters. They should have learnt their craft through producing canvases in the manner of Poussin, Claude Lorrain and
Richard Wilson.

Nursey was certainly, by this time, well acquainted with Constable;
for a month after the *Letter*, being up in Town he dropped into the
painter's studio and gave it as his opinion that ''the picture of Willy
Lott's house . . . promises well in masses et cetera and tones''*.

Next summer Constable, on his annual visit to East Bergholt, at the
request of the Rev. F. H. Barnwell an antiquarian parson at Bury,
came over to Woodbridge on the 31st July to paint the picturesque little
church of nearby Brightwell, quaintly refashioned in the unlikely years
of the Commonwealth†. His commission completed he remained a further five days in the neighbourhood, on the 3rd of August making a
drawing of Woodbridge across the Deben from Sutton Hoo‡. He may
well have become one of the many artists who, like his great friend
David Wilkie, several times in these years enjoyed Nursey's hospitality
at The Grove. In a thank-you letter of 1816 the young Scot wrote of
''the happy days'' enjoyed there when he brought with him his, and
Constable's, ''old friend Stothard'', the Academy's Librarian. Other
letters tell of bringing his mother who found everything there ''extra-
ordinar''§.

Constable's Brightwell visit of 1815 is probably the occasion when he
made acquaintance of the Pulhams, for Mrs Pulham was also of the
local artistic circle. Certainly in September of the next year the attorney was able to write the great painter on familiar terms. He asked him
to pay an urgent visit to Brightwell once again¶, this time to take the
likeness of its ''venerable Clergyman before he goes hence and is seen
no more,'' for he would not be alive, he was almost certain, in
November. It was all to be done to oblige a young lady whose ardent
wish it was to have his portrait. The scheming lawyer knew the contents of the parson's will and that the protégée would ''be much
benefited by the death of her friend''. Everything most discreet. No
names put into writing. In fact the Rev John Clarke recovered to continue in the incumbency a further fifteen years, actively farming in
three parishes and keeping a cellar of ''fine flavoured Port . . . which

---

* *John Constable's Correspondence*, ed R. B. Beckett (Suffolk Records Society, Ipswich 1962) I,
101.
† Recently identified and acquired by the Tate Gallery.
‡ Beckett has this noted in error as being of Sutton Hoo from Woodbridge.
§ British library, MS Additional 29991.
¶ *John Constable's Correspondence*, ed. R. B. Beckett (Suffolk Records Society, Ipswich 1966) IV,
88.

realised very high prices.'' A bachelor of 82 he outlived Pulham and his last will made no mention of the ardent young lady.

From the hastily arranged sittings at Brightwell Vicarage there sprang a close association between the Pulhams and Constable. They called on him when in Town visiting their son James Brook Pulham, notably for the Academy of 1817 where hung the young man's portrait by his father-in-law Pierre Violet, Louis XVI's miniaturist escaped to London from the Revolution. Next spring the attorney commissioned the masterly portrait of Mrs Pulham, for which she sat in the London studio.

His method in acquiring his first Constable landscapes seems to have been not so admirable. That July he wrote Constable to say that an anonymous acquaintance of his (names he never mentioned) wished for two of the artist's paintings: one must be of Dedham Church. If they could be sent to Woodbridge, with the lowest prices, he would see what he could do for him. Two months later he reported that the anonymous gentleman liked the picture but not the price. Liking it himself he would take it instead ''and keep the price secret'' if Constable would reduce it to 20 guineas. The other he would also take ''and leave the price to you knowing that you will not hurt a poor lawyer''. It is unfortunate for Pulham that Davy gives him a bad reputation, for it raises the thought that the undisclosed client was from the start the attorney himself, beating down a poor artist. A few months later the indigent lawyer was commissioning a marble bust of himself by the sculptor Goblet that was exhibited in the 1820 Academy.

Devious as the attorney was he can be praised for his early admiration of Constable's landscape painting. When calling at the studio he had seen versions of the artist's *Helmingham Dell* on which he was working and said he must have one. That which Pulham later took was to play a cataclysmic part in Churchyard's career as an artist. It went down to Woodbridge in 1826 and the lawyer had from then, four years ''ere I go to my long home'' in which to enjoy the ''handy works'' of which he told the painter he was ''so fond''. He died on 2 May 1830, having seen to it that his will, so different from that of lawyer White, should give away the least possible information about himself. Close as an oyster he left everything to his wife except what it would cost to provide a number of ''mourning rings to those I have mentioned to her''. As usual, no names.

While there were in the neighbourhood these comings and goings of celebrated London artists, Churchyard was pressing on in his determination some day to match them at their level. The progression of his art is difficult to trace with certainty, for he dated almost nothing throughout his life. In his early years after qualifying he had worked at improving his skill by copying the Cromes that he owned; copying "with such faithful exactitude", Loder said, "as on more than one occasion to deceive the most eminent connoisseurs!" In him "he revelled and delighted" as the one who opened up the path along which he too made his way: no longer the idealised classical patterns into which Poussin and Claude Lorrain fitted their grand landscapes but the scenes of Norfolk wrought into splendid compositions of Natural Landscape Painting.

With young George James Rowe, son of an ex-army surgeon come to practise in Well Street after Waterloo, Thomas struck up a painting friendship that continued through life. Rowe, trained in London and nearly seven years the junior, must have been attracted as were other bright ambitious young men, by the still youthful enthusiasm, and already considerable achievements of the lawyer-painter. Three lines only by a single historian of the minor painters of the 19th Century seem to be all that is written about Rowe's landscapes, shown through more than thirty years in the major London exhibitions: nothing about his engravings during forty years of living in the Capital, nor of the close on eight hundred sketches, now stored in the vaults of the Putnam Museum, Davenport, Iowa (with some by his friend Churchyard as well). Col. Grant describes his Woodbridge watercolours as depicting "the sweet scenery of the country in a mellow style, tending to the browns and ochres of the old Norwich School." There are some apparently early sketches from nature by Churchyard that could be similarly described, giving a feeling of time arrested; a placid winter afternoon with the sun obscured in a spread of cloud, below which it lights a broad streak of "the orange and pale violet evening sky". Not only does it seem that he could match what was being painted in Norwich at the time, his great *Kyson Point, Woodbridge* shows how thoroughly he understood the earlier achievement of Old Crome himself.

To become known, showing at the Exhibitions was essential; that of the Norwich Society was a natural choice. Churchyard was first off the mark in 1829 with three *Studies from Nature* and a fourth *Sketch from Nature*. He did not offer them for sale but they caught the eye of the reporter on the *Norwich Mercury* who thought them as good as those of the professionals and wrote "There are some pieces worthy artists by several amateurs particularly two sketches from nature by Mr. Churchyard". On the strength of this first sending-in he was elected an Honorary Member of the Institution and his name appears in their annual lists from 1829 to 1833. Not so his pictures. Nor did he ever attend their Artists' Conversatziones presided over with such aplomb by Old Crome's son, the genial and extravagant John Berney Crome.

After so encouraging a start, not to have exhibited there again would seem strange were it not typical, in all Churchyard's ways, of his distaste for repetition. Moreover, having been declared equal to professionals in the provinces he now sought to match himself with those in the capital. In 1830 he sent to the exhibition of the Society of British Artist at Suffolk Street a watercolour, *A Sketch in the Neighbourhood of Woodbridge, Suffolk* and two oils, *A Cottage at Bredfield, Suffolk* and *A Lane at Melton, Suffolk*. This season Rowe was in the lead, for in addition to Norwich, he was accepted at the Academy itself. Next year Thomas achieved the like ambition, being represented at Somerset House in 1831 by *A Drawing from Nature*. At Suffolk Street, too, were a couple of his watercolours, *Landscape* and *Sketch from Nature*.

A Drawing from Nature, Sketch from Nature, Study from Nature: it was the natural painting of landscape that throughout his life continued to be Churchyard's unceasing concern.

VII

The collapse of his fortunes

THE ONLY new piece of Churchyard information to come to light in the twenty years following the death of the last of his daughters appeared in the *East Anglian Magazine* of June 1947. A Mr E. C. Jennings of Felixstowe wrote a letter saying that he ''owned some delightful little water-colour drawings of Thomas' '' and also a priced 1866 catalogue of the lawyer's collection of pictures auctioned after his death.

''I also have a catalogue of his father's effects which were sold April 2nd, 1832. His father, although a lawyer, must have been an above-the-average painter judging from the number of his own oil paintings in the sale''. The pamphlet read ''The Catalogue of the Modern Household Furniture, Paintings, Drawings, Prints, Valuable Law and other Library and effects of Mr Churchyard, Seckford Street, Wood-bridge,'' (the name had been changed from Well Street a short time earlier) ''to be sold by auction by B. Moulton on Monday, April 2nd, 1832 and following day''. It was a sale not of Jonathan's effects, he had been dead six years, but of his son Thomas's.

There was itemised a thoroughgoing sell-up that would leave the family, blessed already with five small children ranging from seven years to three months, denuded of the household necessities of life. Their dining-table, set of mahogany chairs, carpets, hearthrugs, beds, chests of drawers, washstand, Ransomes Patent mangle, child's dining chair, a cradle in the Nursery, the connubial bedstead from Bedroom No. 1 — all were to be disposed of in Monday's auction. Tuesday saw the sale of the attorney's extensive library including the valuable reference books of the law office. These were in forty-two lots made up of a great number of Reports, Precedents, Commentaries, Pleas of the Court, Jacob's Law Dictionary, works by Reeve, Watlings, Impey, Sugden, etc. Without them it was difficult to see how the bread-winner would be able to continue to practise.

That so much should be going under the hammer conjured up the picture of a desperate plight. It gave rise to an immediate assumption that the disposal could only have been forced upon Churchyard in an effort to stave off pressing creditors. "His near bankruptcy sale" was the designation that an early writer gave it. The guess became adopted as an established fact and now, dramatised as "the collapse of his fortunes", the phrase is freely copied from pen to pen.

In the hunt to discover what more could be found to shed light on the unexpected happenings of 1832, it was noticed in the Rate Book that after the sale of its contents the Churchyard home in Seckford Street came into other occupation. Thomas and his family were not entered anywhere in the town in the year's rating list drawn up at Easter 1833. The next mention of his name to be noticed in 1947 was in Pigot's Directory 1839, where under Woodbridge is shown the firm of Churchyard, Meadows and Everitt, Solicitors, Market Hill. Romantically minded writers filled the vacuum by postulating seven years in the wilderness: "Churchyard's Hidden Period" during which he kept well out of sight of Woodbridge, practising as a junior partner somewhere where his debts were not known, till he could at length afford to return and repay. A sojourn perhaps near London or in the West Country that would account for a number of paintings by him of scenes in Sussex, Devon and Somerset.

The true nature of the events of 1832 is very different. The explanation of what was in train is to be found in Ben Moulton's preliminary newspaper advertisements of the forthcoming sale. It was to be of "The Genteel Household Furniture, Valuable Law and other Books, Paintings and effects of Mr Churchyard, Seckford Street, Woodbridge, who is changing his residence and his profession". He was on the point of abandoning the calling of an attorney and becoming full time a painter in London.

Moulton, in his advertisement, included only a few sketches and prints and a couple of paintings from Churchyard's collection. One, a *Cupid and Psyche* by Violet must have been a post-wedding present from the Pulhams. As the close old lawyer was now dead the picture's being publicly sold could give no offence to the donor, buried beneath an imposing tomb with urn and armorial bearings, prominent in St Mary's graveyard. It was not these pictures, though, that Moulton billed as being the chief attraction in this part of the sale. They came as merely a tailpiece to "A collection of Landscapes, Marine and other pieces, in oil and watercolour by the Proprietor". Today's collectors accustomed to the typical eight by ten inch Churchyard landscape oils would be startled in identifying his "*Deben looking towards Martlesham Creek*", 36 inches by 50. There were several others 19 by 24. With Churchyard about to set himself up as a professional landscape painter it was a helpful hand by his sporting companion to suggest the "Proprietor's" works as the most important pictures in Tuesday's sale.

The wild risking of a young family's future in the uncertainties of an artist's life, was a decisioin that had been come to after thoughts first raised maybe three years earlier. Thereafter there followed the strangely isolated series of his sending into the Exhibitions — Norwich 1829, Suffolk Street 1830, The Academy 1831. If the long-standing Woodbridge belief that Churchyard once sketched there with Constable is well founded, the May of 1830 is the most likely date. When lawyer Pulham died that spring Constable hurried down to buy back from the widow the *Helmingham Dell* and maybe the two earlier landscapes, presumably to prevent them going into an auction in the country, where there was risk of damage to his reputation were they to be knocked down at paltry bids, unappreciated in a local sale. He did not return to London before spending some time sketching in the neighbourhood*. An outing with Churchyard would have provided further stimulus to him, having come, already thus early, to understanding something of the East Bergholt master's urge to paint the day, not merely the place. One of the "Proprietor's" oils in the Seckford Street sale was titled "*Landscape and figures — showery weather*".

The change of residence and profession followed, in fact, not from a collapse, but from an accession of fortune. The *deus ex machina* who provided the solid means that could support the family for a year or two, come what might, was none other than the traditional, rich bachelor uncle from away. It was in the Spring of 1829 that the Will was proved of Young Tom's godfather, Charles Churchyard, gentleman, of 29 Cornhill, London, the banking house where he had passed all his adult life. He was the second son of Jonathan the elder and some time before 1793 had gone up to the City and entered the service of Mason, Currie, James and Yalleby as junior clerk.

Curries had been a small bank with a staff of only four when Charles joined it. In ten years he rose to become Chief Clerk, a position of considerable importance next to the partners, and one that he filled for the succeeding quarter of a century. The esteem in which he came to be held is testified to by the fact that when, at the end of 1827, he retired from his rule over then fourteen juniors, he had been allowed to continue to live on in the private quarters at 29 Cornhill.

It was not unusual for the Chief Clerk in a City house of the standing of Curries to become a man of substance. Charles was no exception. Part of the wealth thus acquired he invested in land in the neighbourhood of Woodbridge. First he bought a "freehold estate, farm lands

---

* Holmes has its church tower titled in error as "Woodford".

Kyson Point, Woodbridge. Oil on board, 56 x 23cm. The Rev. E. C.
Charlesworth

Lawyer's Lane, Melton. Watercolour, 24.7 x 17.1cm. Christchurch
  Mansion, Ipswich

and marsh in the Parish of Ramsholt;'' later Brooks and Lynns Farms lying in Clopton and Burgh. Finally he added Bakers, also in Clopton, the parish in which his sister Ann owned their father's old farm, Floreys. James and Isaac at Pettistree became tenants of them all. The gradual building up of such a Churchyard holding is typical: there was close rapport between the brother who had taken the London Road to the City and the rest of the family who had remained in the rural heartland.

When Charles came to make his dispositions he adhered to the Churchyard practice of keeping things very much in the family. He left his youngest brother Isaac of Pettistree, yeoman, the three farms he had owned longest, together with ''£1,000 standing in my name in the 3½% annuities in the Books of the Governors and Company of the Bank of England.'' James had only Bakers Farm but in addition a compensatory £2,000. To his spinster sisters Ann and Hannah he left £1,000 each, free from the control, debts or engagements of any husband with whom they might marry: an ultra careful provision by his lawyer, for both were already well into their fifties. For the rest of their lives they were to have also the interest on a further thousand pounds each in the four per cents. At their death this capital to go back into his estate, of which Isaac was the residuary legatee.

To his nephew Thomas of Woodbridge in the County of Suffolk, gentleman, he bequeathed £500 sterling, while a further £500 was to be invested ''for the benefit of my Great Nephew Thomas, son of Thomas, to pay and apply the dividends and interest for the maintenance and education of the said Thomas till 21, then to his absolute use.'' A few days before his death, Charles had kindly thoughts about some of the clerks and servants with whom he had been associated so long at Number Twenty-Nine. A codicil distributed about £600 among seven recipients.

However fancifully Churchyard may, before 1829, have dreamed of becoming full time a professional painter, his uncle's bequest on top of those of his grandfather and father now made the attempt possible. He had enough to support his family for the time that it would take to establish himself in the art world. In the public exhibitions of the three past years he had been able, he must have thought, to equate his achievement with that of the professionals, but to achieve fame he must work in London. The adventure seems to have been well planned with Rowe, his painting companion, for both made their first moves at almost the same time. Mr Giles auctioneer and appraiser, advertised that on 15th July 1831 at the White Horse on Market Hill he would sell ''a hundred lots of Prints, Drawings, Paintings and Grease Drawings of Mr George Rowe, Drawing Master, who is leaving the town.''

Seven weeks after Rowe's sale Churchyard added to his resources by

turning into cash the splendid paintings of the English Landscape
School that he had started to collect in his bachelor days. The auctioneer Mr Cana aiming at a more distinguished clientele than did Mr
Giles "had the honour to announce to the Nobility, Gentry and the
Public, that he had been instructed to sell by auction at the Crown Inn
on Monday 5th September a small but very choice and valuable collection of Paintings, the property of Mr Thos. Churchyard; consisting
chiefly of Works of some of the most esteemed Masters of the British
School — Gainsborough, Morland, Old John Crome, and others; but
containing a few brilliant Paintings by Old Masters, splendidly framed
and in fine condition". The walls of the little rooms at Seckford Street
must have been even more gloriously arrayed than the brief sights of
them in the portraits show.

The pictures were fit companions for the rows of handsomely bound
books standing on the shelves there — six volumes of Voltaire's
Philosophical Dictionary; seven of the Orations of Demosthenes and
Cicero; fifteen of Hume and Smollett's History of England; twenty of
Buffon's Natural History; the complete poems of Byron and all
eighteen volumes of Sharpe's Elegant Extracts. This was the comfortable establishment that Churchyard was giving up on the chance of
establishing himself in lodgings in London, there to demonstrate
something new in the portrayal of his ancestors' countryside. Non-
chalantly, the householder did not concern himself to stay in Woodbridge and learn then and there how much the very choice and
valuable paintings and the handsomely bound books fetched. He had
gone away on a sketching visit to the Wiltshire Downs. On September
4 he was at Market Lavington and a few days before or after had been
in Dorset in the Blackmoor Vale, doing watercolour drawings near
Marnhull and Gillingham.

The prevailing mood of the Norwich School had been calm. The
excitement that impelled Churchyard to his rash move may perhaps
have sprung from his having grasped the fount of Constable's inspiration — the movement of "Light and shadow upon landscape" and his
endeavours "to arrest the more abrupt and transient appearances of
CHIAR'OSCURO IN NATURE . . . to give one brief moment
caught from fleeting time a lasting and sober existence"*.

The sale of April 1832 whose rediscovery has given rise to such
fundamental misunderstanding of Churchyard's story, was, accordingly, only the final move in the steps that he was taking to change his
whole life. Many in Woodbridge must have thought the dashing young
man crazy. Ten years a lawyer, outshining all the other local attorneys,
he was now off to London, not as a portrait painter, an art which

* *John Constable's Discourses*, ed. R. B. Beckett (Suffolk Records Society, Ipswich 1970).

people respected and would pay for, but going for landscapes — all a matter of chance that nobody had commissioned. With five small children, the youngest a baby of twelve weeks, Harriet's parting with the household stuff suggests that for the time being she and the family remained behind to share grandmamma Churchyard's ample and amply provided house at Melton.

The bachelor Rowe had delayed his departure and sent up his 1832 Academy picture still from his parents' home at Woodbridge. It suggests that when his married friend had at last made all his more complicated arrangements, they left together after Thomas's second sale and shared a London studio.

Churchyard could hardly have chosen a more inopportune time for setting forth to stake out a claim in the placid field of the arts. People's heads were filled with political excitements and within a month of the Seckford Street sale the tension over the passing of the Reform Bill brought in the dramatic Days of May, when for a week many in the country believed that Wellington would be coming back to rule by the sword. Instead he had withdrawn in hauteur and later, in eclipse plumage at the start of the shooting season, was reported as enjoying at Sudbourne "with other distinguished Noblemen and Gentlemen the pleasures of the field and the princely table of the Marquis of Hertford". At the Hall it was just as at Coningsby Castle and Beaumanoir: "the noble, the beautiful and the celebrated gathered together in rooms not unworthy of them"; to which "the guests came not merely to slaughter the Duke's pheasants but to hold council on the prospects of the party." The agent at Sudbourne was able to inform My Lord Marquis that the poachers were likely to have not such an easy passage when brought up before the Woodbridge bench in future. The little pettifogger who had been getting so many of them acquitted had given up and gone off somewhere to be a painter.

Charles's disposal around the family presaged a bright financial future. Thomas was the sole descendant in the second generation of Jonathan the elder. His four uncles and aunts at Pettistree were all childless. Isaac, youngest of them, 47 in 1832, would likely remain a bachelor. There were great expectations. Time, however, was not altogether on the painter's side. Churchyards were, most of them, a long lived lot and many years were to pass before he was to know how the final accounts of that old family fortune would be struck. It was otherwise with his new profession, where, in only a few months he experienced the collapse of his hopes.

VIII

Little Country Town

"God made the country, man the town,
And the devil the little country town".
Suffolk saying.

IT WAS to number Seven, Upper Stamford Street, London that Churchyard went. Stamford Street had been developed only a few years before, running westwards from the Surrey end of Blackfriars Bridge to the newer Waterloo Bridge. Much of it has now been rebuilt but there remains an impressive terrace of Regency houses and in one similar to these he played out the gamble of establishing himself as a great landscape painter. The Lambeth rate book of 1832 shows as householder living near the beginning of the street (house numbers are not given) a "Jno. Obbard". The families of Obbards living in London in those days can be numbered on the fingers of the hand and one of them owned a glass and lead factory in Blackfriars Road, a few minutes walk away; so it may be that Thomas lodged with a close relative of his sister-in-law Susan of Horseferry Road.

What early moves he made towards establishing his name, beyond sending a very few pictures to the exhibitions, remain undiscovered. In 1832 there had been an oil and a watercolour of his at Suffolk Street but in 1833 beset as ever with restlessness and change, he threw in his lot instead with the New Society of Painters in Watercolour, founded a twelvemonth earlier, and exhibited a single item *Lane Scene with Cattle*.

What success came to him in this new profession does not appear. The inescapable conclusion is that the gamble was a failure. If, as he was almost bound to do, he submitted landscapes to the Academy in 1832 and 1833 they had been marked with the fatal chalk cross by the Selecting Council.

Equally depressing was news of difficulties overtaking established landscape painters well known to him in the smaller world of East Anglia. The affairs of Perry Nursey who, like himself, had exchanged the safety of a learned profession for the chance of an artist's life, and more recently given up landscaping for architecture, were going from bad to worse. From Norwich came the news that John Berney Crome •was in Queer Street. In less than a year's time both were declared bankrupt.

Before either of these cases became *in extremis*, a disaster occurred that struck home so very closely. It was the catastrophe detailed in the *Morning Chronicle*'s report of the sale at Christie's on 28th June 1833. ''Another lot we may notice, as its public estimation may serve to teach a little modesty to the Royal Academicians in their demands. A good sized *Dell Scene* by Mr Constable R.A., in his usual style, and we would say preferable to anything he has in the present exhibition at the Academy, was knocked down at fifty shillings''.

Churchyard knew the Helmingham picture better than almost anyone, for it had hung in lawyer Pulham's house for four years till 1830 when Constable came down to Woodbridge to buy it back. Although it had been secured so that it did not go for a song amid a disposal of surplus furniture in a little country town sale, an auction by Cana or Moulton could not have rated it as low as a beggerly two pounds ten. Yet this was the figure, so he read, at which connoisseurs now valued it in the most noted of all auction rooms.

What he did not know was the extraordinary series of mischances that brought about so bizarre an outcome of the *Dell*'s sale: how after its new owner's death it had been sent in too late for cataloguing, so that several enthusiastic Constable collectors who had come to do battle for it had left the rooms thinking it was not in the auction after all; how at the very end of the day when it was offered verbally from the rostrum it failed to interest those few remaining, who in view of the way it was put up doubted its authenticity: how Mr Christie, sensing the position, hurriedly knocked it down at fifty shillings to a friend of the late owner, thinking he had thus saved it for the widow whose property it then was.

All this would have come out had Constable not been dissuaded by his friends from suing the *Chronicle*, whose critic was the ''assassin'' who for several years had carried out a vendetta against him and his painting. Knowing nothing of these things Churchyard was left believing that if this was as much as the public nowadays would pay for an important landscape nearly two and a half feet by three, by an accepted Academician, there could be no livelihood for an obscure disciple just starting out and at such a distance behind. His notion of changing from lawyer to artist may have matured only slowly over three years or longer. The decision to revert from artist to lawyer was altogether more precipitate. At the time of the second exhibition of the New Watercolour Society in 1833 he had still every intention of continuing full time as a painter. He is listed in the catalogue as one of the professional artists who had paid next year's subscription in advance. Before the third exhibition opened he was back in Woodbridge practising once more as an attorney: Rowe was back too.

The interlude could not have improved his image as a shrewd country town lawyer. To a remarkable degree, however, he seemed careless of what people thought. Loss of face did not drive him to seek fresh surroundings any more than it had done over his marriage. It was otherwise with his painting where though working at it most days of his life, to all intents he eschewed public exhibition ever again. During the more than thirty years that he pursued his way towards an honourable place in English Landscape Painting, virtually his only critics were his friends, his family and himself.

In haste to get re-established as a Woodbridge attorney, Churchyard had been driven to take a makeshift office in Quay Lane, adjoining a coal and corn merchant's premises. Suitable as it was for the poachers, something in smarter professional surroundings was needed to reinstate himself in the eyes of more important citizens.

Already by the second week in November he was busy dealing with the Will of his father's cousin Isaac Churchyard, the butcher on Market Hill who was clearly not going to last more than a few weeks. For the next quarter of a century he was plagued from time to time with the affairs of that unlucky branch of the family. From the point of view, however, of the historian it was a fortunate association, for it brings to light some contemporary sightings of the lawyer in his last years, and of the household after his death, that have not been found in any other source.

This Isaac was second son of Henry the butcher of Ufford, eldest of the six boys of Charsfield, who had made an even more promising start in business than his brother Jonathan, but had died early of smallpox in the family's sad year of 1785. Isaac had been already into his thirties when he married Sarah Smith of Woodbridge. Two years later, in the summer of 1807 he purchased for £540 a butcher's shop, dwelling-house and slaughterhouse on Woodbridge Market Hill. The auctioneer's announcement had described it as extensive, valuable and good accustomed; but Isaac might have taken warning from the fact that it was billed as being part of the Estate and Effects of Mr George Cole, bankrupt, and the place had remained unsold in the assignees' hands for two and a half years.

A daughter Susan was born in 1810, a son Isaac in 1816 and when the boy was only three months old their mother died. A few weeks later the butcher made his original Will and, looking well ahead, left to his Young Isaac when he attained the age of 21 the premises, with a charge on them to provide a legacy of £200 to Susan.

In 1824 he married again: another Smith, Lucy a country woman of Great Bealings, half his age. In 1830 an only child of this second marriage was born, a boy christened Henry after his grandfather. The November of 1833 found the butcher now 62, failing. His lawyer kinsman by then returned, was called in to deal with matters that had been causing such anxiety of late. His affairs were found to be in sorry shape. It would be necessary to revoke not only the gift to his executor Isaac of Byng Hall but, more serious, the charge in favour of Susan as well. To soften the blow when the Will would be read, the attorney framed the necessary words of explanation. The excisions had had to be made ''by reason of my property being greatly diminished by recent losses. And whereas since making my last Will I have married a wife and have issue of her one infant son and I am desirous of making out of my little property some provision for their support, Lucy to be permitted to occupy the aforesaid dwelling house and butcher's shop for 3 years for £15 only, that she may carry on and establish a business.'' There was nothing else for her beyond a legacy of £20.

Next day worse was to ensue. The lawyer discovered that the butcher had made use of a hundred pounds out of a legacy left for the children of the first marriage, by an Aunt Rolle, the said legacy to be paid upon their coming of age. It had already gone in educating his son Isaac and apprenticing him as a druggist and chemist. Nor was this all. There was a promissory note to Isaac of Byng Hall for a further £50 similarly expended. As Young Isaac, the indentured druggist, was still a minor he could not give a release and the two debts had in consequence to be charged on the ill-omened premises. Isaac died on the 25th of the month. There was no provision for the infant Henry beyond the hope that Lucy could run the business successfully and so bring him up. Very practically she employed her brother Robert Smith to deal with the harsh day to day work. It was a promising start but the unkind fates had further calamities in store for this star-crossed branch of the family.

By the time Churchyard resumed practice the Game Laws had been altered root and branch. The Acts of 1829 and 1831 abolished the Qualified Person and substituted for him the holder of a Game Licence. They did little to improve the lot of the farmer. Landlords owned the sporting rights and inevitably withheld them from their tenants. An article in *The Times* spoke of ''cartloads of hares sent to market knocked on the head and sold to game dealers and fishmongers at ninepence a piece to the landowner's profit, each of which has done half a crown's worth of damage to his tenant's farm . . . They dare not complain or they would be looked upon as dissatisfied characters, and be got rid of at the termination of their leases.''

The new laws were complicated in the extreme. Whether the wrongdoer was liable to be searched, detained, fined, imprisoned or transported — each of these depended on a multitude of different circumstances: whether the offence were by day or by night, on week-day or Sunday; the nature of the bird or beast and what was being employed to take it. Had it been taken already or was it still being searched for; was the taker the proprietor of the soil, tenant, servant or trespasser; was it on open land or enclosed; on a public road or path; did the miscreant give or withhold his name, attempt to avoid capture or offer violence: was he acting by himself, with a companion or in a gang? A gamekeeper could not detain on the highroad, a policeman could not enter the fields to make an arrest. Churchyard rapidly got it all to his fingertips and so was able to expose the most unexpected defect in an indictment: to display every fact in a light surprisingly favourable to his own case.

His move from the inappropriate Quay Lane was achieved by entering into partnership with a young attorney Edwin Church Everitt, who had qualified only as recently as August 1832, and had opened with an impressive address in Thoroughfare. Before a year passed, the growing practice of Churchyard and Everitt needed more ample accommodation. Marsden House near the start of Cumberland Street* was taken, Everitt to live there and set part of it aside as their law office.

Churchyard chose to live at Melton, renting The Beeches, one of the pleasant short red-brick terrace of three that marked the western end of the built-up village. It stands on the north side of the street at its junction with the lane to Hasketon. The Beeches looks sideways across Lawyer's Lane, at the distinguished home of the Wood family on the opposite corner. The Churchyards's double-fronted house is now much hidden by the six great conjoined trunks standing before it, that must have been considerable timber already at the time the family were living there.

It was at the Beeches that the sixth child Elizabeth was born on 2nd July 1834, which suggests that her father may have returned from London at the end of the previous September. In March 1836 there arrived another daughter christened Harriet after her mother, and following her in December 1837 a second son, Charles, who survived only till the next autumn.

Late in 1834 another slice of the family fortune came the lawyer's way — £500 under the will of his aunt Ann of Byng Hall. She had had a head for business, like her brother in the City. In addition to having earlier taken over Floreys Farm from her father's executors, she had borrowed of Charles's executors and persuaded Hannah to join with her in investing in the purchase of Hill House, Ufford, a good red-brick

---

* Now named Marston House in lower half of Thoroughfare, now Cumberland Street.

Georgian residence that they let to Sparrow Toms, Esquire. Beside the bequest to her nephew the lawyer, she left Floreys to James; £500 and her moiety in Hill House to Hannah; remainder to Isaac — everything kept in the family and on its way eventually to Thomas.

The decade the followed his abandoning his new profession and returning to the law is to a real extent Churchyard's Hidden Period, spent though it was in the far from hidden world of Woodbridge and Melton. Less is to be seen of him in person then than in any like stretch of his adult years. With the exception of his bidding at a local auction, a call at the office by John Charles Constable, a wedding party at his house and a birthday one there too, there are no occasions when he is brought forward into the limelight. Further afield he did not go entirely unnoticed. Fulcher's Sudbury Pocket Book for 1835 carried a vignette *Melton Spring* titled as by Churchyard, engraved by Hawkesworth, a busy London illustrator of topographical books and the like. It owed its appearance to an introduction by his friend Barton, still tirelessly contributing his verses to such evanescent repositories as the annual Pocket Books that in those days served as handy yuletide presents — a diary to give a friend for use in the forthcoming year.

In Ipswich that Christmas, grandmamma Hailes found herself having to fix up schooling for the two recently-returned sons of Captain John, soldiering with the 4th Native Infantry in India. An unbeneficed cleric, the Reverend Woodthorpe Collett, cousin of the Headmaster of the Grammar School, had advertised that he wished, in his home, to board with his own sons, who were going to the school, ''a few young gentlemen, those of tender age for preference''. This seemed an arrangement well suited to the needs of the young Hailes — John Clements, nearly nine and Charles Metcalfe just seven. So, while boarding privately with the Collett family, they daily entered the larger world of school; going each morning to the old dormitory of the Ipswich Blackfriars, still as it was when their father, a new boy, had passed the winter of '02 in it. With Young John on one of the lower forms sat Edward Byles Cowell, the finest scholar of that generation. Teaching himself Persian, and sending up verse translations of its poetry to the *Asiatic Journal* while still a schoolboy of fifteen, he later taught it to FitzGerald, seventeen years his senior, godfather of the *Rubáiyát*.

At midsummer 1836 the Headship of Woodbridge Grammar School fell vacant and Collett presented himself as a candidate. An Old Boy of the School and nephew of one of the many sisters of the Reverend Thomas Carthew, it is not surprising that he secured the election. The two Hailes moved with him and stayed for a couple of years before passing, the one through Addiscombe, the other through Cheltenham, into the service of John Company. Fifty years later Major-General

John Clements Hailes writing down for his cousins some recollections of his Woodbridge schooldays could tell them little about the town. "Boarders had no associations with the day scholars or allowed to mix with them''.

In the brief three or four years since his return to the law, Churchyard had quickly re-established himself in good standing in the upper echelons of professional Woodbridge. In 1836 his contemporary Rolla Rouse, attorney, also practising in Woodbridge and living in Melton, entered the Middle Temple and was called to the Bar. His wife was Elizabeth Jane, daughter of the Reverend Philip Meadows, rector of Great Bealings. Her eldest brother Daniel Charles, recently qualified as an attorney, came to Woodbridge to take his brother-in-law's place. Within a few months he sought to become a junior partner of Churchyard.

This was a feather in the cap of the cattle-salesman's son. The Meadows considered themselves as being decidedly distinguished in the locality, having been lords of the manor in Witnesham since Jacobean times. The young man's grandfather and great-grandfather had for half a century practised as solicitors at Botesdale. In deference to David Charles' standing the partnership was styled Churchyard, Meadows and Everitt. With three partners, Everitt's house in Cumberland Street no longer gave them adequate elbow room and at the end of 1836 a separate law office was opened on Market Hill, within sight of the shop where Lucy was trying to establish herself in business as a butcher.

There for nearly five years the practice continued. Churchyard's professional hours remain behind a closed door but there are a few sightings of him in private life. On 17th July 1837, from the Beeches, his wife's youngest sister Mary Elizabeth of St Nicholas, Ipswich was married to Henry Clarke of that parish, well-to-do proprietor of a shoe factory in the county town. It occasioned a considerable gathering of young Churchyards and Hailes. The Rev Mr. Collett brought the two young pupils from Woodbridge School and signed the register as one of the witnesses. Into the next century there continued a close association between the cousins though their fates interposed long periods when they could not meet. At the end of the year came sad news for the Hailes boys. Their mother had died in Hissar. She was thirty-six, the same age as Aunt Clarke.

IX

The Death of Constable

IN THE same way that Churchyard was collecting John Cromes in the artist's lifetime, so was he buying works by Constable. Although those contemporaries who knew his painting knew of his debt to Crome, only his close friends understood Constable's influence on him. The tenuous memory of the great painter's visits to Woodbridge has supported the idea that he and Churchyard once sketched together — "used to sketch together" the bolder have declared. There could have been such a day when Constable was in Woodbridge to buy back his paintings from Pulham's widow, for he certainly then made a drawing of the church tower that Churchyard portrayed so often. A paper, however, has been preserved* that points to a much closer association than a few hours sketching together would account for.

When the last Miss Churchyard died, the sole remaining member of the family was her ne'er-do-well brother Charley, then 85. Forthwith a second cousin of theirs, Miss Annie White of Peasenhall, hurried to Woodbridge and "took all letters and family papers with her from this house as she knew that Charlie Churchyard would not be in the least interested. Unfortunately she was elderly at the time and soon became unable to deal with them as she had wished."† To this judicious breach of the strictly judicial is due the saving from a bonfire of a sheet of writing paper that tells of young John Charles Constable, with one of his uncles, calling on Churchyard and giving him a verbal account of his father's death that had taken place only ten days earlier.

The lawyer had learnt of the great painter's end from a paragraph in the *Morning Herald* of April 3rd 1837. He cut out the report that was headed "Death of Mr Constable R.A.". Some of it read strangely.

---

* Manuscript collection, Victoria and Albert Museum.
† Mable Redstone.

"Mr Constable began his career in life at a point very remote from the paths of art, he was originally a miller, near Woodbridge, in Suffolk." The error over his provenance shows how little his career had caught the public's attention and it is ironic that the reporter should have fixed on the Churchyard Country instead of the Vale of Dedham as being the locus of which Constable said "these scenes made me a painter."

The manuscript paper in Churchyard's handwriting is dated 11th April and records, with all the precision of a lawyer taking instructions, the exact scene at No 35 Charlotte Street on the night of 31st March as described to him by John Charles. There is every mark of its having been written down as soon as the visitors had left; in a determination to get the account on to paper in exactly the right form; words deleted and others substituted as he wrote swiftly along; only one slip of the pen corrected afterwards. It opens: "11th April young John Constable and his uncle Golding called and described to me the last hours of Constable." Golding and his brother Abram had gone up from Bergholt to the funeral at Hampstead the previous week. There seems to be no account preserved of events in the Constable family during the ensuing couple of months till young John Charles started to keep a diary on 27th May. It records Golding's return to Suffolk that day. Two months in London would be an impossible stay to be endured by Uncle Golding, an innocent countryman with no ability whatever in life, save that of being a good shot, and who could only with the greatest difficulty ever be induced to be away from Bergholt at all. John Charles, 19, at home "brushing up" for entry to Cambridge, had been so overcome by the shock of his father's dying in his presence so suddenly and so unexpectedly, that he had been unable to attend the funeral. When it was over, it would not be surprising that he should be persuaded by his uncles to return with them to Suffolk within the week, and make there a recovery from his breakdown. 27th May must be Golding's second departure from London after he had accompanied his nephew back to Charlotte Street at the end of a health-giving stay in the Vale.

There was a particular reason why, when in these parts, John Charles should have visited Woodbridge: it enabled him to confer with his cousin the Reverend Daniel Constable Whalley about going up to Cambridge that Michaelmas. Four years earlier, when Daniel himself had graduated, there was talk of his preparing John for matriculation. Mr Whalley had then been licensed as curate of St Mary's Woodbridge at £50 a year and although succeeded in 1835 by the Reverend John Jubilee Reynolds, had remained unbeneficed and in lodgings in the neighbourhood. As late as the summer of 1838 he was still at hand to act as officiating minister at a couple of weddings in the parish church.

Although it was natural that the presence of Daniel should bring uncle and nephew to Woodbridge, it is remarkable that John Charles should have called at the attorney's office and narrated in such detail the event that so short a while before had brought him to a state of nervous prostration. He could hardly have put himself to the pain of communicating this to a mere acquaintance. It becomes understandable if he were seeking out and unburdening to one who was sufficiently well known to himself and his father to be regarded as a friend. For John Charles to be already acquainted with Churchyard it is pretty certain that their meeting place must have been at Charlotte Street.

The son's description of the painter's last hours differs in several respects from that given by Leslie in his "Memoirs of the Life of John Constable." There the painter is reported as having, upon his return home, eaten a hearty supper, had his bed warmed and read himself to sleep between ten and eleven. A little later John Charles back from the theatre and preparing for bed, was called to by his father who had awakened in great pain. He refused to have Mr Michele his doctor summoned but had taken rhubarb and magnesia and drank copiously of warm water, both of which produced sickness. "But the pain increasing, he desired that Mr Michele, his near neighbour, should be sent for who very soon after attended. In the meantime Constable had fainted, his son supposing he had fallen asleep; Mr Michele instantly ordered some brandy to be brought, the bedroom of the patient was at the top of the house, the servant had to run downstairs for it, and before it could be procured, life was extinct; and within half an hour of the first attack of pain. A post mortem investigation was made by Professor Partridge in the presence of Mr George Young and Mr Michele, but strange to say, the extreme pain Constable had suffered could only be traced to indigestion."

Young Constable's account as written down by Churchyard ran thus (Deletions show in brackets): "It appears he retired to bed about eleven after eating bread and cheese and drinking cold water for his supper taking with him a book for the purpose of reading (he felt) shortly after he called his Housekeeper Roberts and desired to have some figs as he was thirsty having no (figs) fruit of that sort some french plums were brought which he ate: he fell asleep but woke complaining of heart-burn and (his son) took from his son a dose of magnesia and rhubard he complained after of exhaustion and giddiness and was sick (bringing up cold) sickness seemed for a time to relieve him but his heart-burn returned and he wanted more magnesia and drank copiously of hot water; his heart-burn still (continued his son persuaded him) continued — after a time he suddenly got out of bed and sat on the side of it in a stooping (possi) position, then went and sat on a chair, rose up again approached (over) the bed raised his hands to his head (muttered) uttered some words and (in the) twisted over on his side (recling) on the bed — after this he never spoke the extremeties became

59

cold and after a gasp or two he expired.

Mr Partridge of King's College ⎫
Mr Young a surgeon ⎪
Mr Drew ⎬ present post mortem
Mr Mechele (sic) ⎭

all healthy but blood did not coagulate which accounts for discolourment of body''.

This is the authentic account, related by the chief spectator on the heels of the event. The differences from that in the *Life* arise from the fact that well before Leslie completed his work, John Charles had been buried in Jesus College Chapel, victim of the dread scarlet fever. The biographer had accordingly to rely upon information put together by ''Mr Michele, in a letter to me, describing all he had witnessed''.

In fact Michele had witnessed nothing. John Charles did not so much as mention him to Churchyard for he had not arrived till Constable was finally unconscious. Perhaps the doctor felt some pique at not having been called earlier by this youth, with his smattering of medical knowledge. The young man was, indeed, in the course of acquiring a modicum at London University, feeling that it would help him in parochial duties after he had graduated and taken Holy Orders. Certainly he knew enough never to have supposed, as the doctor alleged, that his father had fallen asleep. The physician's feelings of self-importance are to be gathered from the jargon in which he dressed up the idea that had the brandy he instantly prescribed been at once available it might perhaps have saved him. He told Leslie that ''it is barely possible that the prompt application of a stimulant might have sustained the vital principle, and induced reaction in the functions necessary to the maintenance of Life''. He had ignored mentioning the presence at the post mortem of Mr Drew, the Constable family's trusted apothecary for more than twenty years.

The note of John Charles' visit is a strange document. The need for rehearsing the exact and earthy details of Constable's last movements is not apparent, whether it arose from the son's wish to tell them or from Churchyard's to hear them. Whatever the case, the record was almost the sole piece of his own writing that the lawyer did not throw away. It was not the only memento of the great painter that he preserved. Two carefully treasured scraps of Constable's writing were also found among his papers. He had much later begged of James Brook Pulham a simple note from the artist to him. The two had formed a close aquaintanceship as neighbours in Charlotte Street and Constable had written his friend when about to leave London to spend Christmas with his family whom he had installed, for the benefit of his wife's health, in lodgings by the sea.

"Dear Pulham,

I go to Brighton to-morrow and John in Suffolk — it is a sad thing thus to run away from one's work.

My best regards

Ever truly yrs

John Constable

23rd Decr 1825"

The second relic was something more memorable: a letter that Constable had written to his engraver David Lucas. It was the covering note he sent on 17th May 1831 with the latest plan for making up the sets of plates for his *English Landscape*.* That Churchyard should have been able to possess it is remarkable. With this one exception, every single scrap of paper that the painter had ever written to Lucas, including those that carried frustration and hopes, unjust reproaches and the apologies for them, was faithfully preserved by the decayed engraver till the day of his death in Fulham Workhouse in 1881.

When Churchyard had first called on him, it may have come out in conversation that both were sons of graziers. Something in common between them, less adventitious, must have operated to cause the attorney to be favoured with this unique gift. When in 1846 Lucas published a further set of Constable engravings, the artist's old colourman, George Fields, commended them in the preface for the fact that Lucas, operating for so long in close intimacy with the painter, "had imbibed to a degree otherwise unattainable the peculiar spirit of the master." It must have been because, in turn, the engraver saw in Churchyard something of the same discipleship that he gratified him in that unparalleled fashion.

* See Appendix.

X

In His Elegant Way

MUCH OF what is known of Churchyard in middle age stems from his friendship with Bernard Barton, confidential clerk at Alexanders Bank. They had dealings with one another in the course of business, and contact more personal, month by month, as members of the Book Club. It was not long before the painter-collector infected the poet, fourteen years his senior, with a great fondness for owning pictures "especially such as represented scenery familiar to him, the shady lane, the cornfield, the village, the sea-shore". It was the discussion and appraisal of new acquisitions that gave the occasion for evenings of toasted cheese and porter, well before the Three Chief Wits came together to converse over the same fare.

Some verses written by Barton early in 1839 paint the best surviving portrait of Churchyard in middle age, at home at the Beeches. They were lines written to celebrate his forty-first birthday of 22 January. In them he is to be seen a thoroughgoing paterfamilias; keeping a good table, and with decanters well-filled on the sideboard; addicted to the weed; a devotee of field sports and, like Moulton, out on the stubbles the first morning of the season. Out, too, at every opportunity with sketch book or palette, catching at the feel of the country scene; connoisseur of landscapes of the English School, on his walls the Cromes, Wilsons, Morlands and Frosts that he had quickly acquired to replace those sold before he went off to London. Joining them now were the Constables he had begun to collect more recently.

These are the verses "To T.C. — at Forty-one" that Churchyard read before a bright fire in his keeping room at The Beeches that Tuesday morning three weeks into the New Year:

> On the birthday of a King,
> Or a Queen, let Laureates sing;

And to recompense their lay,
Quaff their sack, or pouch their pay;
In such odes I see no fun;
Here's to Tom — at forty-one!

If a Poet's wish could tell,
Doubt not I would wish thee well;
Yet what could best wish of mine
Give — but is already thine?
Wife and bairns, surpassed by none —
These are thine at forty-one!

With a good house o'er thy head,
And a table — amply spread;
With a fire-side warm and bright,
Faces all in smiles bedight;
Thus may Life's sands sparkling run
As they do at forty-one.

With good paintings on each wall,
Holding sense and sight in thrall;
Morlands, Constables and Cromes —
Good as grace much prouder domes,
Sip thy wine and bite thy bun,
And so welcome forty-one!

With good pictures of thy own,
Wearing Nature's tint and tone;
And a love for others, too,
Be they but to Nature true.
What with brush, and dog and gun,
Thou'st still young at forty-one!

May old age forbear to mar
E'en a puff of thy cigar,
Or impair thine eye or hand,
Or o'ercloud thy household band;
But may every boon be thine
Friendship's blessing would assign.
Now my Birthday rhyme is done —
Good-bye! Tom! at forty-one!

The Woodbridge Laureate's lay was not without its recompense, for
later that day he was invited to the Beeches to join in the Birthday's

evening festivities. He was shown a notable Old Crome that Churchyard had just brought home from one of his legal journeyings. On occasions such as these, Barton had to have at once someone with whom to
share the news. Next day he penned a letter* to an Ipswich acquaintance, William Stevenson Fitch, postmaster, druggist and antiquary,
lamenting his own standing in the picture-collecting fraternity. "To
buy Pictures would soon beggar a Banker's Clerk. I get cut out by
every brother Collector. Here's Churchyard, the Sol$^r.$ has just picked
up a Crome that throws my two into the shade, for just the price of one
of them — a turn in a woody lane, with an old Clay Cottage in a sun-
shiny background — just the picture I have been dreaming of for years
— is he not a lucky fellow? But he has 6s.8d. for looking at a Man, and
the chance of going about when such things are to be picked up. He
says there are many of Crome's in & about Yarmouth."

Barton's verses make no mention of his friend in the professional
sphere, nor are there to be found many sights elsewhere of his performing in Court at this period. Newspaper accounts in the eighteen
thirties and forties of "Proceedings Before the Woodbridge
Magistrates" still give little beyond a list of convictions and sentences.
They can be sometimes as bald as "About 80 cases entered for hearing:
nothing of note transpired." Only the unusual is reported in any
detail.

To hear him it is necessary to borrow from accounts of later years.
The best is by Loder writing his obituary. Fully twenty-five years the
advocate's junior, Loder was too young to have known him at forty-
one. Nevertheless it cannot be doubted that the attorney with whom he
was well acquainted in the late eighteen fifties, was already displaying
the same courthouse manner in the late eighteen thirties, acquired as it
was by nearly twenty years in practice before the magistrates of the
little country town.

"Very many of our readers yet hear ringing in their ears his clear
and nervously eloquent delivery of some nice legal distinction, an eloquence that not only enchanted all his hearers, but often lent a positive
grace to the dry details of many an uninteresting case. His addresses,
whether to the Bench or the Jury, were distinguished by a refined and
dignified courtesy, so that whatever he advanced always commanded
at once the attention and respect of his audience. Many a luckless
wight has had cause to thank him for hair-breadth escapes from the
penalties of the law; his thorough knowledge of the intricacies of his
profession enabling him often to convert defeat into victory, and turn
the trembling scale in favour of his client. United to this, his manner
was polished and gentlemanly in the extreme." It is the sense of style

* British Library, MS Additional 33964.

one would expect, knowing that years after the lawyer's death Fitz-Gerald when he saw his first aconites would recall that "Mr Churchyard (in his elegant way) used to call them New Year's Gifts." Glyde adds to the portrait by Loder: "Churchyard had not the advantage of an imposing appearance. He was a small though rather stout man, with light hair and fair complexion." Small certainly — "my little friend" and "Le petit Churchyard" FitzGerald called him; but the slight boyish figure of the Well Street portrait and the keen features that Harriet sketched in the late 1850s suggest that stoutness only came to him towards his end. If ever Glyde did himself see him it would not be till then, for he was still hairdressing in Ipswich to within a few years of the lawyer's death.

This is perhaps the place to relate Glyde's Labourer's story of his dog and the sausage rolls, seeing that it has been fastened upon in one version or another as being one of the few action shots of Churchyard that has survived. "His readiness to rejoinder may thus be illustrated. Churchyard's retriever went one day into Mr James Barritt's the confectioners, and ate a quantity of sausage rolls which he managed to knock from the counter to the floor. A few days after, the Quaker seeing the lawyer coming up Church Street stood at his door, and stopped Mr Churchyard. After relating the damage done by a dog in his shop, he cautiously enquired of his friend Thomas what remedy he had in the case. "Oh" said Churchyard, "you can recover against the owner of the dog." "Then hand me eighteen pence" said the Quaker, "for it was thy dog". "Very well," said Churchyard, "I charge you six and eight pence for advice, and the balance due to me is 5s. 2d." Similar stories have been related of other keen-witted lawyers elsewhere, but this Woodbridge story is a fact."

Such a tale is universal and Glyde's vouching for it as a fact is on a par with the "genuineness" of the Farm Labourer's *Autobiography* and with his posing as "Aunt Kitty of Lowestoft" when addressing a series of admonitory articles to The Young Women of Suffolk.

It is a pity that the anecdote is not original for it portrays just such a man as Churchyard must have been. It first appeared as Woodbridge news in a weekly column of the *Suffolk Chronicle* in 1861 under a heading "The Lawer and the Quaker — The Spaniel and the Baker" and opens "Friend C—, I am come to ask thy advice concerning a dog which came into my shop and ate and destroyed sundry pies and pastry to the amount of five shillings." Glyde, remembering having read it some thirty years before he wrote the *Autobiography*, relates a number of details differently, but the drift is the same. One cogent reason, if such were needed, against pinning the incident upon Churchyard is the knowledge that the *Chronicle*'s Woodbridge reporter at that time was several parts a knave.

The Farm Labourer's account of Churchyard's dealing with the poachers brings in another misapprehension about his legal practice. He certainly defended so frequently in cases under the game laws that Glyde is right in saying he became known as The Poacher's Lawyer. From out the long generations of his yeomen forbears — unqualified persons — and now with kinsmen taking leases on a nobleman's estate, Thomas no doubt found pleasure in court in scoring off the landed gentry in the Commission; every one of whose hares had done the Churchyard farmers that half-a-crown's worth of damage before being knocked on the head and sold for ninepence. Glyde's statement, however, that "he was essentially a poor man's advocate" and "very considerate in his charges" is mistaken. It was his having so many fat briefs, so many 6s. 8d's falling into his hand "for looking at a Man" that enabled him to accept some of the poachers' defences where the diverting points in the case were of more attraction than the size of the fee. There was always the chance of some comical surprise from a countryman unacquainted with legal processes, as when he put his client into the box to elicit from him the facts necessary for his defence and was met with "I have nothing to say to you at all."

In any case, not all poachers had to rely upon a poor man's advocate. Frederick Gowing who had served on the Sudbourne estate and after the 1831 changes in the Game Laws managed to obtain a licence to sell, was well able to afford the best attorney available. He could, at any time, dispose in Ipswich of a hundred pheasants taken in one night. He used illicitly to supply leverets, likewise pheasants' and patridges' eggs, directly or through agents, to noblemen, MPs., magistrates and clergymen whose own stock of game needed replenishment. Confining himself to day poaching he never had to go to prison, paid only £300 in fines throughout a lucrative lifetime's occupation and was usually defended by Churchyard.

Pre-eminence in forensic skill made him the most sought after attorney in the district for every sort of case, whether to defend against a serious accusation, or to push a charge against someone at whose hands a complainant believed he had suffered wrong. When there were grave matters of fact where elucidating the whole truth was of paramount importance, he was the attorney *par excellence* to draw it out in examination or cross-examination.

It was so in the Extraordinary Case of an Attempt to Poison, that took the headlines in 1840. The child of a Woodbridge watchmaker had had poison put into its victuals so its mother declared. When all other probabilities had been eliminated suspicion pointed at the father, Israel Peter Smyth, who was represented by Churchyard. Mr Carthew appeared for the wife but his adversary so cross-examined her that at the end of a minute investigation which occupied many hours on three different days, she was brought to admit to having sworn falsely in her original depositions that had served to incriminate her husband. "The magistrates opined that there was not the slightest grounds to suppose Israel Peter Smyth guilty."

In the few cases in these years reported at length for their comic rather than their serious content, it was just as certain that Churchyard would be the attorney concerned: retained equally by persons of high or of low degree. Such was the affair of the rival bellringers of Tunstall, where he was briefed by the Churchwarden Mr John Flatt of Dunningworth Hall, a large landowner in the parish. The Rector had by subterfuge got rid of the regular Company and substituted others in their place. The Warden espoused the claim of the dispossessed and cut down the six bellropes. The Rector procured plough lines and the bells were again rung by the usurpers.

Flatt, in virtue of his office, directed that they remain silent but the substitute band turned up to defy him. Accompanied by his servant as witness he went up into the ringers' chamber and cut down the new lines. William and John Groom whom the rector had recruited into the rival Company abused the Churchwarden in a shameful and blasphemous manner. William pushed and shoved about, and John kicked him from behind all the way down the tower stairs. Churchyard having secured convictions, the Grooms were each fined the full penalty of £5, allowed a week for payment, in default of which two months imprisonment in Ipswich Gaol. The whole affair had "created some disturbance and it was late in the evening before the crowd had dispersed." To complete the village's entertainment that day it fell out that the Rector had incurred a charge of assault for having roughly set going an innocent locksmith sent to repair damage done to the church door in the forcible entry.

Mr Churchyard in that side of the law where his nimble mind and suasive oratory made him so outstandingly successful, was prone to make little distinction between a weighty case and one that was *de minimis*. Each was there to be won, whatever expense of time it involved. On the five occasions where in the course of 1841 he is particularised, the reporter comments in the same style. "After a long hearing of the case the Magistrates dismissed the complaint" (defending against a claim for damage to lawyer Carthew's gate) — "after a long hearing Mr Churchyard failed in attempting to prove the complainants drunk" (collision between a cart and a trap) — "Mr Churchyard appeared on behalf of Leggett but after a long hearing the Magistrates convicted" (assault) — "this case occupied a considerable time, Mr Churchyard having appeared on behalf of the blacksmith" (drunkenness) — "the case occupied a considerable time" (defence of a poacher).

At a rare sitting of the Sheriff's Court in that same year there was "a protracted hearing lasting about five hours." It was to determine who had agreed with whom, and where, to buy what quantity of potatoes for delivery when and at what price. Despite the time involved the patient reporter, like Loder twenty-five years later, appears to have been similarly enchanted by the positive grace lent to the dry details. "Mr Churchyard appeared for the plaintiff, Mr Jackson of Ipswich for the defendant, to both of which gentlemen, for the ability displayed in the management of the cause of their respective clients, the greatest praise is due." Churchyard secured the verdict.

It may have irked the junior partners that their principal should be enjoying himself in a not very profitable way in court while they were left with the steady duller work of the office. The more so as his picture collecting must at times have taken him far from Woodbridge. Morlands, Wilsons, Constables and Cromes were not to be picked up locally. Visits needed to be paid to London, Norwich, Yarmouth. To Birmingham even. After their years of running the day to day law business Meadows and Everitt were well able to be their own masters. Everitt was first to leave, departing in the September of 1841 for Great Yarmouth. Churchyard took over from him Marsden House, thus giving himself office and family home under the same roof — a splendid Georgian red-brick building of five bays, three stories high and with the most elegant doorcase in the town.

Before he left Melton there had been born to Harriet a daughter Catherine in 1839, and finally in 1841 another boy, whom they registered Charles James Isaac, remembering the well-to-do great uncles and the long line of bearers of the family talisman. All the children were then at home, except Young Tom away at boarding school. To supervise the daughters' education there was Ann Bird a resident governess aged 20. The two female servants were one 25, the other 20. The family Bible recorded of the children that "All have been vaccinated, all have had the measles except Catherine and Charles James Isaac. Young Tom has had the measles and whooping cough."

Less than a couple of years later *The London Gazette* announced that on 6th April 1843 the firm of Churchyard and Meadows was dissolved by mutual consent. Churchyard, for the remaining twenty-two years of his life practised entirely on his own. Advocacy brought him into court far more often than any other Woodbridge lawyer; how much of his time he gave to the traditional work of a small town, family solicitor is not known. He certainly kept himself free of any standing appointments that carried with them routine commitments. He was the antithesis of the more typical John Wood junior, three and a half years his elder, who could proclaim himself in the local directory as solicitor, clerk to the magistrates, clerk to commissioners of taxes, clerk to

Seckford Charity, clerk to the Burial Board, clerk to Helmingham Turnpike Trust, perpetual commissioner for taking acknowledgements of married women, commissioner in Chancery, commissioner Common Law Courts, agent to Guardian Fire and Life Insurance Offices; office Church Street. Churchyard's entry read baldly ''Attorney, Cumberland Street''.

His name was never listed among those holding insurance agencies. All the other attorneys in the town held an appointment from one or usually two of the Fire and Life Offices. With a good thirty of them competing for business in Woodbridge the companies had to go outside professional circles; so that beyond the three auctioneers, a stock and share broker and the Post Office Clerk, they had to depend upon a motley assortment of chemists and corn merchants, a grocer, a wine merchant and a cabinet maker. Churchyard chose not to be tied. His preference was always for a different day; a different case whose conduct was a work of art complete in itself. His advocacy, his painting, his picture buying were all pervaded with the same disposition. Barton sensed it when he wrote of Tom's ''restless craving after novelty.''

XI

Fellow Wits

On Saturday I give supper to B. Barton and Churchyard. I wish
you could be with us. We are the chief wits of Woodbridge. And
one man has said that he envies us our conversations! So we
flatter each other in the country.

> FitzGerald to the painter Samuel Laurence
> 21.12.1843

Woodbridge came in mid-Victorian days to experience some love-hate
relationships with the two younger of the oddly assorted trio of Chief
Wits. Contrariwise the eldest of them enjoyed throughout the second
quarter of the century the town's never varying affection and admiration. The place knew itself to be celebrated through the length and
breadth of the land, and in America too, as the home, much senti-
mentalised and sung about, of Bernard Barton the Quaker Poet.

> For more than forty chequr'd years
> Hast thou not been my home?
> Till all that most this life endears
> Forbids a wish to roam.

In return its inhabitants found more than one occasion for signal-
ising him. A schooner built and launched on the Deben in 1840 and
trading from her quays was given his name; causing him no little
amusement when she appeared one time in the Shipping List of arrivals at some far-off port as the Barney Burton. Four years later White's
first Suffolk Directory added ''Poet'', in brackets, after his name in its
list of Woodbridge gentry. The ''nutshell of a house'' which he had
earlier occupied was known as ''Poet's Cottage'' long after he left it.
''Barton's Cottage'' is the name painted over its doorway in
Cumberland Street today.

He had come to Woodbridge in 1806 with only a narrow education and just out of an apprenticeship to Samuel Jesup, a Quaker shop-keeper at Halstead. He married his master's niece, Lucy, and joined her brother in his coal and corn merchant's business in Woodbridge. Lucy died giving birth to their daughter a year later and Barton left the town for a twelvemonth to recover from his sorrow. From such unhelpful beginnings he returned, and in the course of forty years of unremitting work at the desk of the Quaker brothers Dykes and Samuel Alexander, rose to be their confidential clerk and succeeded in drawing to himself by dint of indefatigable versifying, letter-writing and conversation, three great companies of acquaintances — his readers, his literary correspondents and his friendly neighbours.

The poetry he wrote is today forgotten and unreadable. In 1812, at 28, he published anonymously his first *Metrical Effusions*, printed by a Woodbridge bookseller. Literary aspirations, that were to haunt him all his days, prompted him to send a copy to Byron with a question to which he hoped the answer would be "Yes, you are better fitted to be a poet than a bank clerk." In the "Stanzas Addressed to some Friends going to the Seaside" his muse had given forth such strains as

> The stroll after breakfast, when all are got out;
> The saunter, the lounge, and the looking about;
> The search after shells, and the eyes gleaming bright,
> If cornelian or amber should come into sight.

Accordingly one can but feel that his Lordship gave good advice when he replied "Do not renounce writing, but never trust entirely to authorship."

The lure of the inspiring word "Authorship" led Barton six years later to publish under his own name a second venture, having in advance enrolled a diverse body of a hundred and twenty-four subscribers ranging from William Wordsworth, Esq of Rydal Mount and Robert Southey, Poet Laureate, to James Pulham, not in the highest repute.

For Barton good poetry meant verse conducive to goodness: it was painful to him that the Romantics should write so well and live so ill. Boldly addressing "Stanzas to Percy Byshe Shelley," he pleaded

> Ere it should prove too late, thy steps retrace;
> The Heights thy muse has scal'd, can never be
> Her loveliest or her safest dwelling place

A further six collections in the next eight years established Barton with a multitude of earnest readers as the foremost writer of pious verse, unexceptional in its goodness of heart, of rhyme and of rhythm; gladly received into thousands of homes by single-minded believers who admitted his volumes as their only books of poetry.

Upon almost any subject Barton could drop into a mood that he felt to be poetic inspiration: A Stuffed Eagle; Zechariah XIV.7; A Poet's Memorial to Robinson Crusoe; hundreds of deaths, birthdays, views around Woodbridge; "To Sir Samuel Fludyer on the devastation effected on his Marine Villa at Felixstowe by the encroachment of the Sea". Near the end of his life when, though a Whig, he opposed the repeal of the Corn Laws, he sent up his views to Sir Robert Peel in the unlikely vehicle of a couple of sonnets. Improving reading as his volumes might be, nevertheless that a Quaker should have written poetry at all was a matter of regretful surprise to the stricter of his silent brethren, one of whom upbraided him for using the word November in a poem when he should have referred to it as Eleventh Month.

Barton's letter-writing was even more voluminous than his poetry. His missives went impartially to literary lions most of whom he never met, and to friends around Woodbridge he was likely to encounter next day. Among the former were Lamb, Byron, Scott, Southey, Mrs Opie, Lord Jeffrey, John Linnell, William and Mary Howitt, Letitia Landon, Mrs Hemans, Allan Cunningham. Of a few of them he made acquaintance in the flesh during his visits to London in the publishing years. Charles Lamb he visited on several occasions. In this there was a close Woodbridge link for James Brook Pulham was a fellow clerk of the essayist at the East India House, and when business in Leadenhall was not pressing would pass the hour doing landscape sketches and at one such time drew Elia's likeness.

It is this particular exchange of correspondence that must keep Barton for ever remembered as the recipient of some of the best letters Lamb wrote. The Quaker had raised with his newly-made acquaintance the old idea canvassed with Byron ten years earlier. The reply brought the celebrated Keep-to-your-bank-and-the-bank-will-keep-you letter, with its "Throw yourself on the world without any rational plan of support beyond what the chance employ of booksellers would afford you!!! Throw yourself rather, my dear sir, from the steep Tarpeian rock, slap-dash headlong upon iron spikes." There ensues the cascade of humour upon the miseries of Grub Street compared with "the stable foundations of Leadenhall".

Barton's letters often strive to be the sort that would be preserved in the expectation that some time in the future when their writer was dead, they would be collected and published. Lamb saved none, though he initially enjoyed the exchange that continued through eight years. But he tired of it eventually and left the latest missives from Woodbridge unanswered. "Barton is dull enough" he said, "but not nonsensical. He writes English too."

To all for twenty miles around who had any literary pretentions, B.B. introduced himself: from such diverse writers as the Miss Charlesworths — Maria whose *Ministering Children* had so enormous a circulation, Elizabeth author of *Historical Reveries* — to the Rev John Mitford who preferred landscaping his grounds at Benhall Rectory to carrying out any clerical duties there and preferred, most of all, living in London for the greater part of twenty years editing the Gentleman's Magazine. Acquaintance, too, Barton made with anyone of note in the neighbourhood, from Clarkson, the Abolitionist, as an old man to George Airey, the future Astronomer Royal, as an undergraduate; to William Cubitt, knighted later for his work in building the Crystal Palace.

With less exalted correspondents near at hand Barton was less stilted, though here, too, there are sometimes the unnecessary literary allusions and flourishes, the determination to bludgeon the recipient into listening. But there is also any amount of good chat, indeed the letters are often a mere extension of recent conversation, sometimes dashed off to a caller who had left only an hour before. It would be a loss not to have, for instance, the description of a scene at the Quaker school at Brook House to which he was obliged in early days to repair for meals, his own nutshell higher up the street providing space for sitting and sleeping only. The room in which he was trying to write was more crowded with young Friends than a poet waiting upon quiet thoughts might have hoped for. ''All hands are busy round me to clap, to starch, to iron, to plait — in plain English 'tis washing day; and I am now writing close to a table on which is a bason of starch, caps, kerchiefs &c; and busy hands and tongues around it.''

Outside the circles of those with whom he conversed through the Post Office was the throng of persons going about Woodbridge with whom Barton could exchange an inevitable pinch of snuff and pass a friendly word or an evening's talk in person. His determined reading and excellent memory made him worth listening to at dinner table at the Hall, while he was equally at home in everyday talk in a farmhouse parlour.

Early in 1837 the Quaker, so adept at forming literary acquaintances, had made himself known to Edward FitzGerald and secured an introduction to the latter's friend of school and college days — William Bodham Donne, reviewer, wit, and the Lord Chamberlain's Examiner of Plays. The Quaker had heard that living with the Donnes at Mattishall in Norfolk was great-aunt Mrs Bodham, then 89, cousin of the poet Cowper. She it was who had sent him the painting that inspired *On Receiving his Mother's Portrait*, Barton's favourite lines of his favourite author. For him to be able to meet Great Aunt Bodham, Cowper's ''gentle Anne,'' was the very coming together of letters and life. The pious literary pilgrimage that ensued was, he said, one of the most lived-over-again hours of his life. "I believe I am more proud of having sat on a Sofa with her, than having, or being about to have, a ship named after me."

FitzGerald, 28, was at this time living with his parents at Boulge Hall, three miles from Woodbridge. At Bury St Edmunds Grammar School and Trinity Cambridge he had made lasting friendships with notable writers and scholars — James Spedding; Thackeray; W. B. Donne; John Mitchell Kemble; W. H. Thompson afterwards Master of the College; John Allen who became Archdeacon of Salop and, a little after his Cambridge days, with the Tennysons whom he had known in College by sight only.

The succeeding half-dozen years he had spent reading much, writing little; drifting around between his home, his brother-in-law's house across the Waveney, and his own lodgings in London: to an aunt in Paris; to his father's estates at Naseby that encompassed the battlefield, and at Castle Irwell near Manchester that overlay his coalmines.

In 1837 he moved from the Hall to the cottage at its gates. Here he got up early, ate a very small breakfast, stood at his deak reading or writing all morning, then, having put on his tartan shawl, walked with his dog. "He did not visit the gentlefolks as he hated a set party." Instead he would often finish a day by spending the evening with the Bartons. Talk across the fireside in the small study at the Bank House, inevitably centred on the sort of bookish matters that fill his earliest letters to the Quaker — comments upon Carlyle and Goethe, Homer, Quarles or Addison. Most admired of all were Crabbe's *Tales of the Hall* and to accompany them, toasted cheese and gin and water; only one thing, FitzGerald said, was wanting to make up the square of comfort — a pipe, that Barton abhored: "one night, devote your little room to that" the visitor pleaded.

It was these occasions that made E.F.G. aware, from the pictures hung on the walls, that his host had a second enthusiasm: a consuming interest in paintings. From London he wrote to Barton wishing he were there to view with him the Old Masters. There is dilettante comment on Salvador, the Poussins, Raphael, Rembrandt and the Venetians. "I am sure their greatness would not diminish your pleasure in your own small collection. Why should it? There is as genuine a feeling of nature in one of Nursey's sketches as in the Rubenses and Claudes here".

Commenced in the light of Churchyard's advice and growing in response to his exuberant promptings, the Small Collection contained, by that time, works well above sketches by local dabblers with a genuine feeling for nature. When the Quaker died, Ben Moulton, could, in his advertisement of sale, call attention to two important works — *Norwich Market Place* by John Sell Cotman and *The Flight into Eygpt* by Mad John Martin of *Balshazzar's Feast*. The auctioneer went on to list landscapes and portraits by more than a dozen celebrated painters of the English and Dutch schools. No small achievement for a badly paid bank clerk. At the best of times the amount he could lay out on paintings was slim. "£3.10s is pretty nearly a fortnight's board etc. for my Household — will he give me credit till I get in my rent at Christmas?" he asked in 1843, when a tempting piece at that figure was dangled in front of him seven weeks before quarter day.

Through mention of Churchyard, FitzGerald became aware that it was the attorney's opinion in things artistic upon which Barton relied. "Maybe you have asked Mr C. to come and give his judgment upon it over toasted cheese." "Lay in a Double Gloucester" E.F.G. commanded Barton and signed himself "Philocaseotostus: which is a Lover of Toasted Cheese". That evening a slice was cut and stood on a "Footman" facing the coals till it was roasted, first one side then the other.

The lawyer was slower than the poet to enter into fellowship for as late as the November of 1841 he was still referred to somewhat distantly in a FitzGerald letter to Barton as "your friend". Six months before that, however, the writer already knew of Churchyard's picture-buying excursions to London, and said he was prepared to join forces with him on one such.

FitzGerald himself had been a picture buyer from the time of his first occupying The Cottage, bringing back from London every now and then some piece that had caught his eye. Churchyard's infectious enthusiasm in searching diligently for unrecognised masterpieces quickly spread to his new acquaintance. But E.F.G. found it to be altogether too great a disturbance to his composed way of living. "After this year I shall bid complete adieu to picture *hunting*, only taking what comes my way. There is a great difference between these two things" he told Barton in the spring of 1842, "Who can sit down to Plato while his thoughts are roaming to Holborn, Christies, Phillips, etc?" It was a resolution he found he was unable to keep. Within a year of his becoming more closely acquainted with Churchyard not only talk about books, but talk of the great masterpieces of Raphael and Rembrandt gave way to news of acquiring the sort of works of the English School that could be hung at the Bank House, Marsden House or Boulge Cottage. He soon fell to the never-failing excitement of the sale rooms: "Going today to look at some pictures for auction at Phillips' — oh Lord, Lord."

There is what at first sight seems to be some tiresomely heavy humour, contrived by FitzGerald in the early letters to Barton. Two pounds, he once said, was his "ultimatum" for a Constable. Four or five is the sum at which he secured treasures to which he gave the most optimistic attributions.

There was pretence, too, of his taking over the lawyer's role as supplier from London of tempting additions to the Small Collection: a "picture of dead chaffinches which Mr C. will like, it is so well done: I expect you to give high prices for these pictures — mind that: and begin to economise in household matters. Leave off sugar in tea and make all your household do so." In Norwich he had bought "a fine head, as I am not particular I call it a Giorgione" and went on to boast he would "sell it to old Rogers at a vast profit" — Samuel Rogers, wealthy banker, man of letters and art collector.

All this nonsense had its point. It was a private joke between Fitz-Gerald and Barton at Churchyard's expense. Connoisseur that their friend was, lover of fine paintings brought home to be hung for his delight on the walls at Marsden House, it became apparent to them that he nevertheless might well come later to sell them at a profit. Something bred in the bone of the cattle dealers came out in the blood of their more aesthetic descendant.

He had not been entirely forthcoming to his two fellows about these ins and outs during the early years of their acquaintance. A sly question is addressed to Barton by FitzGerald from town in a letter of February 19th 1842. "There are three genuine pictures of Gains-borough now to be seen at Conduit Street. I understand: the property of some Suffolk man . . . do you know whose they are? I dare say Mr C. does" As time went on and they understood one another more fully, no secret was made about the pictures sent up to London from Marsden House for resale. In the April of 1844 FitzGerald looked in at Christies to see Churchyard's Linnell sketch come up for auction. In subsequent years he was enlisted to report to him on the state of the London market and what pictures were being offered. Even at that later stage when all was well understood between them, Churchyard, when on important buying or selling business of his own, did not let his two companions know what he was up to. FitzGerald was driven to complain about such secretiveness. He had deliberately reserved all his picture expeditions till his friend came up to town and yet, in the April of 1844, "I have not seen Churchyard: had I known his put up I could have called on him." The lawyer on that occasion did have other business to attend to, for on the 15th he presented himself at Doctors' Commons to prove the late grandmamma Hailes's Will. Next year he was equally unforthcoming and FitzGerald wrote back to the Bank House, "Tell Churchyard I am *angry* he did not come and see me. There he was gadding over London for three days".

XII

Riches So Heaped Up

BARTON reputedly never threw away a letter. Of the surviving seventy or so from FitzGerald between 1839 and 1846 more than three-quarters deal with the all-absorbing sport of picture-hunting. The unidentified Woodbridgian who envied the Wits their brilliant intellectual exchanges, would have been surprised to know how large a slice of the conversation was given to discussing their latest successes or disappointments in the art-dealing world.

One of the regular bulletins sent to Barton by E.F.G. when staying in London was what he called his weekly "Report on the Fine Arts to be laid on your table on Sunday morning;" for letters could be collected from the Post Office on the First Day by those who, like the Bank, had private boxes there. The purpose of these Reports, Fitz-Gerald told the Quaker, was "that you might have something to reflect upon in your silent meeting." Immediately feeling that the jest was misplaced he had added "(N.B. This is very wrong and I don't mean it)".

The bulletins give glimpses of joint excursions when he and the lawyer were in Town together. When the latter was at home in Wood-bridge they contain frequent injunctions to Barton: "Ask Mr Church-yard" or "Tell Churchyard", for he was more likely to get a reply via the Quaker than if he wrote to the lawyer direct. Barton consoled himself by remembering the "Old Proverb, where two men ride the same Horse one must needs go behind — so touching Picture-buying I give up all rivalry with Tom, and make up my mind to ride on the crupper." FitzGerald admitted that he and B.B., discussing the authenticity or otherwise of a doubtful Constable, could only "pro and con it like monkeys together." For an authoritative verdict on the picture it must be referred to "our great judge Mr Churchyard."

The painter's youthful devotion to Old Crome that led him to be "the first who even ventured a 'long price' on his works," continued throughout his life. Norfolk and Suffolk were still, at this time, the natural hunting ground for them and as lookers-out he had at Norwich George Rossi and old Wiggers; at Ipswich the brothers Owen and Joseph Roe. They were not entirely reliable. On one occasion Owen, at Churchyard's request, had gone over to Lackford "somewhere sideways of Bury", to view some pictures coming up for sale and had reported "all was naught. The dog was there, though, on the day of the auction" wrote Barton, "and his Brother too, the fatsy. Tom implored the latter to bid for him," when he heard there was in fact an outstanding Crome to come under the hammer. Roe secured it and Barton reckoned he must have gone to £30 or £35.

To find Constables one needed to visit London so that FitzGerald, staying often at his rooms in Charlotte Street, was early able to exult over examples secured. Although he had seen in these purchases "a dash and felicity in the execution that gives one a thrill of good digestion in one's rooms, and the thought of which makes one inclined to jump over the children's heads in the street," he had still not understood the spring of Constable's inspiration. Writing that encomium to his friend Frederick Tennyson, he had in the next few lines decried what he felt to be the artist's "faults" — the trees "splashed with the sky-mud, which (according to Constable's theory) the Earth scatters up with her wheels in travelling so briskly around the sun." Fine writing, but mistaken. A year later he brought the two pictures to Woodbridge and with his eyes opened by Churchyard, broke out into "How inferior are all the black Wouvermans, Holbeins, Ruisdails & Co. to a fresh Constable with the dew on it." Two more years of insight accorded him by the great judge, and he made amends for his earlier cleverness by writing to Tennyson "I respect the man who tries to paint up the freshness of earth and sky." His lawyer friend was attempting the same himself.

In the January of 1842 where at one London sale all the pictures went cheap and at the next all went dear, E.F.G. had at both seen "that fat fellow Rowe of Ipswich." Although Roe may have been commissioned on those occasions, there was no need to get him to bid in the October, for the lawyer was then in Town himself. Reporting back to Barton, FitzGerald added as a postscript "Churchyard does not write because I have told you all the news". That Churchyard did not write was no isolated happening. There were occasions that justifiably exasperated his friends.

All that is told of the 1843 jaunt is that there had been an encounter with a she-dragon, who had an early Gainsborough over which they had been unable to come to terms. Late that October FitzGerald had been in Norwich for a concert: "Also bought a picture of course." It

Portrait, at 29 Well Street. Watercolour, 31.5 x 26.8cm. Christchurch
Mansion, Ipswich

Trees in the Wind. Watercolour, 26.8 x 38.2cm. The Rev E. C. Charlesworth

A touch of Autumn, Wilford Hollows, Melton. Watercolour, 22.3 x 33cm

was the alleged Georgione, sold him by Rossi who had mentioned "that Mr Churchyard had been in Norwich, and bought two Cromes off him. I suppose you have been tempted with these before now."

At this point the curtain rises on a scene, remarkably well lit, that displays in detail Churchyard's picture-hunting over the next twelve months. The script is contained in a bunch of two dozen letters* written by Barton to a "seemingly intelligent person at Ipswich of the Name of Wodderspoon". John Wodderspoon, in his thirties, described himself as having "a literary engagement upon a newspaper" in the county town. He had been author three years earlier of a flowerily written "Historic Sites of Suffolk" to which Barton and Elizabeth Charlesworth were invited to write some lines of Introductory Verse, he having no difficulty in contributing more than a hundred, she nearly three times as many. The reporter's connection with the picture-hunting activities of the Wits was marginal: he was serviceable in such things as getting some of the Quaker's purchases framed, or in arranging for repairs to Barton's "Great Crome that got that unlucky poke". Once he ventured gingerly into suggesting, via B.B., an exchange of his *Ambleside View* for T.C.'s Cotman *Tower* — "but it was 'no go' Tom wouldn't bite . . . he rated his Specimen of Cotman very highly . . . much more so than I do . . . it looks like a dis-interred well . . . that bit of brickwork." It was the *Norwich Cow Tower* that Wodderspoon had off Churchyard later.

Barton's first letter in the batch, dated Quakerwise 11.3.43 and to be interpreted as the Third of the Eleventh Month, was sent off in seasonable "muddy, muddle-headed weather." Its news was that "Tom Churchyard had pick'd up two new Old Cromes, but I can't report on them for I have not had time to run in & look at them." They were those bought from Rossi a fortnight earlier. After Norwich he had before the end of the month visited London, and returned with a large Bassano: "A size or two bigger, Than my wapping nigger." The Lawyer had been dazzled "with its exotic hints and hues, but that fancy can't last long with him" because of the fact that "he'll find none such in Suffolk Nature."

One evening a few days before Christmas Barton was invited over to Marsden House where a splendid surprise had been prepared for him. There, hoisted on the dining table, with a chair behind it and in front, a lamp on either side, was a "Great Wilson." Before it the poet had "sate, nearly two whole hours in admiration." Certainly very fine, he pronounced it. There was glee, too over the fact of its having been secured largely by exchange, without much money to boot. "Worth a Cart load of such Pictures as he gave for it" Barton considered, and felt

---

* British Library, MS Addition 37032.

that his artful friend had much the better of the bargain — "he has jew'd the Jew."

When the novelty of having the Wilson began to wear off, Churchyard started to fret over the fact that its acquisition had denuded him of "his finer Cromes, or what he thought such." He must have an outstanding work of the Norwich master to illumine his walls again. Some considerable time earlier he had found for Barton what the Quaker always called "my great Crome," and it had been agreed that if ever it came to leave the Bank House the lawyer should have the first opportunity of resuming possession. Then just returned, repaired, from Ipswich, it must be got back to Marsden House. Now was the moment, before Barton, who had become accustomed to its absence, should fall too deeply in love with it again. Churchyard overwhelmed him by offering for it the Bassano; a small Wilson; "the sweet little *River Scene* by Crome, which was an earlier and older favourite than the Great Crome; & the Romneys". Temptation of this order could not be resisted. The Small Collection at the Bank House was a safe repository in which Churchyard could leave a picture for a time, with the opportunity of suggesting a swap to have it back later. The Bassano eventually returned in just such a way.

Getting up to London had now become much easier than in the past. In 1842 the Eastern Union Railway had brought the line down as far as Colchester and the Quicksilver and Retaliator coaches from Woodbridge connected with the trains there. In the early spring of 1844, Churchyard travelled to Town and brought home a Constable oil, a painting of Higham village. There was no question of its authenticity for he had bought it off Leslie himself, in whose possession it had been for several years. It was just the thing with which to tempt B.B. who "had a long higgle with Tom, ere we could get through." £17.10s. was the final figure below which the lawyer refused to part. Seven pounds ten was all the money Barton could lay his hands on. He bethought him, though, of a debt of £10 that Fulcher owed for some verses in one of the Sudbury Pocket Books and which had been mentally written off as irrecoverable. He must have the picture, so there was nothing for it but to dun the publisher. This was crowned with only partial success for "Fulcher only bled to the extent of a five Pound flimsy, in place of a ten." The final makeweight that could balance the scales came when Churchyard agreed to another of the familiar swaps: "so I threw in another little Picture which cost me five pounds 10 or 12 years ago."

"So Churchyard has caught another Constable" FitzGerald wrote laconically in reply to Barton's excited news of the Higham trophy. "Did he get off our Debach boy that set the shed on fire? Ask him that." The question has found itself several times repeated in the

FitzGerald analects without bringing a reply. The answer however is
"Yes".*

Barton salved an uneasy conscience over his recent extravagance by
reckoning that he had a Constable for £12.10s. because but for this
transaction he would "never have dunn'd F. at all. Even at £17.10s. I
cannot think the thing dear, when Tom gave £50 for the *Dell*, and forty
guineas for the *Summerland*." But for Barton's loquaciousness, and
Wodderspoon's hoarding of the letters, it would never have been
known that these world-famous paintings once shone out from the
crowded walls of the house in Cumberland Street.

A *Helmingham Dell* had played its part in Churchyard's grand crisis of
a decade earlier. Despite the deep troubles associated with the version
painted for lawyer Pulham he did not hesitate to bring home its fellow.
It went later into Barton's Small Collection, perhaps the subject of
another of the higgling swaps, for the price was outside the Quaker's
range. "What is the exact size of your *Dell?*" FitzGerald asked him, "I
have seen one or two frames likely that might suit your picture well." If
Barton's answer had been preserved it could have helped art-historians
unravel the provenance of this version.

The *Summerland* had been painted years before and exhibited in the
Academy of 1814 as *Landscape: Ploughing Scene in Suffolk*. It is a conspec-
tus of the light-drenched land Churchyard knew from his Dedham
schooldays — the Vale spread out below; distant glimpses of the Glebe
Farm; of Stoke-by-Nayland churchtower on the horizon and Stratford
St Mary Church among the trees. Like the *Dell* it had been engraved
for the "English Landscape." Its time at Marsden House must have
been short, for by September 1846 a new owner was writing to David
Lucas asking him for some details of its previous history.

It was in the April of 1844 that for a second time, "Tom has been to
Town since and visited the Gent of whom he had two of his three larger
Constables." The "gent's" identity Churchyard had not disclosed.
From that excursion he brought back "Two more lovely pictures", an
Etty "group of Angelic Heads and a glorious sea-scape by old Crome,
Yarmouth Jetty, as it was some sixty or seventy years ago — its end
crowded with figures looking on a lot of fishing boats just come in —
the masts and sails of which are just piercing above the extremity of the
crowded promenade . . . all the right side of the Picture is sun and sky
both glorious, and a capital bit of beach." FitzGerald was in London at
the time of these acquisitions, but Churchyard had not at first let him
know where he was putting up. Once the purchase had been made he
had disclosed himself, and been pressed by his friend to return with
him to Charlotte Street "but he would not." It was just punishment,

---

* See p. 95.

E.F.G. reckoned, that he had in consequence missed first cut at a meal prepared for entertaining some artist acquaintances the following day. "Tell him he would have had this tongue to eat" was fired after him in the Weekly Report for that Sunday.

Wodderspoon, subjected to this spate of news about Churchyard's acquisitions, commented that Tom C's rage for picture-collecting was enough to craze himself and his friends too. Barton, with one of his unnecessary flourishes agreed: "Thou wert *no far wrang* as the Scotch say" but did not take the hint. On the contrary he speedily wrote once more in the middle of May telling how Churchyard had "actually brought home, this blessed week, six more new Pictures." There were two Morlands; a Crome Twilight about the size and tone of the Bergholt Twilight sketch by Constable; another little Constable — a gem!; a large Crome bigger than my Hethel Hall — it is a Heath Scene, Mousehold Heath, near Norwich, as fine as Wilson and a Water Nymph by Etty . . . unencumbered by any redundant drapery — yet the whole redeem'd from indelicacy by the downcast delicacy of expression in the Countenance." The Quaker considered that many would quarrel with its nudity, and demur at hanging it up at home. Churchyard had no qualms about displaying it before his school age children.

Barton's head remained full of thoughts about the Constable view of Higham, acquired after the long higgle. He was prepared to break his long-held habit of taking "almost as little exercise as a milestone, and far less fresh air", by hiring a conveyance to see "my little village itself." This was probably the occasion when the lawyer drove him to the Vale accompanied by a party of the Charlesworths and their young friends. Before returning to Woodbridge he "set up his easel behind Flatford Mill to paint Willy Lott's house" which brought the Constables' workmen to say "this looks like business." They remembered Mr John sketching there about Waterloo time: since those years no one had come to paint those immortal scenes at all.

FitzGerald lingering on in Town wanted his friend to come up for another excursion with him — "I have as yet bought no picture" — and was "sorry to learn that he would not do so . . . I could give him bed at the end of this week if he would even yet come". Churchyard changed his mind, and before the end of June invested during this "London trip" in some contemporary paintings by a promising artist from Suffolk who had that year been patronised by the Queen and the Prince Consort: bringing back "Sundry *Bright* memorials of the same" said Barton, unable to resist the pun. He and Churchyard must have known of young Henry Bright, thirteen or fourteen years before, apprenticed in Woodbridge to a chemist, but giving to drawing whatever time he could get.

The Quaker, who a month earlier had complained of the "ceaseless influx of new objects for admiration'' and declared ''if he don't stop I will go to look at no more of 'em'', soon resumed his normal tune. He was rejoicing that ''Tom has picked up another very fine Crome — Old Buildings by the side of Norwich River — one of the loveliest specimens I have yet seen of the Old Man . . . A magical master-piece of Art and more entirely faultless than the *Yarmouth Jetty.*'' Churchyard cherished it unsold to the end of his life.

The year had moved on as far only as July when, from somewhere, once again not disclosed, Churchyard secured perhaps the best known of all his Cromes. It was *The Windmill*, now in the Tate as *Mousehold Heath: Mill and Donkeys*. Barton, describing to Wodderspoon its more obvious details, caught its true appeal: ''A sky full of air over all''; and thought it ''the very truest piece of Nature I ever saw . . . Will it ever have done raining Cromes? Tom is insatiable and would, I believe, swallow the versal world, could it be cut into Cromes''.

That autumn Churchyard was concerned in an aspect of the law with which he was unaccustomed. Being somewhat different it was an excitement, something to be looked into with zest. He was to act for Barton's cousin John against Dr William Moore of Church Street Woodbridge, in a libel suit to be heard in the Ecclesiastical Court at Norwich. ''Billy is cited to appear there in early December and Master Tom is in deep consultation with eminent Civilians in Town and Proctors at Norwich, bending each mental power to the terrible feat of trouncing the doctor for his base slander. Tom is a shrewd, cute little fellow, but this branch of the law is rather novel to him, so that besides reading, study and reflection on his case, he is sifting and searching *a priori* in every direction''. These preparations took him several times to the cathedral city and Barton, punning again, told Wodderspoon that when the lawyer was there ''upon this *foul* business it was not in his Nature, despite the errand, to forget the *fine* Arts!''

From a visit early in November he brought back from ''trafficking again with Signor Rossi & Wiggers'' two Cromes — ''splendid large one of Sea shore &c and a small one, a perfect little gem'' and in addition a couple of Dutch paintings. ''Also, what is more in thy way, a fine Water Colour Drawing by Cotman of Norwich Market Place on a Market Day — well worthy of being engraved were it not for the cost.''

Churchyard cast his net wide. Wider even than these letters to Wodderspoon report. For Barton, writing in October to Ellen Churchyard away at school, told of another five paintings brought home, beyond those mentioned to the Ipswich newspaper man. Later, in November, was the Lackford sale when the fat Roe acted for Churchyard and secured a Crome that it would be splendid today to recognise. Barton thought it ''as good as Canaletto . . . one could fancy it was taken on a Boat on the Norwich River, and almost in the heart of

Norwich. On both sides are Houses and Warehouses, some low with gable ends, some loftier and of more respectable bearing, all lifting up their walls, roofs and chimneys, into a lovely sky, with their reflections beautifully given in the water, & a breathable sky over all, & in the distance the river is arched over by a Bridge, which Tom calls the Norwich Bridge of Sighs.'' Mr Churchyard in his elegant way.

Less than a week later Barton dashed off another note to Wodderspoon with some perceptive words upon what he saw as the achievement of the *Norwich Market Place* watercolour (Later the picture became his own noteworthy possession). ''It goes some way to shake my faith in the exclusive *power* of Oil painting.'' Two more letters in early December make sidelong allusions to other painting matters and there is news of Barton's swapping Crome's *Hethel Hall* to Churchyard for a copy of a Wilson. ''I have tried to make everybody beside myself like the Hethel Hall but no body will!'' In the report three weeks earlier of the capture of the *Norwich Bridge of Sighs* there had been, in addition to the sense of wonder, a touch of desperation. ''That fellow Churchyard is an out and outer for Cromes . . . Old proverbs tell us you can have too much of a good thing.'' So, perhaps, thought Wodderspoon for if there were more letters of this sort he ceased keeping them. The final one in this batch concludes by opening up a scene in which henceforward the three Chief Wits appear from time to time in company with a kindred spirit on occasions when conversation other than about picture-hunting filled the evening.

The paintings that Churchyard brought back to Marsden House in the twelve months from December 1843 make up a hoard of almost unbelievable richness. Nine of them may well be world possessions today. The *Windmill* is in the Tate: in the Mellon Collection the tumbledown *Houses by the Side of Norwich River*: almost certainly there too is the *Yarmouth Jetty*; for Barton's splendid description makes it likely that his friend's was indeed that finest version of the harbour scene. *Spring Ploughing* must be Constable's original version exhibited at the Bicentenary Exhibition. The *Helmingham Dell* could be that in the Nelson Gallery, Kansas City; while the ''sweet little river scene'' is certainly the Norwich Castle Museum *Scene on the Wensum* of which Churchyard himself made a splendidly exact watercolour copy before he parted with the original. Of the Cotman watercolours, the *Cow Tower Norwich* was shown from a private collection in the 1982 Exhibition at the V. & A. That tour de force of *Norwich Market Place* is in the Abbot Hall Gallery, Kendal.

There were, too, the ''Great Crome'' thought to be his *Glade Cottage*, once believed to have gone down in the Titanic but now known to be safe in private hands; and matching it the *Hethel Hall*, exhibited more than once at an earlier time but now lost sight of. The other purchases of that year unidentified could have been a collection little less precious — the *Higham Village*, the *Bergholt Twilight*, a large *Mousehold Heath* as fine as Wilson, the *Norwich Bridge of Sighs* as good as Caneletto; the Brights, Morlands, Ettys, Wilkies, the Dutchmen and still more Cromes and Constables. Could the paintings all be assembled, some viewers might feel as Barton did: "the eye, the mind, the heart itself grows weary of the prodigality spread before it — begger'd by the very accumulation of riches so heaped up."

It has to be borne in mind that by this time a great number of fake Cromes and replicas were on the market, and recent research suggests that Churchyard's collection contained some of dubious authorship. However, it is unlikely that he was often deceived into bringing home a goose for a swan. He had bought Cromes twenty years earlier when their fame was only local, and had served his own apprenticeship to landscape painting by studying and copying the hand of the master.

1844 is the only year for which an account of Churchyard's picture buying has survived. The inventory of 1854, the catalogue of the 1866 sale and a scatter of remarks from various quarters make it certain that similar activity spanned his adult years. A prodigious procession of masterpieces must have followed one after another on his walls.

XIII

Boulge and Bredfield

THE SUPPER in December 1843 that had been the occasion of Fitz-
Gerald's coining the phrase, the Wits of Woodbridge, was a celebration
on, effectively, the Eve of Christmas. That Saturday night was the twenty-
third when Churchyard drove Barton over to the now legendary Boulge
Cottage. "A hut with walls as thin as a sixpence: windows that won't
shut; a clay soil beneath my feet: a thatch perforated by lascivious sparrows over my head." It had been conceived in perversity in the days of the
previous owners of Boulge Hall. Colonel and Mrs Short had reached a
season in their marriage where neither spoke to the other, except through
the medium of remarks at the dinner table addressed by him to the dog,
by her to the cat. The lady had built the cottage as something to which she
could withdraw when life at the big house became more intolerable than
usual.

Mrs Faiers and her husband, who having served at the final defeat of
Napoleon had come to be thought of as the Waterloo Veteran, took care of
FitzGerald's housekeeping. The quiet, studious melancholy into which
the place had passed under his tenure was interrupted from time to time
by the bizarre hospitality he lavished upon a few well-chosen friends.
Beyond his two picture-hunting companions only the rector of neighbouring Bredfield can be reckoned as an honorary Wit of the first water — the
Reverend George Crabbe II, son and biographer of the Poet of
Aldeburgh. "One of those happy men" FitzGerald said, "who has a
boy's heart throbbing and trembling under the snows of sixty-five;" a
heart "wild but not going astray — liable to sudden emotions, to sudden
and sometimes unreasonable likes and dislikes . . . much of the noble and
Cervantic humourist in him." When asked at a later time what he had
thought of the Great Exhibition the parson replied "Thought of it, my
dear sir! When I entered that vast emporium of the world's commerce, I
lifted up my arms and SHOUTED for amazement."

The four were indeed a consort of opposites. In years they spanned from thirty-five to sixty and while Crabbe, as FitzGerald later said, was "as much a boy at seventy as boys need be at seventeen," he himself had seemed at twenty-six "always like a grave middle-aged man."* Barton was the obsessive friend of all, whereas "the Boulge Hermit" when one time greeted by a Woodbridge dissenting minister with "Good morning Mr FitzGerald" had replied "Sir, I do not know you." Churchyard and Barton had been bred up with no relatives other than yeomen and tradesmen: Crabbe and FitzGerald both of Trinity, Cambridge, had notable family and literary connections. Fitz-Gerald never had to bestir himself to earn a living for a single day, setting no store on money but disposing a large fortune: Crabbe, well enough off to build himself a new parsonage house upon presentation to Bredfield, enjoyed also the living of Pettistree. Barton and Church-yard, working till the day of their deaths left, as to money, nothing behind in this world more than they brought into it. All professed and called themselves Christians: the Quaker the single-minded believer, outside any formal creed; the vicar a polemical defender of particular brands of faith, whom E.F.G. twitted upon being "a good deal in the secrets of Providence"; the lawyer several parts a dissenter; FitzGerald apologised for by his literary executor as being "more than half his life a prisoner in doubting Castle."

These were the choice spirits who numbered Churchyard as one of themselves. Only a few widely scattered remarks by them about him at that time have survived. One brief sentence in a FitzGerald letter sheds a bright illumination: "Though a lawyer, the most sanguine of men" is a key to some of the contradictions in his life. Barton found how exasperating he could be when time was of the essence. Wanting a little work to be done on an unfinished oil sketch of Cotman's he demurred — "were I to put it into Churchyard's hands I might not get it out again these seven years: Rowe would do it in seven days." One evening when FitzGerald had looked in at the Bank House and promised to be "back in ¼ or ½ an hour" the Quaker feared that "he may have gone to Churchyard and if so I may not see him for an hour or two — or maybe not at all."

The verve with which the four came together has long been savoured in one of Crabbe's acceptances of an invitation to an evening at The Cottage. It is likely to have been in reply to the equally jocose:

> Dear Crabbe,
> When from your walk you've rested
> And your dinner half digested,
> Prithee, then set off again

* George Crabbe III.

> Through the dirty roads and rain,
> And win your way with courage here
> To smoke cigars and drink small Beer.
> Churchyard I expect and Barton;
> But should they fail — here's I for sartain;
> Who, as e'en my foes do boast,
> Am always in myself "a host."
> And so expecting you to see
> I'm your obedient E.F.G.

Crabbe's acceptance, told by Barton to Donne "as nearly as my memory serves" ran:

> As sure as a gun
> I'll be in at the fun;
> For I'm the old Vicar
> As sticks to his liquor;
> And smokes a cigar,
> Like a jolly Jack Tar:
> I've no time for more,
> For the Post's at the door;
> But I'll be there by seven
> And stay till eleven,
> For Boulge is my Heaven!

These evenings of well-being and good talk commenced sometimes early enough to include dinner, sometimes were a post prandial affair over oysters with perhaps some of the audit ale sent FitzGerald from Trinity. The host might be indulging in one of his bouts of vegetarianism, "muching apple or turnip and drinking long draughts of milk."* Whether so or not, as the evening wore on there was certain to be more and more tobacco smoke, particularly that rising above Crabbe like clouds of steam. "The Radiator," E.F.G. called him.

The scene within which all this was enacted has its classic description.† "The chaos of the room is vividly in my mind. Large pictures standing against the walls. Portrait on an easel; books, boots, sticks, music scattered about on a table, chairs and floor. An open piano with music, lumber everywhere." It is not surprising that Crabbe summed it up to his son as "all very hospitable, but not comfortable."

Glimpses of evenings at The Cottage as have become known are few. Almost all the papers recording them that chance has preserved were, as before, scribbled by the loquacious Barton — four letters to Crabbe and two to Wodderspoon. To them falls to be added a brief remark by

* F. H. Groome, *Two Suffolk Friends*, 1895, 71.
† J. Glyde, *Life of Edward FitzGerald*, (London 1900) 51.

FitzGerald to his friend Bodham Donne and a shopping list sent to the Bank House. Almost all are clustered into the few weeks between 26th November 1844 and the following February the twentieth.

In the earliest of them the Quaker had told Crabbe he would be happy to bring Churchyard, "or rather to be brought by him to thine any evening. I want him to see the Portrait of thy good Father — very much; . . . he is a very pleasant and intelligent chap — and equally at home in Law or the Fine Arts." Barton went on to repeat the letter he had written Wodderspoon a fortnight earlier about the forthcoming case at Norwich, and could not refrain from sharing with Crabbe a humorous touch that Churchyard had told him concerning "the curious constitutional working of the Spiritual Court Of Judicature. You do not do it for filthy Lucre's sake, or from any vindictive feeling to the culprit — but out of Christian Love and regard for *his Soul's health*." Introduction to the lawyer in person had, however, to be postponed. Despite the attraction of Phillips' portrait of the Poet of Aldeburgh, a genial dinner, with FitzGerald also present, cigars and smoking for a good three hours, Churchyard was adamant that he must remain in Woodbridge, sitting in the lamplight of his office putting the final touches to the slander case against Doctor Moore.

With that disposed of the visit could take place. Such good news Barton must share with someone. He was writing to Wodderspoon on 12 December to tell him of the swapping of Crome's *Hethel Hall* for the Wilson copy and could not refrain from adding that "Churchyard, FitzGerald, &c" (that is himself) "are to dine with the Rev Geo. Crabbe tomorrow at six, and then there is to be such a Cigar Divan held, as makes me hold my nose at the mere thought of it!" Later in the month there was another dinner party at the Vicarage when Barton had to retire to join Crabbe's daughters in the withdrawing room, "more than wroth with cigars and smoking — did they not cheat me of a good three hours of thy Company?"

Into the New Year, on 29 January 1845, FitzGerald writing to Donne threw in a last sentence: "Barton comes and sups with me to-morrow, and George Crabbe, son of the poet, a capital fellow." Next day but one after the meal the talkative Quaker wrote to his fellow guest merely for the purpose of going over with him the details of the party they had enjoyed: "The mutton of our Hero of the Cottage was capital — his Wild Ducks ditto — the Port fine — Porter prodigiously potent — His Pickles had the true Bredfield pungency — but the odour of that room was really awful — talk of my tippling Port! marry the clouds such a trio as yours can and do blow would do more to make me drunk than all the Wine I could be induced to swallow." Mention of a trio of smokers denotes Churchyard's being present; it was he who usually drove Barton to any gathering away from Woodbridge.

In the autumn of 1845 a different bill of fare was planned for an evening at Boulge — that "midway place where happy spirits may alight between Bredfield and Woodbridge." FitzGerald wrote to Barton adjuring him to "bring up with thee a pound of Derby Cheese, for a toast: some oysters, with knives; that thou mayst eat. And I will pay thee the cost — I have a fowl hanging up: and if my father's cook arrive, as I think she will, tonight, she shall handsell her skill on the fowl. For I doubt Mrs Faier's powers of Bread-sauce — I doubt she would produce a sort of dumpling. But Sarah knows about these things."

At the end of January 1846 a letter of Barton's to Wodderspoon told him that "the Cottage Hermit comes to me tonight and Churchyard is to meet him — We will pledge thee in a bumper of something." All other bright and coloured evenings that the four spent at the Cottage or the Vicarage or in Woodbridge itself, the darkness has obliterated them. As with other of Churchyard's continuing activities, light has only been shed on them for a brief and arbitrary spell. One final glint comes from a letter of FitzGerald to Edward Byles Cowell, relating his hurried return to Bredfield in the October of 1857 to attend Crabbe's funeral. He told him that when it was over he took away from the Vicarage "as a Relic . . . a little silver Nutmeg Grater which used to give the finishing Touch to many a glass of good hot Stuff." Since neither he nor Churchyard kept Barton's letters the chance is lost of hearing about other occasions when the little grater had been used to such admired effect. Barton must have written talkatively about it to someone for it served as another coming together of letters and life. It "had belonged to the Poet Crabbe."

A further picture of the Churchyard household at this time is preserved in a batch of the Quaker's letters, covering once again only a short span: eleven weeks in the autumn of 1844; three lengthy moralising screeds to Ellen Churchyard.

It was a time of high family fortune. Beyond the fees that came into the lawyer's hand from his many appearances in court, there was the recently inherited capital that had passed to him on his mother's death in 1843 — the old home at the bottom of Melton Hill, Blocks Barn Farm at the top, the remainder from her share of his father's personalty. Harriet, too, had received under her mother's Will a quarter share of grandmamma Hailes' estate in the spring of 1844. In consequence Churchyard, with an uncharacteristic display of prudence, decided to take out a life insurance policy with the Norwich Union Society for a thousand pounds, annual premium £36.16.8. Furthermore the girls ought to be educated in a manner befitting the daughters of Woodbridge's liveliest attorney. And so, in the first week of August Ellen, Emma and, presumably, Laura were despatched to join the twenty-six girls already at the Boarding Academy of Mrs Maria Jay, 52, Southgate Street, Bury St Edmunds; one of a baker's dozen of such establishments for young ladies in that social capital of Suffolk.

Ellen, just short of her eighteenth birthday had already outgrown the tutelage of Miss Ann Bird, but it was felt to be only proper that she should for one term enjoy, as a finishing touch, what was henceforth to be the regular education of all her younger sisters. Becoming a schoolgirl again was by no means to Ellen's liking. It was an occasion entirely suited to Barton for delivering homilies full of sound sense and laudable advice to a young lady; urging her to be a good girl despite her not unnatural sense of revolt.

After an elaborately contrived preamble, his first letter of 6th August went on: ''I am not going to preach thee a sermon, my dear, so let not my little Nelly be frightened on that score.'' If not a sermon, it is difficult to know what the missive can be called, for it proceeds: ''There is always something yet to be learnt, and old proverbs tell us none are too old to learn, at eighteen, or even under it, this may fairly be assumed; and at such an age a sensible and well disposed girl may be supposed, if not very vain and conceited (which my Nelly is not) to have become aware in what respect her education has been most neglected, and what deficiencies she feels most conscious of. With all these aids to reflection, & resolution too, I really think the six months absence from home, though I am well aware of thy hearty love for it, may be turned to good account, both for body and mind, and I don't despair, my dear, of thy coming back a wiser, happier girl, and in improved health and spirits. So my dear Nell make the best of these six months, as a dutiful, sensible good temper'd & true hearted girl should, and come back to us as much like thy old self, improved, as may be — when I talk of improved, I do not mean in mere accomplishments, which though I would not under value, are not all requisite to finish one's education. The true end of all learning, my dear, whether in or out of School, is to teach us how to live; and what we are living for — and at thy age with so many whom thy example must more or less influence, this, my love, is a lesson which must daily & hourly come more home to thy heart & head.''

Such was but a quarter of the moralising to which the long letter ran. Not nonsensical but dull. Still, Ellen kept it to the end of her life and responded to his hope of ''merely a few lines to tell how thy time is spent & whether my writing to thee can give thee pleasure or encouragement.'' In the consequent exchange of letters Barton sat down ''to scribble a line or two'' (a good five hundred words) to give Woodbridge news. ''Pa was out sketching so I only saw mamma and Charley, the latter took care to call my attention to his new hat''.

At the end of October Barton was already writing about the end of term and "lots of new things for thee to see on coming home". He himself had picked up one or two pictures by barter "& thy father says I have made a good exchange." Edward had bought none. "But as to pictures thy Father is the man to pick them up, it seems to rain down pictures for him."

The letter catches one of the few surviving glimpses of the now matronly Mrs Churchyard. Barton had seen her at supper the previous night. "Ma very poorly with a bad headache: muddled about her Servants & they have had Workmen about the house and yards for ever so long which has altogether kept her in dibles,* as the Suffolk folk say:" The Quaker's screed ended with asking Nelly to give his love to Emma and Kate. Kate must have been a slip of the pen for Laura, since Catherine was only just five.

A few weeks later Barton was exercising himself in putting together after a lapse of nine years, a selection of his later poems, *Household Verses* that were to be published in July of the following year. To his great satisfaction he was able to inscribe it gratefully to The Queen, by Her Kind Permission. In letters to his friends there is suppressed excitement at thus drawing near The Lady of Windsor. Between the covers of the volume members of the Churchyard family gained entrée to The Castle. Ellen, home from Bury St Edmunds, could now take charge of domestic arrangements when Mamma was poorly, muddled about her servants, in dibles. One of the final poems Barton included was something very recently written in the young woman's praise. Telling Crabbe about "my new Book" he informed him "I copied out fairly for it this morning a Piece to Tom Churchyard's pretty little daughter Nelly commemorative of her skill in making pies, puddings, tarts & bread. And is not that a dainty dish to set before a Queen? — at any rate I mean it to go, as a most appropriate item in a Book of *Household Verses.*"

To a Very Young House-wife

To write a book of Household Song,
   Without one verse to thee,
Whom I have known and loved so long,
   Were all unworthy me.

Have I not seen thy needle plied
   With as much ready glee,
As if it were thy greatest pride
   A sempstress famed to be?

---

* Vernacular for vexations.

Have I not ate pies, puddings, tarts,
　　And bread — thy hand had kneaded,
All excellent — as if those arts
　　Were all that thou hadst heeded.

Have I not seen thy cheerful smile,
　　And heard thy voice — as gay,
As if such household cares, the while,
　　To thee were sport and play?

Yet can thy pencil copy well
　　Landscape, or flower, or face;
And thou canst waken music's spell
　　With simple, natural grace.

Thus *variously* to play thy part,
　　Before thy teens are spent,
Honours far more thy head, and heart,
　　Than mere accomplishment!

So wear the wreath thou well hast won;
　　And be it understood
I frame it not in idle fun
　　For girlish womanhood.

But in it may a lesson lurk,
　　Worth teaching now-a-days;
That girls may do all household work,
　　Nor lose a poet's praise!

The Young Housewife's father caught royal notice by the book's two illustrations. For frontispiece it had his *Gainsborough's Lane, on the Orwell*, while vignetted into the title page was *Scene on the Deben*, a couple of barges at Tide Mill Quay, both paintings delicately transcribed by J. C. Bentley, the busy London Engraver.

XIV

Bury St Edmunds and Botany Bay

JUST AS 1844 is the *annus mirabilis* for its sights of Churchyard as picture hunter and Woodbridge Wit, so is it notable also as showing him at work on legal matters of great weight. In contrast to the scant mention by the press at this date of cases at Petty Sessions, newspaper accounts of proceedings at Assizes give pages-long verbatim reports of evidence, cross-examination, barristers' addresses, judges' summings up. FitzGerald's question about "our Debach boy that set the shed on fire" is a reminder the Churchyard was consulted by many around Woodbridge who came to be committed for trial on charges of serious crime; preparing the briefs for their defending counsel, some of whom were destined to become luminaries in after years.

Glyde, with his usual near misses, says that Churchyard prided himself upon having given Sir Fitzroy Kelly, Solicitor General and Lord Chief Baron his first brief as a newly called barrister. This could not have been so, since young Kelly had already practised for a year or two on the Home Circuit before he came into Churchyard's sphere upon joining the Norfolk. It is likely to have been Judge Dasent. John Bury Dasent, of a family long prominent in the West Indies, his father Attorney-General of St Vincent, was the genial young wit of the Norfolk Circuit in the eighteen forties. Like Thomas, he was for ever embroidering his briefs with sketches of brother lawyers, witnesses, sometimes prisoner at the bar, sometimes the Judge or Chairman. One of his jests at a Suffolk Quarter Session is said to have been retold in Punch. The local press reported it thus, "A learned counsel fell into the arms of Morpheus, spectacles on nose and pen in mouth. A talented gentleman of the long robe — clever with his pencil as with his oratory — took a sketch of the object before him. When finished he did it up in an envelope and addressing him by name 'Here is a note for you from the gaolor'. 'Capital' said the awakened barrister when he opened it, 'I will take this home and have it framed and glazed.' " On an occasion in a lower court when Churchyard was noting down on his blue paper some evidence being given, one of the witnesses had deposed "I was in the family way". At the side of the sheet he quickly sketched the simple countrywoman's face and completed his drawing by adding her shape in the way he imagined it to have been at the time. It is not surprising that he and Dasent found themselves to be kindred spirits.

There were weighty cases in which they collaborated in 1844, one of the most desperate years of the hungry forties. "A whole county is on fire" opened a leading article in *The Times*, headed *Suffolk Incendiarism*. "Between 20 and 30 trials for arson and threatening letters stand for hearing at Ipswich alone", and the writer estimated that for every prisoner brought to trial, nine perpetrators had gone unapprehended. The ricks and buildings of farmers who were Poor Law Guardians were the main targets; it was they who had to bear the brunt of the opprobrium over the working of the new regulations for poor law relief and its being withheld from the able bodied — "the natural, though the bitter fruits which, with the mass of men, always will and always do spring from hopeless penury and distress" as *The Times* leader had summed up the position.

It was the universal panic over the nightly fires, and the determination of the judiciary to stamp out this terrifying crime by exemplary sentencing, that led to the Debach boy being charged with one of the most serious crimes in the calendar. His case came up at the Suffolk Lent Assize at Bury, dignified with all its traditional panoply of "High Sheriff, Under Sheriff and their retinue of Officers, Marshals, and Trumpeters: the Javelin Men in Liveries of naval blue with pantaloons of Oxford grey and buff waistcoats." William Wayley, the Debach boy, was only ten.

Churchyard had prepared the ground for the defence with his usual thoroughness. He had made his enquiries about the farmer's shed and had found that in one vital respect what the farmer's wife had said in her depositions, was clean contrary to what she had originally told the parson. Dasent had, in consequence, been able to enjoy himself in making much of this in cross-examination, where he brought the woman to contradict not only herself, but the only other prosecution witness as well. Under pressure she "could not remember" what she had told the rector, could not remember having offered a new slop or half a sovereign to Wayley's eleven-year-old friend, James Crane, to worm the story out of the accused. The young friend indeed gave evidence that William had told him "he had set the shed on fire but wished he had not, and then turned away and cried." Mr Justice Patteson not unnaturally considered the prosecution had quite failed to establish a case of the grave crime of arson, and asked the jury whether they needed to hear the defence. Without its being called the charge was dismissed.

Churchyard and Dasent had no success in another case at that same Assize involving two men and a woman of the travelling people accused of stealing a cash box from the Woodbridge Cock and Pie, where they had lodged the previous night. Traced to Debenham they were found to have on them 24 sixpences, 25 shillings, 5 half-crowns, a bright farthing and a black bent one. The black farthing was identified as was also one of the sixpences with a hole in it, likewise the incriminating cash-box which they said they had found under a hedge at Bealings. The chances of the accused being able to clear themselves were slim. Nevertheless it was worth everything that poor people had to fee attorney and barrister whose thorough knowledge of the intricacies of their profession might enable them to turn the trembling scale in their favour. A verdict of guilty could be cataclysmic. The gypsies Eliza and John Smith of previous good character were sentenced to transportation for ten years. James Scott, who had a previous convinction for stealing, was sent to Botany Bay for life. The Assize concluded and next week Churchyard went up to London to prove his mother-in-law's Will.

At the Summer Assize that year with its heavy calendar of incendiarism he briefed Dasent in a grave case. James Friend, 27, of Tunstall was accused of sending a threatening letter to his employer, William Cockrell of White Cross farm. The writing, sealed up and held in place by a stone, was found by the farmer's son in the stackyard. On the outside in place of an address were the words: "Farmer you Premisas will Sone Be Set on Fire. 1844". Opened it read: "Farmer, ve are starven, we wol not stan this no longer, this gang is 600 80, rather than Starve we are turment to set you on Fire, you are Rongan the Pore of there living By imploying thrashmans Sheans, this Promsas will sone take Plase if you dont oltar, thare is Plenty Grown in this cuntry to suport the Pore, you must not Be surprised if you se your Primsas on Fire and Stok all Barnt. There will Be si6 on Fire in one time."

Friend was typical of the men with whose life style Churchyard was acquainted unlike any other attorney — the drivers of his father's droves to Smithfield; the labourers at Blocks Barn, Byng Hall and Clopton; the poachers and keepers; the countrymen he met while shooting or sketching in the fields and meadows. It was natural that it was to him they should come to make themselves understood when in trouble with the law.

The prosecution had all the facts on their side. Friend had gone to a neighbour's house to borrow writing materials and to pen something there; the half of the sheet he had not covered he had torn off and left behind. It was still there and Loder, as an expert witness, identified the two parts as fitting together. The Registrar of Saxmundham recognised the fist as correspnding with Friend's entries of the deaths of two of his children. There were sufficient letters impressed on the seal to connect them exactly with the motto on his watch-fob, ''Forget-me-not''.

His lawyers used all their ingenuity. Mr Dasent objected that the Act specified houses, barns, stacks. The letter said premises, therefore the indictment was not framed within the statute. This the judge over-ruled. At the end of the prosecution, the defence submitted that nothing had been adduced to show that the letter was intended for Cockrell and that there was accordingly insufficient evidence for the case to be put to the jury. This also his lordship would not accept. Dasent was then driven to making much of the improbability that Friend who had a steady job on the new-fangled threshing machine would be the one to threaten his employer with arson because of its introduction. The jury had no hesitation in bringing in a verdict of guilty. Friend was stood down till the end of the Assize.

On Saturday 27th July all those convicted of offences concerned with arson were addressed by Baron Alderson. ''In a voice quivering with emotion'' he besought them to reflect upon their crimes and to repent while life and time was spared to them. What had it availed them to have brought misery to happy households; to have encompassed the deaths of unoffending animals — ''the horse that perished in the stable, the kine that died in their stall, the sheep that fell in their quiet fold, the faithful dog in his kennel . . . Many of you, perhaps, think that the punishment of transportation is but slight. Fearful, dreadful mistake! It is a punishment that makes my blood run cold when I think of its deprivations and its horrors . . . You will be exiles from your families and your friends — for life — aye! for life most of you. You will have to dwell under the lash, under privation and great labour, in a land where you will find nothing but unmitigated villainy around you. Among your fellows you will find no mixture of good and bad, nothing but the *bad* altogether; creating a foretaste of that hereafter, when the bad are appointed to dwell tormented for ever. There in that far distant land to which you will be sent you will find a hell upon earth, the thoughts of which, as I before-said to you, make my blood run cold, but to which nevertheless, however, unwilling, however pain-ful, I am bound to send you, though with reluctant heart and unwilling mind.'' All the incendiaries suffered transportation to Botany Bay for life.

Mr Justice Williams then dealt with those who had merely threat-ened. ''I say there is too near a connection between the fires that have happened and these letters, to allow me to pass over without a sentence of great severity such an offence as this. I sentence you James Friend to be transported to such place as Her Majesty shall, by her Privy

Council, think fit to direct, for a space of fifteen years.'' The defence
had done what they could but on matters of fact it had been a hopeless
case, and there was as yet no Court of Appeal to which Dasent might
take the two points of law on which he had been over-ruled. Churchyard returned to Woodbridge to admire and copy his *Windmill* that he
had brought home a few days before the Assize opened.

XV

Living on Borrowed Money

IN JANUARY 1846 there was a bad sale of some pictures that the Quaker and the lawyer had sent up to the London auction rooms. On hearing the news FitzGerald, Christmassing at his niece's near Beccles, wrote tersely: "I am not surprised . . . his Morland deserved more but was very likely not to get more, because of its size . . . I think those Cupids met with their deserts" — Etty's *Angelic Heads*, most likely. That spring saw the last of their joint excursions, though from time to time afterwards FitzGerald would look in at Christies and write to Barton as to whether there was anything worth buying. "Pray tell this to Churchyard who wanted to know about it."

Some stray Barton letters to Wodderspoon in July 1847 tell of cold water poured on the Wits' enthusiasm. They related a visit to Woodbridge by FitzGerald's "poor quarrelsome friend Morris Moore. A strapping sandy-haired fellow thinning on top and with a thick moustache of that same on his upper lip . . . Very learned on pictures of the older School." He was the *Verax* who shortly before had been writing a succession of vituperative letters to *The Times* upon the *Abuses of the National Gallery*; smiting Eastlake, the Keeper, so severely (albeit on no very good grounds) as to cause his resignation.

Barton found him pleasant and intelligent, but joined FitzGerald in wondering how he managed to make a bare living from a percentage earned now and then on pictures which one or other of the nobility and gentry got him to buy for them. For he made life difficult for himself by his outspokenness in abusing the Old Masters that his clients thought their best possessions, and finding fault with their bad taste in getting such rubbish. His last evening was spent with the Wits at Churchyard's. Moore made no bones about his views on East Anglian painting. "It was all plain to me he regarded it as if it were the work of a sort of rude and half civilised Barbarian . . . The two he abused most were

the Cotman drawing of *Norwich Market Place* and the Constable *Dell* —
both of which he averred to be as bad as they could be — villainous in
perspective, drawing, colour & everything. I believe the Man was
perfectly honest in his scorn & hatred of them.''

By this time money troubles had begun to cloud the outlook for both
FitzGerald and Barton. Since 1843, E.F.G.'s father had been increas-
ingly concerned over his five miles of flooded coal mines at Pendleton.
At the earlier time ''with the aid of the powerful engines at work, Mr
George Stephenson, the celebrated engineer, has no doubts of effec-
tually clearing the pits of water, and ere long having this fine colliery in
full working order.'' By the end of 1847 hopes were wearing thin and
creditors losing patience. In the succeeding January E.F.G. had to
write to Barton in some anxiety as to whether his cheque on Coutts,
that depended upon his father's allowance to him, would be met. In the
middle of May he was asking his friend to let him have in London a
Post Office order or a cheque for £5. That autumn John FitzGerald,
with two houses in Portland Place, country seats at Brighton, Boulge,
Little Island Waterford and Castle Irwell Manchester, failed with
liabilities of £190,000. ''The coming diminution of wealth and reputation would not make the slightest difference to me,'' E.F.G. wrote Barton in August and referred him to Churchyard who was aware of the
intricacies of the family trusts. FitzGerald had told his legal friend
something of his plans and doings — a reversal of the usual chain of
communication — for it was no longer proper to trouble B.B. ''Only
partially well: is altered during the last year: has less spirits, less
strength; but quite amiable still''.

Writing humorously to Donne, the Quaker reflected upon the enthusiasm of his employers for the freeing of the slaves in the West Indies
while remaining blind to the servitude of their confidential clerk at
Church Street, Woodbridge. ''Our Friends are reputed a rich sect, and
they are a liberal one in their way. To the distant Irish they give
thousands, to the Negro Cause ditto!'' Then, quoting against them the
popular anti-slavery slogan put into the black man's mouth, he continued ''*Am I not a Man and a Brother*? But I can never sue them *in forma
pauperis*, or even drop a hint that I stand a fair chance of falling from
my perch and dying in clerkly harness. This growl and grumble is only
for thy private ear.'' It was prophetically near enough to the way in
which he went off.

He had suffered some loss of means the previous year, so that his
daughter, now forty, would be ill provided for. The Alexander partners
felt, presumably, that they had done all that was called for by peremp-
torily forbidding him, in his declining weeks, to do any duties in the
Bank after his four o'clock dinner. FitzGerald, busy with lawyers in
London, came home for a few days ''to spend Christmas with Barton:

whose turkey I accordingly partook of.'' A few weeks later he reported him as looking ''very demurely to the necessary end of all life. Church-yard is pretty well; has had a bad cough for three months. I suppose we are all getting older.'' The lawyer was fifty-one and he himself still in his thirties — ''always like a grave middle-aged man.'' These two were to live many years longer, but Barton's headstone in the burial-ground of the Woodbridge Meeting House soberly records his death ''19 of 2 mo. 1849.''

To lighten Lucy's financial difficulties, FitzGerald assisted her in editing a selection of her father's letters and poems and supplied to the volume what he called his ''little dapper memoir.'' Great exertions were made to enrol subscribers, as the result of which nearly nine hundred names appear — every nobleman in the locality and many more from all parts of the kingdom; politicians and pillars of the Church; whole Quakers families of Alexanders, Peckovers, Rowntrees, Gurneys: scores of Barton's friends in the flesh and from his widely scattered correspondents such names as Harrison Ainsworth, Dickens, Kinglake, Lockhart, Thackeray, Wordsworth. FitzGerald took ten copies, Crabbe twelve and Churchyard six. It is to be hoped that chance may yet bring to light the grangerised copy, shown by Ellen to E. V. Lucas, that FitzGerald made, ''calling in the assistance of Mr Churchyard and two of his daughters. A very charming volume . . . rich in watercolour drawings of the Barton country, some of these, par-ticularly of the Deben, being of great beauty.''

For many hundreds of subscribers and their friends the arrival of the volume was the first time they had come across the word Churchyard serving as a somewhat macabre surname, for it is almost unknown out-side East Anglia. They saw it titled as that of the painter of the three Marvy engravings that illustrated the book. Outstandingly *The Valley of Fern*, that accompanied Barton's favourite poem, showed them to what levels this unknown artist could attain.

The next year, 1850, Churchyard was drawn into departing from his resolve not to show his work in public again. The ambitious Mayor of Ipswich, Thomas Baldock Ross, had determined that the Borough should no longer lag behind Norwich culturally and proposed the in-auguration of a Suffolk Fine Arts Association. Churchyard's devotion to painting made it unthinkable that he should decline to sit on the Exploratory Committee or to act as local secretary for Woodbridge: the only local secretary who was himself a painter, (others were concerned with Art at shopkeeping level — printers, booksellers, picture-framers), the only local secretary invited to the Main Committee. Francis Capper Brooke Esquire of Ufford Place, bibliophile with one of the finest private libraries in the kingdom, magistrate and game preserver was asked to move the Association's foundation. There was great enmity between him and Churchyard at Sessions and perhaps his opening remarks were meant to cut his neighbour. "The primary object, I believe, is to improve the taste of the artists who have already produced works of art." An inelegant piece of English, but not one that caused the Poacher's Lawyer to be put off by its imputation.

The Exhibition opened with great éclat and under distinguished patronage at the New Lecture Hall, Tower Street, on 28 August. "Lighted by gas, the hall had a brilliant appearance". Throughout its continuance excursion trains were run from Bury, Colchester and Norwich, and because the hours of ten to five were "inconvenient for the young men in shops and for the working classes, the opening was extended into the evening one day a week . . . The London artists seem to have contributed the bulk, next in order come the Norwich artists" — Thomas Lound, David Hodgson, the Ladbrookes, the Middletons, James Stark, Mrs Stannard. With all but one of them Churchyard had exhibited on their home ground twenty-one years earlier.

His own showing exceeded that of any other painter: ten oils and six watercolours. Altogether ten are straightforwardly titled *Sketch from Nature*, four others have "Sketch" along with some other words. Unhappily nothing is to be gleaned from the local reporter, all at sea with this assignment. He mentions two of the oils: "146, *Dead Pheasant, a Sketch* has a very natural appearance and is very creditable to the artist. We cannot commend his *Sketch at Melton, No 149*". Of his watercolours there is the bare "We may also notice 210". Meeting with such scant recognition it is not surprising that he did not send in to any further annual exhibition the Suffolk Association staged before expiring after that of 1854. In 1852 there must have been a rift with the Norfolk painters who stayed away and staged the Norwich Exhibition on the same dates as Ipswich.

Churchyard apt at being different, sided with his newly re-found friends and sent in eight "Sketches" and "Studies" to Norwich, all of them within walking distance of Woodbridge save one at Dover. As in 1829 the *Norwich Mercury*, with a reporter experienced in art shows, fastened on to his pictures in particular. "The smaller works are many of them excellent. Among these we may note the fresh and natural sketches by Mr Churchyard". Again this showing falls into his pattern of "once in a lifetime". Four more similar exhibitions were mounted in Norwich in that decade but he chose not to send in. It was not till a few weeks before his death that he exhibited anywhere again.

Something racier on Churchyard's Ipswich submissions might have appeared in the two hundred lines of doggerel by "Peter Pindar Jnr." had not

The landscapes so num'rous (been) and so good
I can't speak of all e'en if that I would . . .
(Thomas W)'s respectable in his own scope
But Clarke, Dr William, is all yellow soap.
E. Smyth and T. I have no wish to blame,
But really you both should feel some tinge of shame;
Nature to each has been lavish of gifts,
And yet you are always a-painting makeshifts.

Scattered hints are all one has to go on in trying to visualise Church-yard's achievements in these half-way years of his painting. The naturalness of the dead bird commended itself to the Ipswich reporter but not the "Natural Landscape Painting" of the living sketch at Melton. Living, such scenes certainly were, for the Norwich critic found his sketches fresh and natural. These were not the qualities that commended themselves to the Suffolk picture-buyers of the day. They found themselves more able to admire the contrived landscape paint-ings — splendidly contrived as many were — of artists such as the Smythe brothers, where one is conscious almost always of looking at their placid and imagined places on any late afternoon in early autumn. Churchyard was aiming less at a highly finished composition than an expression of the natural scene as he had glimpsed in *au premier coup* on a day never to be repeated. Barton had noticed this, telling Donne that "Churchyard will dash you off slight and careless sketches by the dozen, or score, but for touching, re-touching, or finishing that is quite another affair." The Quaker put this down to laziness and want of pains. FitzGerald saw further into it when he declared that "all Painters except the best *are* best in their slight sketches done in a heat."

Even he missed the kernal of the truth. Churchyard understood, as few then did, that such sketches done in a heat could in fact be a satisfy-ing order of painting in themselves. Even Constable, it seems, thought of his own in this genre mainly as raw material for scenes to be painted in the grand manner: certainly his contemporaries valued them at no more than a few shillings as bundle. Only looking back at them through eyes accustomed to impressionism have they come to be treasured at hundreds of thousands of pounds.

By no means all Churchyard's painting at this stage was slight, as a few dated pieces such as a Norwich Cathedral of 1847 clearly show. It would not be rash to think that at the time of the Ipswich exhibition, already in his fifties, he had come to his accepted style. Within it trees, above all, were his abiding interest — the conflicting curves of young saplings, the grotesque pollards of ancient oaks and willows. In com-pany their rounded forms were used to tie in or cut off areas of his com-position: single they could be painted analytically, each with its own

103

particular leafiness. In these last he indeed answered Major Hart's encomium: "He knew exactly where he wanted to put his brush, he never
put it down twice and he always put it in the right place." The oil *April
Day, Old Melton* has the movement of Constable. The wet leaves of ivy
on the old oak glisten as the wind brings along another shower and for a
last brief moment a gleam of sunlight runs over a strip of meadow as
the clouds race and the young willow sways away from the north-easter
and the coming rain.

The water colour drawings, so many times more numerous than the
oils, are sometimes impressions rendered as mere splashes of colour,
sometimes are highly organised while yet retaining the first careless
rapture. Typical of these latter are *The Pond* or again *Across the Meadows,
Martlesham*, full of minor interest, with two dozen young pliant willow
saplings in the background, its foreground dominated by the bulk of
the contrasting old pollard.

In the spring of 1851 there had been the taking of the Census. It
shows that the Churchyard household lacked Young Tom now farming
at Ufford, and Harriet and Kate away at boarding School in Bury. In
Thoroughfare, the Return records Lucy, widow of Isaac the butcher on
Market Hill, now aged 50, as a Lodging House Keeper. Misfortune
had dogged her efforts to maintain the business left by her husband.
For ten years she had had the active help of her brother Robert but at
10 o'clock on the night of 3rd January, 1843, as he "quite sober" was
driving the two of them home from an evening at Ipswich the mare
slipped on the ice in going slowly down Drybridge hill. The spot was
known to be "a great nuisance — some women of loose character there
make an invariable practice of throwing large quantities of waste water
on the road." The horse fell so suddenly that the breechings broke and
both occupants of the trap were thrown out with great violence. Smith,
a very heavy man fractured his skull and was killed on the spot. For the
next five years Lucy managed to keep the business going till in the
April of 1848 she was declared bankrupt.

The census enumerator at Boulge was a young master-miller from
the next-door village of Debach. Calling at The Cottage and asking the
Head of the household for details in person he was given Christian
Name: Edward. State: Unmarried. Age: 42. Born: Bredfield, Suffolk.
"And what shall I put for your occupation, sir?" "Living on borrowed
money."

Over the three years leading up to 1851 FitzGerald's letters to
friends had been well sprinkled with abuse of the persons who were
handling his affair arising out of his father's bankruptcy. "I have been
trying to hurry on, and bully lawyers: have done a very little good with
much trouble" — "hoping to get some accursed lawyers to raise me
some money on what remains of my reversion" — "They utterly failed

in any part of the transaction except for bringing me in a large bill for service unperformed'' — ''fresh squabbles with lawyers.''

The firm was White and Borrett: John Meadows White who had gone up from Halesworth to practise in London, and Thomas Borrett married to Laura Tuthill, a cousin of his partner's wife: both ladies drawn from the legal network of that little country town. The prayer to heaven Robert Gostling White made on behalf of his numerous family in that strange will of 1813, had not gone unanswered. His eldest son, Robert, had become an Oxford Doctor of Divinity, Fellow of Magdalen and Professor of Anglo Saxon. John, the second son, had risen to great eminence as a parliamentary attorney and author of a number of law books. His firm became solicitors to the Tithe Commissioners for England and Wales, solicitors to the Copyhold Commissioners and to the Ecclesiastical Commissioners.

They had advanced from Great St Helens to more and more distinguished addresses; Lincolns Inn Fields; Whitehall Place. Gentlemen of the law practising in such eminence had a reputation to sustain. It was shaken by a typical FitzGerald scoff. After three years of protracted and abortive consultations with them he finally lost patience and accused them outright of trying to cheat him. They replied with a threatened action for traducing their good name. E.F.G.'s rejoinder, had it come out in Court, would have produced a nickname to last for all time. Instead it led to a prompt and quiet dropping of the action. He related his triumph in a letter to Donne; it is likely that Churchyard was let into the joke, seeing that he had known the Whites since his days when articled at Halesworth. Traducing the good name of White and Borrett? FitzGerald wrote them saying that he had no concern for whatever their name was. For aught he cared they might style themselves Bite and Worrit.

XVI

The Book Club

BEYOND THE evenings Churchyard spent in the unpredictable comings together of the Wits, there were those arranged with clockwork regularity in which he joined a gathering of other friends — the monthly meetings of the Woodbridge Book Club. Founded in 1793, subscription a guinea a year, its purpose was to circulate among members the best new books and current magazines and for the gentlemen who comprised it to meet on the Thursday of the full moon, entertaining by rotation in their own homes.

The membership was nominally confined to a dozen, thought at times the number was stretched to include a few more. Any candidate proposed one month was admitted only "if the ballot four weeks after shows that those present be unanimous in their approbation, but not otherwise." The company that had passed muster constituted a slice of the substantial men of Woodbridge. Corn merchants, millers and maltsters were always prominent with two or three from the professions; usually a doctor, auctioneer or architect; the Congregational minister or a curate of St Mary's. Few of the shopkeepers came up to requirements. The gentry were not interested. After long years of association one might be allowed to drop into honorary membership, paying an annual guinea not to be subject to fines for missing the meetings.

The bill for Club Nights was ordained straightforwardly to be "Before supper port and sherry: at supper cold beef and horseradish sauce: cold cheese after supper as usual." There were fines of 6d for failing to arrive on time at 7 o'clock and a shilling for absence. An annual dinner was held at the Bull at 4 o'clock with as many bottles of wine ordered as members present "And when the last of such bottles of wine shall be brought in, the Chairman shall inform the company, and any further orders shall be at the expense of the person giving them."

Barton writing to tell Wodderspoon about his friend acquiring the "very fine Crome — *Old Buildings by the side of Norwich River*", gave him also an account of the annual dinner the previous afternoon. It was an oppressively hot Midsummer Day — people "gasping and panting" — so that "of 17 members only nine had courage to go to it." Port and sherry taken by so small a number would not "make it answer to Salmon (the landlord) who got up a capital dinner." So the company was "reduced to drinking Champagne, Hock & Claret instead — how the fellows did drink. We sate down at four & by eight o'clock when I left them I fancy they had drank nine or ten bottles of the wines I have nam'd, besides two or three of port and sherry for ones of the older members who had no liking for thin potations." Later the function was moved to the New Year; absentees fined five shillings and after the repast the books and magazines that had run their course around the club were auctioned by one of the company.

Like the new members, new books were proposed at one meeting, voted upon at the next. "No book to be proposed after ten o'clock." It does not follow that till that hour the conversation had been purely literary. Even Barton, very much the man of letters, expected nothing remarkable in that direction. He described his old acquaintance Thomas Heard, tenant farmer of Seckford Hall, a founder member and still going strong at eighty-six, as "really a pillar of our literary temple, not that he cared greatly about books, or was deeply read in them, but that he loved to meet his neighbours and to get them round him."

The earliest surviving minute book of 1845 is just in time to show the meetings as Churchyard had known them under the old régime, still with several senior members going back almost to the foundation. The before-supper port and sherry were taken as a leisurely affair, with many a sixpenny fine recorded through the strict time-keeping of the venerable secretary. He was Mr Thomas Giles, retired from auctioneering, whose tenure of office stretched back more than fifty years to the club's inauguration. Seldom absent, never late, he was by then in his eighty-eighth year, "his faculties perfect (hearing excepted)". A brief four day's illness in 1846 carried him off and the minutes of the next meeting, recording the members' sense of great loss, went on to praise his remarkable tranquillity, even temper and large share of plain good sense, with a most retentive memory. It spoke of the beautiful hand that he wrote and the remarkable correctness with which he expressed himself. A bad word was never uttered by him, nor an unkind word of a neighbour.

The old gentleman had become set in ways that no one would have questioned while he still remained, but on the same evening of their obital esteem the members lost no time in changing the name to the

Woodbridge Social Book Club and in altering the hour of foregathering from 7 o'clock to 8. Thomas Temple Silver, ironmonger of Church Street, primly-dressed radical and unitarian, succeeded to the secretaryship: one who "cultivated the social virtues by which Man is attached to Man . . . he thus materially assisted to unite his neighbours in pleasant companionship."

There was one meeting each year on which no forfeits were collected. Invariably there was a farmer in the Club: at this time Mr Robert Hillen of Ferry Farm, Sutton — and June or July came to be chosen as their night for acting host. Such occasions rarely produced any absentees and no one was ever late, for the Club hired a brake and all arrived together. When Mr Nathan Walker succeeded Hillen at Ferry Farm the summer excursion was superseded by a September "Feast of St Partridge." They seldom ordered books or balloted for new members at such gatherings, instead the minute book would sometimes depart from its usual recital of mere business and report "a very pleasant evening spent." There was an occasion when it was recorded of Mr J. J. Brown, hatter of Thoroughfare, that he had been "charged by a Bull but made an heroic defence with an umbrella."

It was early, too, in the new secretary's reign that Churchyard took a liberty he would scarcely have done in Mr Giles's time. One night when in the Chair with the minute book before him, he amused himself by making three thumbnail sketches inside the cover. "By our artist" is added good naturedly in Mr Silver's handwriting. He reproduced them as the trio on the right hand side of his *Convivial Evening at Woodbridge* that has wrongly been thought to be a meeting of the Wits themselves. It conveys the impression of the Club's being together for pleasant companionship rather than that by that time they greatly cared about books. Probably after ten o'clock.

As to the books taken up, the minutes supply a complete catalogue of all that passed through Churchyard's hands from 1845 to 1865. Foreign and far away places and our countrymen's accounts of their leisurely travels in them, were an unfailing interest to the stay-at-home Woodbridgians. Such works bulked largest in the purchases, conjuring up for their readers the Highlands of Ethiopia, Borneo, the Oregon Territory, My Home in Tasmania.

Suggestions were by this date scrutinised less narrowly than in days twenty-five years earlier when, with its strong Quaker membership, the club had blackballed Lamb's *Essays of Elia*, for what the Friends had considered to be some levity on religious matters. Now members usually had their suggestion agreed to, even though it was an oddity which the main body may have had no intention of reading: *Nasology* by E. Warwick or Lieut Col Reid on *The Progress of the Law of Storms*. Not everyone could expect to have sufficient staying power for such works as the *Life and Letters of Niebuhr*; the *Life of Mary Anne Schimmelpennick the Moravian* or the 20 volumes of Allison's *History of Europe*.

The lighter relief provided by the lady novelists probably did not greatly occupy the gentlemen. It was intended for the womenfolk of their households, who did a considerable part of the reading of the Book Club's choice in any case. For them there was the pleasant distinction of having the latest volumes delivered to one's house by a neighbour's servant. It was a cut above the necessity of going down to Loder's shop where his Circulating Library was housed in a large niche at the side, with a small office at the back selling patent medicines and a glass case of books for sale with its smell, "the bitter-sweet of unsold classics and first editions".*

Over and above those works of their day that have now dropped into limbo, the members of the club interested themselves in what has stayed to make up the accepted body of early Victorian literature. The weekly and monthly circulation of *The Athenaeum, Cornhill Magazine, Chambers Edinburgh Journal* (Churchyard was first on the list to receive it) and the *Westminster Gazette* kept them fully abreast of works that stirred the world of writers and critics in London. Dickens' and Thackeray's latest were going the rounds in Woodbridge as soon as in the metropolis, while *Lavengro*, Mayhew's *London Labour*, *Uncle Tom's Cabin*, *Sybil*, *Silas Marner*, *Tom Brown's Schooldays* or Coventry Patmore's *The Angel in the House* (one of their rare ventures into poetry) were taken up upon publication.

As for the sales after the annual dinner at the *Bull*, apart from securing *Punch* — even sending in bids after he had slid away into becoming an honorary member — Churchyard did not buy a dozen books in twenty years. It was less than for anyone else.

There was little need for him to add to his literary possessions. At home he had a wide-ranging collection of books which any gentleman could call his library. Beyond the hundred or so works on painters and painting there were Lemprière's *Classical Dictionary*, *George Selwyn and his Contemporaries*, *Paul et Virginie*, four volumes of Erskine's *Speeches*, Paley's *Evidences of Christianity*, the *Life and Works of Cato* in six volumes; translations of the *Comedia Divina* and *Orlando Furioso*; Howitt's *Visits to Remarkable Places*, Ogle's *Chaucer*, *Plautus*; a folio of Sidney's *Arcadia* and Kirby's *Suffolk Traveller*; Milton, Sheridan, Dryden, Goldsmith and half a hundred writers more. Byron, whose poetry so appealed to him in the summer of 1824 and with whom he parted when he changed his residence and his profession, was back on his shelves in seventeen volumes.

In the auction of 1845, beyond his buying *The Life of Martin*

---

* Christopher Morley, *Thorofare* (London 1943), 26.

Chuzzlewit in its original twenty numbers it was not surprising that he should secure Cunningham's *Life of Sir David Wilkie* which recalled to him several associations of earlier days. Halfway through the second volume he was reminded of the artist's series of domestic tribulations that drove him for a while to cease painting at the turn of the years 1824 and 1825. Not least was the sorrow that came to his elegant and favourite sister Helen, "doomed to see the man of her choice, whose bride she was to be on the morrow, drop down dead at her side." Churchyard could supply the young man's undisclosed name. It was Perry Nursey's son Robert who had fallen in love with Helen Wilkie, eight years his senior, during a visit with her brother and mother to Bealings Grove two summers before. 1849 saw him make a less predictable purchase, the twelve issues of the *People's Journal* that had been subscribed for, for the sake of its containing Mary Howitt's *Memoirs of Elihu Burritt*, the American blacksmith, originator of the Peace Movement.

On his evening as host in 1852, after a leg-pull by one of the guests who proposed *On the Game Laws*, the choice was Catherine Crow's *The Night Side of Nature*. It was the best collection of supernatural stories in the language to that date: almost certainly Churchyard's proposal, for it was one of those very few books he bought at a New Year auction. Catherine Crowe, William and Mary Howitt, with their friends the Carter Halls who edited the *Art Journal* to which the club subscribed, were all enthusiastic spiritualists.

Next year's meeting at his house was to prove fatal to his continuance with the club. All three suggestions at the supper on 17th August were taken up: *The Story of Nell Gwyn* and the *Autobiography of Benjamin Haydon*, the eccentric painter, both run-of-the-mill choices. It was the third, however, that led to the break with his fellow members: FitzGerald's *Six Dramas of Calderon freely translated from the Spanish*; the only work to which E.F.G. put his name in his lifetime.

FitzGerald had given his fellow Wit a pre-publication copy inscribed "Thomas Churchyard, with the translator's kind regards, St Swithin's Day 1853". He knew, therefore, what it was that he was commending to the club. The work was bound to be a matter of considerable interest to the members. They knew little about the strange, aloof, reading man in their midst, periodically drifting out of the neighbourhood, always coming back to anchor at Woodbridge but making it apparent that he had not the slightest curiosity to know about them. Something would now be revealed of him as a writer, and the one man in the club who was his intimate wanted the members to read him.

But the *Literary Gazette* of 27 August, circulating around the membership, struck a chilling note. It could not conscientiously recommend Mr FitzGerald's free translations, on the ground that they did not give

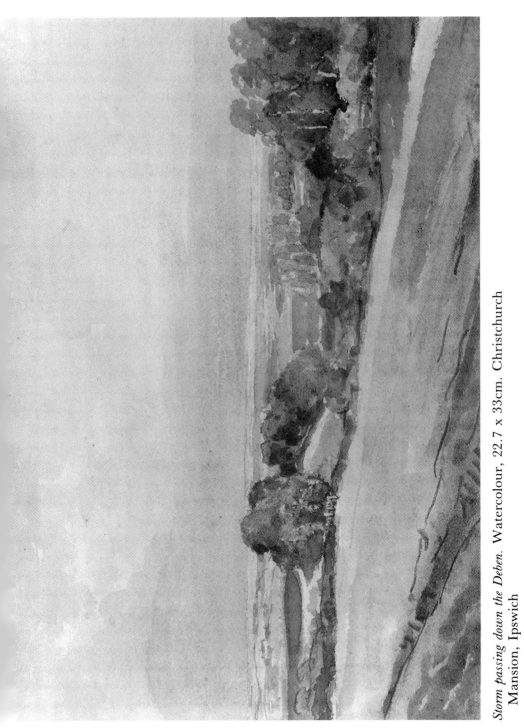

Storm passing down the Deben. Watercolour, 22.7 x 33cm. Christchurch Mansion, Ipswich

Trees by the River Deben. Watercolour, 27.4 x 39.5cm. British

The Pond. Watercolour, 18.5 x 28.4cm. The Huntington Gallery

View on the Deben. Oil on board, 21.9 x 31.1cm. The Tate Gallery

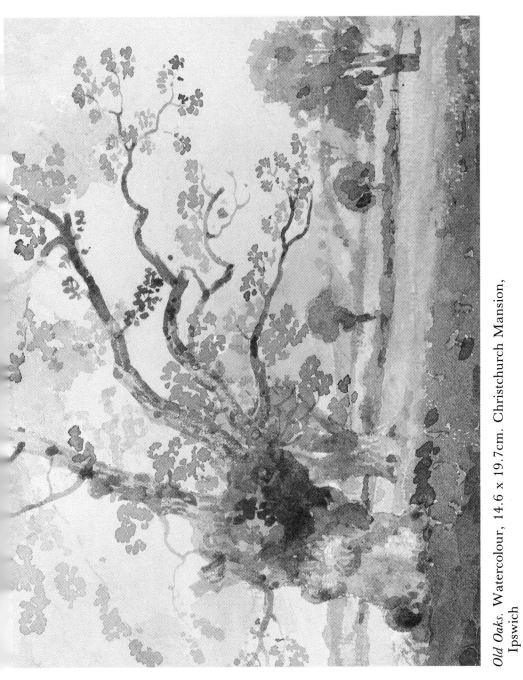

Old Oaks. Watercolour, 14.6 x 19.7cm. Christchurch Mansion, Ipswich

Waning Light, Melton. Watercolour, 18.7 x 27.6cm. Christchurch

Woodland Stream. Watercolour, 34 x 25.5cm. The Fitzwilliam
  Museum

Landscape with kilns, Woodbridge. Watercolour, 19.1 x 29.2cm.

Mr. Michael Wynne-Parker

Shipping at anchor, Woodbridge. Watercolour, 15.2 x 20.4cm. Victoria
& Albert Museum

". . . and that this child may be virtuously brought up . . . ". Drawing by
Churchyard of his wife and Young Tom

"I was in the family way". Sketch by Churchyard in Court

nna en plein air. Drawing by Papa

Edward FitzGerald. Drawing by Harriet

Eliza Capper Brook. Caricature by Harriet

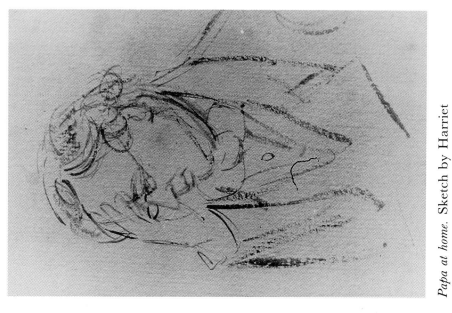

Papa at home. Sketch by Harriet

Cousin Charles, H.E.I.C. Carnatic Infantry.
Portrait by Harriet

Tom Churchyard. Photograph

The Seckford Librarian. Harriet at 89.

a just estimation of the spirit and point of the original. A fortnight later the members read a withering notice in *The Athenaeum*. "We have not taken the trouble to compare these translations with the originals; holding it quite unnecessary to treat as a serious work a book whose author confesses that he has sunk, reduced, altered and replaced much that seemed not fine or efficient . . . supplying such omissions by some lines." This "determined spit at me" as FitzGerald called it must accordingly have impressed itself on the minds of Club as being the informed London judgment, even before the book reached them on its rounds.

After the *Calderon* fiasco the lawyer cut the rest of the meetings of 1853 and the annual dinner in the New Year. In 1854 he brought himself to attend once only at a friend's house. More daunting still was to contemplate having the club under his own roof. At the close of the meeting on 6th September at Mr Edwards' the brewer it was resolved "the next meeting at Mr Churchyard's." The 4th October gathering however, was in fact held at Mr Tills' the corn merchant, Thoroughfare, at the conclusion of which it was again resolved "the next meeting at Mr Churchyard's." Once more he failed them and the 1st November supper had to be spread by Dr Marshall in Castle Street. "No books ordered; the next meeting at Mr Churchyard's."

On 29th November he did at last come up to scratch and keep open house, with books ordered and himself proposing for election his young kinsman James Waspe, helping Uncle Isaac at Byng. But there was a hollowness about the party. The matter-of-fact men of business showed what they thought of his artistic temperament that had led to the repeated evasion of his duty as host. Of the members who should have attended at Hamblin House that evening nine absented themselves.

The hint was too broad not to be taken and this was the last time Churchyard took part in a gathering of his Social Book Club brethren. He was absent from the annual dinner of 16th February when the unhappy *Calderon* copy was knocked down to Ben Moulton for a shilling. At the next ordinary meeting it was reported "Mr Churchyard wishes to be an honorary member." This was agreed to and the place of the little lawyer was filled by a man of herculean frame, Mr Benjamin Gall the chemist and soda water manufacturer, who had had many a ride to Ipswich as inside passenger at outside price, the stage coachman being afraid of making his vehicle top heavy by having him on either the box seat or the dickey.

For the next ten years, apart from the fact that books were delivered to his door and passed on to the next reader on the list, the club went along with its meetings at the full moon, the annual dinner and the Feast of St Partridge as though "our artist" had never been one of its brightest and most welcome ornaments.

111

XVII

Dangerous in a Bad Case,
Irresistible in a Good One

BY THE 1850s the reductions of the newspaper taxes that had kept journals so slim enabled the local press at last to give space to report Churchyard's cases as they deserved. The *Ipswich Journal* and the *Suffolk Chronicle* competed with one another from opposing stances political and sectarian — the one Tory, strong for Church and Queen; the other Whig, all for Free Trade and Dissent, inveighing against the iniquities of compulsory Church Rates and the monstrous privilege of game preservation.

The *Journal*'s Woodbridge correspondent was Alfred Taylor hairdresser, Librarian to the Mechanics' Institute and Post Office Clerk. His barber's shop in Church Street where he "shaved for a penny and cut hair for tuppence" was in the classic tradition a place for collecting gossip. The *Chronicle* was served by a more adventurous reporter — John Dallenger, diligent at ferreting out news and improving it in the telling. The doings of Churchyard throughout the last dozen years of his life became a regular subject for his pen. He it was who pinned on him the story of the Lawyer and the Quaker, the Spaniel and the Baker. Glyde, who knew Dallenger well through their both writing for the same newspaper, sketched him as "an active little man with straight nose, brown hair, grey eyes and keen sarcastic look. His reports for the *Chronicle* were oft times written at the table of a public house, where, though no drunkard, he was to be found working in the midst of convivial company — quoting authors freely and throwing in puns like small crackers between loud talk of his companions, who eagerly drank in his gossip."

He was constitutionally well suited to his paper's radical disparagement of those in authority, for he bore a grudge all his life against society for its disapproval of the way he had entered it, having been baseborn at Ipswich in 1813. Originally apprenticed to an ironmonger, he had ambitions above serving behind the counter and came to Woodbridge determined to lay hold of the skirts of a profession. His initial venture as clerk to Robert Banks, shoemaker and sheriff's officer did not take him far. Winding up petty estates and making seizures for debt gave him a position in which, so the *Farm Labourer* reports, work and pay harmonised; for there was little of either.

From this he advanced to becoming a clerk to Moulton (he christened his son Ben Moulton Dallenger) but soon struck out on his own as auctioneer and appraiser. By 1846 he was living smartly at Wickham Market, renting The Vinery with its three and a quarter acres of grounds; listing in Kelly's Directory his appointments as Clerk to the Plomesgate Union; Superintendent Registrar of Births, Deaths and Marriages; Agent for the Freemasons' Life Assurance Company; emigration agent, auctioneer, appraiser, estate agent and accountant; Secretary to the Mutual Benefit Society, to the Public Room Company.

There is a colourful sample of his journalese reporting the second anniversary of the Loyal Thellusson Lodge of the Independent Order of Oddfellows of the Manchester Unity, celebrated at Wickham Market on the first of February 1848. After listening to an excellent sermon in church from the Vicar in the morning, the brethren emerged two by two and were played round the small town "by the Parham Band dispensing lively airs. The bells from the old gray octagonal tower burst into a merry peal, causing the handsome spire which surmounts it to oscillate to such a degree that the weather-cock at its apex, by its motions appeared to be clapping his wings with joy." Dinner, made memorable by a generous present of Rendlesham-preserved game, was followed, when all the toasts had been finally downed, by a tea and a dance from which the old ladies of Wickham departed homewards wishing that "the Odd Fellows' *Anniwharsary* could come every quarter."

A certain scepticism needs to be entertained about the pen of so ready a writer. He was, alas, a rogue and a charlatan. Before the third *Anniwharsary* came round Dallenger had been detected in nine separate cases of fraud arising out of his secretaryship of the Mutual Benefit Society. In February 1849 he was being examined in London in the Court of Bankruptcy as to the means by which he had put into his own name shares to which he was not entitled, and had so organised them as to be able to borrow from the Society sums he could not possibly repay. The examining Commissioner found that the rules of the Society drawn up by the Secretary himself were "of an intricate character; and no doubt the bankrupt, who was a shrewd man, would endeavour to escape punishment for his misdeeds, but the Court would be convinced that he was not such a person as should again be let loose upon the simple and peaceful inhabitants of this village.'' His discharge from bankruptcy was postponed for at least three years.

Irrepressible lightweight, he bobbed up again before long in Woodbridge where the Plomesgate Union reinstated him as its clerk and where he managed to get appointed also as Inspector of Nuisances and Secretary to the Board of Watching and Lighting. But it was Journalism that was to him the breath of life. An urge to expose the bias of the landowning and clerical magistracy led to his regular attendance at the town's Petty Sessions, so that more is to be heard of Churchyard from him than from the rest of his contemporaries put together. Dallenger's sarcasm upon their worships ''who dispense the criminal law of the land *according to the version of it by that bench*'', was extended to taking opportunities for poking at their courthouse as well. ''The room is scarcely large enough for a decent man's dressing room; the atmosphere generally at a temperature to which the black hole of Calcutta, comparatively, must have been perfectly insignificant; lighted by a nondescript window in a most singular position; the space allotted to the professional men engaged and to the Clerk to the Magistrates at the lilliputian table being about three feet by 18 inches; and without the slightest accommodation for the press.''

He added a touch to this Dickensian picture in his report of proceedings one November day when business was not completed till nearly six o'clock, their worships ''having been occupied some time on two long affiliation cases, in which Mr Churchyard and Mr Jones of Colchester, were engaged, so that candles were necessary. It does not seem that the Woodbridge Division of the County is overstocked with candlesticks; for a great ink bottle did the office of candlestick on the reporters' table — a fit symbol of their profession — until Mr Doughty (the Chairman) perceived it and smilingly ordered it to be removed and some candlesticks to be purchased.''

There were inherent difficulties for the magistrates in their endeavours to dispense in the little country town game law justice that was free from bias. Every hardened poacher, and the unreliability of his testimony in self defence, was well known to them, while they themselves were every one a preserver. A typical case was that of young Charles Goult, a shepherd boy of Hollesley, charged with having set a snare to take game on land over which Captain Capper Brooke of Ufford Place had the sporting rights. The bibliophile-magistrate expressed surprise that the boy was to be defended by Counsel: ''as these are my cases I shall sit in the corner''. Churchyard said the boy had found the snare on the heath and for his amusement had set it in a pit on his master's land where there was an abundance of rabbits. He called Mr Williams the employer to say that the lad's people were most respectable and the boy very trustworthy; he would trust him with

114

anything anywhere. "If the Court thinks the boy set the snare to catch a rabbit they are bound to acquit him of the offence for which he stands charged", Churchyard concluded.

It all went for naught. On the other side Charles Catchpole averred "I am a looker-out for Captain Brooke and saw the boy set the snare in a sandpit. From the height the snare was set and the size of the wire I should say the snare was for a hare." Catchpole's *ex parte* opinion was accepted by the Bench. "We convict you. The fine is 5 shillings and 14 shillings expenses or 14 days in Ipswich gaol. The fine might have been £5 (ten weeks income of the Goult household) "but for your good character." Mr Williams immediately paid. Captain Brooke came out of his corner.

There are numerous cases that confirm Churchyard's sympathy with the deserving (and the undeserving) poor when legal processes acted to their disadvantage in a manifestly unfair way. The proper operation of the law as the vehicle of natural justice was to him as paramount as the proper delineation of natural painting. In a case where he was defending a labourer who had been detected taking away from a farmer's stack 44 lbs of straw worth 8d, he extracted from the owner the admission that the defendant had earlier supplied him with some new potatoes without charge but with the agreement that he should have a bale of straw in exchange. The farmer freely confessed that till that moment he had not realised he had failed to discharge the debt. Churchyard had demolished the case against his client and no word more was needed, but he could not let pass the opportunity of expressing himself upon a matter of principle.

In "his clear and nervously eloquent delivery", he told the court "If I had elected to send this man's case to the Assizes it would have been for the purpose of the Grand Jury throwing out the bill, or of my client being acquitted by a Jury; but I am sure that in leaving it to the judgment of the Bench I am leaving it to more intelligent jurors, and I shall be certain of obtaining an acquittal at your hands. Of all the charges I have had to deal with this is the most extraordinary; and never ought to have been brought into Court. Instead of being a case of felony it is not even a case of trespass, and such cases ought not lightly to be brought against poor men to the damage of their character. It would be a reproach to the law of England if a man could be convicted in a case such as this."

It was a matter of principle too, that brought him to defend in cases such as that in the County Court where John Stannard sued Joseph Cullingford for 2/- damage done to four faggots standing in a driftway. The bundles had been left there for a long time and the defendant thought he was doing no harm in nipping off a few tops, eight or ten inches long, to peg down some verbena. With heavy sarcasm

Stannard, who had seen the depredation, asked the gardener when he was coming to take the rest of the faggots. "Let's have no noise here," Cullingford had replied, "Send the faggots and I'll pay whatever you demand." What was delivered to him was not the faggots but a writ. In cross-examination Churchyard elicited that the complainant valued the four bundles at only 5d each, to that the trifling damage to the tops of a few of them apparently exceeded their total worth. The Judge expressed surprise: "This action is brought as a matter of principle I suppose" (laughter). Churchyard jumped up: "I appear to defend as a matter of principle too, for if such trumpery actions are to be brought, our newly established County Courts will become a nuisance." His Honour said that he quite agreed (Cheers). But as a trespass had been committed he must give plaintiff a verdict of some sort. Judgment would be for one penny with no costs (Applause). Cullingford then spoke up to say that he wished to thank "Mr. Chuchyd who had undertook the case without any payment" (Further applause).

The probability that in cases concerning the taking of game, questions of fact capable of more than one interpretation were likely to be decided against him, caused Churchyard to concentrate upon questions of law, where his ingenuity was unmatched. John Manners was indicted on two alternative charges of being on enclosed land in search of game. The facts were all against him and the case was proved. Thomas held his fire till this juncture when he then raised an objection to the information's having been laid in the alternative. Accordingly a fresh charge was laid for the same offence a week later but in one definitive form only. "This is intolerable" protested the attorney when the case was then called. "Although your worships last week felt unable to proceed upon my objection, that objection only arose after my client had been convicted. By that fundamental rule of English law, *autrefois convict*, he cannot possibly be brought to stand trial a second time. Today's case is bad *ab initio* and cannot come into court." The clerk had to advise the justices that this was indeed the position.

Quick changes of ground in this sort were sometimes too adroit. Sam Newson of Bawdsey, labourer, was charged with unlawfully taking one rabbit on enclosed land on the night of the 4th November. There was no doubt about the rabbit, but the solicitor's examination and cross-examination so confused the witnesses that it raised uncertainty as to whether the offence in fact took place during the hours of night poaching, and so the case was dismissed. The prosecution thereupon laid a second information for daytime trespass in search of rabbits. Churchyard promptly put Newson into the box to swear that he had taken the animal at night. He was not believed, and the bench made the defendant pay dearly for his counsel's misplaced ingenuity. Full penalty of £2:16:6 and in default to be committed to Ipswich gaol for three months. The rabbit would have cost a few pence only at the poulterers.

In 1849 in a case brought by William Garnham, gamekeeper to Sir Philip Broke, for a trespass on Rushmere Heath in search of game, the wrongful intentions of Churchyard's client were all too obvious. It was one of those challenges to the lawyer's ingenuity to which he responded by being at his most dangerous. "I believe part of the heath, Garnham, is in Rushmere, part in Ipswich. Is that not so?"

"That is."

"Have you at any time ever taken part in beating the bounds of Rushmere?"

"No, sir."

"So you cannot swear that this offence may not have been committed within the Liberty of the Borough of Ipswich?"

"No."

"Your worships, the evidence fails to show that under the new acts passed last year you have jurisdiction to hear this case, which may well relate to the neighbouring petty sessional division. It is not safe for you to proceed and I must ask for a dismissal." Case dismissed. Churchyard amused himself by making on the blue paper of his brief a pen and ink sketch of a baffled *Wm. Garnham, Gamekeeper.*

In a parish beside the Deben estuary he appeared to represent the Bawdsey Union Friendly Society. It had a rule that if one of its brethren went sick and claimed on the club he must put in a doctor's certificate, unless living within four miles of Bawdsey Star. When a member living a couple of miles on the other side of the river claimed fourteen weeks benefit uncertified, Churchyard advised the secretary not to pay. The distance, he held, must be measured by road; up the right bank of the Deben, round by Woodbridge and Melton, over Wilford Bridge and to back to the Star by the heath road; a good twenty miles. When the case came into court Thomas was dished by his learned friend Mr Pollard of Ipswich who quoted a judgment in which it was held that a stretch by rowboat across a river was wholly admissible in calculating such qualifying distances. Churchyard was hardly at his most ingenuous when, being thus floored, he jumped up to say that the plaintiff had been observed one day during the fourteen weeks, knocking a nail into a boat. That constituted working when alleging incapacity and he should in consequence be expelled from the Society.

Although prepared to take advantage of every technicality in advancing his client's interest, he would throw up a case in an instant if he discovered he had been misled in his instructions. When in the County Court it became apparent that some pigs were certainly not worth the price his client had informed him, he immediately asked to be relieved from continuing the case. His Honour said that Mr Churchyard had acted discreetly. When holding a watching brief at the prosecution of one Lambert, a groom, for stealing copper bolts from his master, Mr Garrett of Snape Maltings, a marine store dealer was called to give evidence of buying them from the prisoner. "When Lambert offered them to me he said they were all as safe and sound and as true as old gold. I told him not to bring me into more trouble, as I had just been burying my old lady and had trouble enough." Churchyard immediately intervened to say that this prosecution witness had shown himself to be in a false position and ought to be charged as a receiver.

When prosecuting an undefended village woman for stealing six pennyworth of wheat by gleaning in the harvest of 1864 while the sheaves were still standing in the field, he could no doubt have secured conviction. Realising, however, the defence by which he would have secured an acquittal had he been acting for her, he addressed the court to say that he had given the case serious consideration. Although the defendant had clearly committed a wrongful act she should have been sued for trespass and not for theft and he asked permission to withdraw the case. The Chairman said Mr Churchyard had taken a proper course in acting as he did.

At times when in the full flight of eloquence, as over the supposed theft of eight pennyworth of straw, he did not always check himself from soaring into the language of hyperbole. That case, he had said, was the most extraordinary of all the charges he had had to deal with. It was, however, surpassed a year or two later. An attempt to recover a debt in full, behind the back of a deed of assignment, was made to seem almost unparalleled in English legal history. "This is one of the most impudent things — I might say infamous actions ever brought."

In a quieter mood he would often use his artfulness to get the jury on his side before he had even opened the case. One such ploy was to express his regret at having to bring the action; the defendant had undoubtedly not intended to do wrong. When he appeared for the miller of Snape, claiming assault by the local constable it was only from "the policeman having inadvertently mistaken his duty." This too was the line he followed when called to Ipswich to prosecute the Reverend Stephen Rigaud the Headmaster of the Grammar School for administering an unmerited flogging to one of his pupils. "I am sorry to have to prefer a complaint against a gentleman so respectable as the defendant is for his talents, his learning and his high character. I had hoped there would be no defence, that the defendant would have admitted that he did commit the violence complained of and have explained that it was done under some erroneous impression at the time." Churchyard went on to point out his own sweet reasonableness in that he had chosen not to take the case to Quarter Sessions, where conviction would be much more serious than a maximum £5 fine from the magistrates.

He made a similar display of apparent magnanimity when appearing for the inhabitants of Tuddenham against a rate levied for road repairs in the parish. The village's surveyor had supplied them with stone taken from his own land. Such an action, Mr Churchyard threw in lightly, rendered the man liable to disqualification from the office of surveyor for life but he sought to make nothing of this. His only complaint was that the respondent had "mistakenly" overvalued the stone by six pence a load on the 638 loads used.

An alternative opening, the Comic Gambit, would sometimes be employed to put the jury into good rapport with him. When both loser and finder claimed to have had since it was a puppy, a fully grown dog that had strayed and returned, "Mr Churchyard in a humorous address to the Jury stated the facts." A joke could also be thrown in at the right moment in a long case. For hours in an action for trover many witnesses had been called to speak as to what had been intended when one of the parties had specified "a hive of bees". Did it mean the swarm merely or was the hive included in which the swarm was collected? Churchyard was sustaining the former proposition. "When we speak of the House of Commons we do not mean the walls that encompass those gentlemen, nor when we speak of a den of thieves do we mean the den, but merely the thieves. I of course intend no disrespect to our honourable Members of Parliament." The case, together with another that day relating to the empounding of some sheep, kept the County Court judge sitting till "a few moments before eight o'clock in the evening." For the benefit of readers of the newspaper who could not be be present at Churchyard's two forensic performances, Dallenger's report of them ran to a good ten thousand words.

Sometimes sympathy was won by exhibiting in his commencement the great difficulties that lay before him. Briefed at Ipswich to defend Thomas Mortimer, maltster of Tuddenham, against a charge of attempting to defraud the Revenue in a Malt Tax case, where it was alleged he had illegally wetted his grain twice in an endeavour to secure a double rebate of duty, Churchyard opened: "It is always an onerous duty for an advocate to defend against the Government, especially when they have such vigilant and astute gentlemen as the Excise as prosecutors, and it is proverbial that when an acquittal is procured it is said to be snatching a fly from a cobweb." It is satisfying to know that the maltster was found not guilty; a verdict greeted with applause in court.*

Churchyard's acute legal perception and unhesitating stream of

---

* He was the writer's great-uncle.

language was brought to deal with eightpenny bundles of straw equally as with the rights of Lord Rendlesham. Yet he must for a good many years have realised that as a country attorney his talent for the law was wasted. Had his change of profession in 1832 been, like that of his friend Mr Rouse, to practising at the Bar he would, as Loder saw, "have grasped its highest honours". But there were concurrently the honours of Natural Painting still to be striven for. And so, instead of the Inns of Court and one of the Circuits bringing him the chance of coming to national acclaim, he chose to remain concerning himself with the misdeeds and contentions of unknown men and women, seldom far out of sight of the banks of the Deben.

XVIII

Devotedly Attached

THE HOME life of the Churchyard family was dominated by drawing and painting. From childhood the daughters had been their father's devoted pupils. The sole letter from him that has come to light is undated but of about 1850, when the younger children were still at school. It was written one Sunday evening to "My dearest Emma," then in her early twenties, from "her Affectionate Papa." She had been looking after dear Kitty and Charley at Woodbridge and was now to bring them the coming Wednesday to join their parents on holiday. Mamma and Papa were following the Suffolk fashion of the time in making a summer stay at "that delightful bathing place, Aldeburgh."

The marked difference from other seaside resorts that Aldeburgh has always borne had a particular attraction for E.F.G. and for the Churchyards. "Its appearance . . . had been totally changed" from the poet Crabbe's days of Peter Grimes, when "the clay-built cottages gave the place a mean and squalid appearance." None the less it continued to be a place apart, the changes having been brought about by "several families of distinction wishing for a greater degree of privacy and retirement than can be enjoyed in a fashionable watering place".* They had effectively maintained its strange sense of remoteness — a thin strip of town stretching lonely between empty heath and sometimes hostile, sometimes glittering sea. An acquaintance of the Farm Labourer, some "mutton-head carter" driving into it and seeing the ocean for the first time in his life, had caught its true atmosphere when he commented that "there fared to be a rare lot of water for so small a place".

"For invalids Aldeborough possesses advantages scarcely equalled, and certainly not excelled, by any which the more fashionable places of

---

* W. White, *History, gazetteer and directory of Suffolk* (Sheffield 1844), 156.

resort can boast.'' It had set up Mrs Churchyard. ''Mamma is certainly much better in *health*: tongue appetite complexion chest and stomach all right — but legs trouble her she is weak upon them and they swell.'' Thomas too had trouble with a leg: an injury which Mr Gorham the surgeon had ''just looked at and says it is doing *beautifully*. When I lay upon the sofa this morning a great blue-bottle fly kept lighting upon it and would not be driven away. I believe he smelt the raw flesh through my breeches.'' Mr Churchyard not in his usual elegant way. He had, however, turned his enforced idleness to good effect. ''I have made two glorious little oil sketches out of the window — beyond all doubt the best I have done — that is because I had the convenience of a table and painted carefully.''

Their father did not hide his talents from his daughters. He declared that his little oil sketches were sometimes ''glorious''. Often now, when he was out, his daughters were with him in the woods and meadows, painting in his company. Their excursions together became so much a part of the Woodbridge scene that when he died, Loder wrote ''He was devotedly attached to his family, and his well-known form, attended by some of them, will be missed in our daily haunts for many a day''.

There was considerable tramping to be done by the girls when it was to the meadows at Ufford or over the Ferry up to Sutton Hoo: no slight achievement for small persons, several not much above five foot two, impeded with the voluminous fashions of the day, carrying their stools, paint boxes and boards. All at one time or another were present, although Bessie, being a little simple, had not much to show for her efforts. They have left sketches of one another seated intent on their painting, dressed always in neat waisted jackets over wide-spreading crinolines. On their heads straw hats, black or dark brown, with always some eye-catching white lace or tulle folded round the base of the crown. From beneath the brim hung ringlets or, with the senior of them, hair bunched in more sophisticated fashion in a net behind. At the throat a coloured neckerchief knotted neatly or dashingly according to temperament. Laura is seen with their Norwich terrier curled up at her feet: Emma, who painted but little is reading her book, umbrella laid on the shingle beside her, while the others sketch at the foot of some sandy cliffs — Dunwich perhaps.

Although all painted the natural scene, Harriet was more interested in country people; Kate in the comic side of life; Ellen in flowers, nests and birds. Her local views, usually incorporating some buildings, are graceful and full of a calm light: she was, too, an excellent copyist. Anna's landscapes are heavy-handed whereas those of Laura have a dash that comes nearest to her father's style. She was indeed his boon companion, walking arm in arm with him about the town. It was she,

122

who, while still a young girl, one night when Moulton had arrived for dinner, slipped out to his house and told the maid her master had sent her over to collect a bottle of wine from the cellar. The guest in due course praised it. "Well it ought to be good," said his host, "It's yours."

In 1853 FitzGerald had moved a couple of miles nearer Woodbridge, lodging at Farlingay Hall, a farmhouse almost in the town itself. Calls at Marsden House could now be made more easily. On one of these Harriet drew his likeness. E.F.G.'s appearance is known to the world only from the two head and shoulder photographs of 1873 which he called *The Statesman* and *The Philosopher*. Harriet's sketch portrays him less flatteringly and the best part of twenty years younger. He is depicted looking somewhat superciliously at what must be an important oil in its magnificent frame: something probably just brought home by his friend from one of his London excursions.

A picture of family life there, when all the girls had left schooldays behind them, is caught in the "Inventory and Valuation (the latter now lost) of the Household Furniture and Effects of Mr Thomas Churchyard, Solicitor Woodbridge taken and made this 29th day of December 1854 by Benj. Moulton". With two rooms subtracted from the living space by the necessity for the head of the house to have both a Law Office and a Painting Room, it left the Dining-Room, Drawing-Room and Kitchen a crowded stage for the ten women of the household. So that they could dispose themselves in their various roles it was necessary for the Dining-Room to serve extra purposes outside meal times. It had to change to Library, Music Room and Parlour. Heavy, crimson moreen curtains shut it away from the bright outside world of Cumberland Street. Within, it was dusky with the rotund sombreness of much mahogany — Mahogany Dining-Table, Mahogany Cellaret Sideboard (enlivened by a pair of Quart Decanters), Mahogany Book Case with glazed doors, a set of six Single and two Elbow Mahogany Horsehair-seated Chairs, a Music Wagon.

Accommodated in the Dining-Room were, as well, a painted rosewood sofa, a lady's worktable, a six octave piano by Collard and Collard with a pair of music stools for the girls performing duets; a footstool for Mamma when she sat before the painted fender. The dining-table had been chosen for its Patent Telescope Design whereby as soon as the board was cleared its two Shifting Leaves could be pushed away to give some hard pressed space for the drawing, the reading, the needlework or the music of the females occupying the room at any particular time.

The hundred and fifty volumes behind the glazed doors were mainly their father's English and foreign classics together with a good number of books of travel. A few from his many on painters and painting happened to be there that Christmas. Callot's *Miseries of War* may perhaps be seen to fit in with his interest in Elihu Buritt's Peace Movement.

A couple of dozen pictures, strangely contrasted, hung on the walls. Among large and important oils by celebrated painters, four of Churchyard's *Landscape Sketches*, tiny oils, in a single frame and five *Cottages* in another, were hardly in scale. There were half a dozen in larger ones by him also. Accompanying them is one listed as *Crome Landscape*, a further *Landscape* and *Wood Scene*. A *Fruit Piece* by Adrianen excited Moulton into adding "very fine", as though he were preparing a sale catalogue and not a gentleman's inventory.

A *Colebrookdale* listed as by Constable suggests the painter may have travelled to that birthplace of the Industrial Revolution to meet Mr Francis Darby III of the pioneering family. In 1825 Darby "an entire stranger without interest or affection or favour" had written to Constable, buying a pair of his oils of Hampstead Heath in that year's Academy. There is no account of their ever having met but in 1835 the artist, staying at Bewdley, was within thirty miles of that prodigious ground.

Barton had been wrong in thinking, ten years earlier, that his friend would soon tire of the exotic tints and hues of Bassano's *The Vintage*, "a size or two bigger, Than my wapping Nigger", for it still hung admired in the dining-room. Almost no others of those that had so excited the Wits during the course of 1844 were now to be found anywhere in the house. By the time of the inventory they had passed to other owners. The extreme scarcity at this time of works by the Norwich master — six at most — is surprising. Perhaps, as on a previous occasion, Churchyard had recently parted with "his finer Cromes, or what he thought such", in order to be able to buy in their place the chef d'oeuvres that hung in the dining-room that Christmas. They were two full length portraits by Gainsborough of a Lady and a Gentleman. Full length suggests his paintings in the grand manner of the Bath or London periods. They must have dominated the room. Distinguished and unexpected guests looking down upon the family at dinner, it is not known how long they stayed.

Out in the Hall was a rosewood writing-desk, two chairs, a barometer, hat and umbrella stand and a George Frost painting *The Broken Pitcher*. A door opened into the Drawing-Room, less crowded and with the elegance of its furnishings several times remarked upon by the impressionable appraiser. Chintz curtains hanging from brass rings on brass poles were looped back with handsome tassels. The head of the house might relax in his elbow chair of morocco leather, but for the rest of the family it meant sitting straight-backed on yet another set of eight horsehair-seated chairs. For play there were a pair of card tables and a loo table: cards kept ready at hand in a rosewood case. Over one of the tables a crimson cloth was spread at the appropriate hour after dinner and the tea set taken down from the What Not Stand, the only other piece of furniture in the room. It carried also a choice item singled out for admiration by Moulton — an elegant cut glass Bowl with Bronze and gilt stand. No Victorian nicknacks save two large and seven smaller conch shells.

Before the hearth was a handsome bronzed fender and polished fire irons: on the mantle shelf above, three very handsome cut lustres backed by a large chimney glass in gilt frame. The rest of the walls carried a score of pictures, again oddly assorted. Five were after Morland, Wilson and Turner, copies perhaps that Thomas or Rowe or Ellen had made before their originals left the house. Five others were local scenes by Churchyard. There was also a Wilson landscape and a *Birthday Frolic* by Stothard, an etching, a *Fish from Nature*, a *Portrait of Boccacio* and one designated *Mother Bridget.*

Between the front rooms and the domestic quarters stretched the Passage. Cupboards along its whole length held a multitude of tumblers, wine and jelly glasses, spirit bottles; two breakfast and two tea and coffee services, one Rose and Gilt the other Blue, celery jugs, decanters and a great number of domestic odds and ends that included box irons, a crimping machine, copies of Punch for the past eleven years. The wall opposite carried numerous prints, indeed all over the house, up stairways, on landings, in passages, spare corners and bedrooms hung a multitude of such pieces, some strangely mixed. Morland prints of village incidents hung alongside Sir Robert Strange's famous engravings of Vandyke's *Charles the First* and *Henrietta Maria.* Moulton noted large prints after Rubens as being "very fine".

At the end of the Passage lay the Kitchen with its six elm chairs; then the Wash-house and two Store Rooms with the cutlery and the every day blue dinner and dessert services. For special occasions there was a dessert service in blue and gold china; a brown and gilt one for tea. Outside, among the tack in the stable was a side-saddle so that the girls could enjoy their riding when Papa did not need the pony for going out to visit a client, or putting it into the gig for driving over to Halesworth County Court.

Up the staircase was a *Man's Head* by Northcote, local scenes by Dunthorne and Rowe and, eclipsing them all, a *Diana and Endymion* of the French School, four feet by six. The Gallery at the top was spacious too, having room to carry an escritoire, an inlaid work-table, a Pembroke table and a horsehair-seated sofa. On the walls were a landscape by Constable, one by "Gainsbro" and two by "Rhubens"; Etty's *Joan of Ark*; Thomas's own *Dead Birds in the Snow.*

The Best Bedroom No. 1 over the Dining-Room, seems to have been kept for best. It was furnished with two chests of drawers, one of them circular fronted, and a "Winged Wardrobe seven feet wide by seven feet high expensively fitted up with shelves and drawers." A number of choice ornaments were set around — "waxed flowers in a glass case, mahogany knife box, ladies inlaid work-box, handsome carved Pier glass and marble Statue of Venus, very fine". Save six chalk figures, no pictures.

Above the Drawing-Room was the connubial bed chamber with a mahogany four poster corniced in drab maroon. Thrown over it lay a Marseilles Quilt. There was the usual quota of wardrobe, wash-stand, chest of drawers, six cane-seated chairs and a combined Bedsteps and Night Commode. A small Dressing-Room adjoined, having "an Easy Chair forming a bed &c complete". There was a bookcase with 137 volumes — not itemised. Among the pictures were two of Etty's and a few of Thomas's own local sketches including the shooting man's recurrent *Dead Birds*.

The seven young women, in close company throughout the day, were thrown still closer together at night. Two French Beds and one four-poster accommodated them in the two chambers over Kitchen and Painting Room. There was an attic for Charley. Two footbaths are mentioned. Pictures were inconsequentially distributed around these rooms: a *Town in Holland* in one; eleven paintings in another; seventeen oil sketches and a watercolour in a third. A second attic with one bed was allotted to the cook and the housemaid and there was yet a Dark Attic for the lumber that the family could not bring itself to throw away, including their mahogany cot of childhood days.

Along the passage to the back stairs hung an original Morland and a copy of a Wilson landscape. Below was the Office with stools for two law clerks perched at their high desk, six chairs with leather seats for clients and an antique armchair in which the solicitor himself sat at a mahogany writing-table. His law books lined the shelves around the walls that carried only a single picture: *Fish* by Read, 1795.

The Painting Room held a couple of dozen of Tom's collection of more than a hundred books on the art of painting, lives of painters, histories of schools of painting. His choice ranged widely around the years, from old works of the eighteenth century to a recent one by "a Graduate of Oxford" — the two anonymous volumes so far published of Ruskin's "Modern Painters" where the denigration of Constable must have enraged Churchyard. There was a score of oil sketches and drawings of his own, copies of Constable and Wilson; a Constable *Landscape near East Bergholt* and one of his etchings; sketches by Nursey and by Thomas Heaphy, the prime mover in founding the New Watercolour Society with whom Thomas had thrown in his lot during those London months.

The inventory conveys the impression of a gentleman's establishment, well ordered and comfortably founded, but a dun was at the door. For the past three years Churchyard from time to time had found himself out of ready money. In the May of 1851, Alexanders Bank had insisted on his mortgaging to them his life policy as security for a considerable overdraft. When sealing the deed he impressed the wax with the image of a three-master tossed on a stormy sea and with the inscription SUCH IS LIFE.

When the November 1852 premium became due he enquired of Norwich whether it could be met out of the accumulated bonuses declared at £40.16.4. No, they were not payable in full till his death; their present realisable value was £19.4/. In consequence Churchyard had to write the bank on 18th December saying he had taken the liberty of drawing a cheque on them for the £36.16.8. This he would repay as soon as possible; certainly within the year.

In 1853 and 1854 the Alexanders had again to give the necessary accommodation to keep the policy alive but determined to go no further. Next spring Woodbridge was disfigured with ugly posters announcing a sale by auction on 11 April of a Life Insurance Policy for £1,000 on a person now in his 58th year. If Churchyard's difficulties were still not generally known, news of them must now quickly have passed round the town.

At the auction the Bank bought the policy and the Insolvency Court agreed to the assignment, the sum being considerably under Churchyard's total debt to the Alexanders. He himself was designated "an insolvent" and all the family had to leave the splendid setting of Marsden House and live for a time at Melton. This catastrophe seems not to have disturbed either his painting or his practice. Early that August Carlyle stayed a few days at Farlingay, and his host sent the Sage of Chelsea back to London with some of Churchyard's paintings. Three weeks afterwards he wrote to him that on Saturday the 25th he had driven with the "Little Artist Lawyer (who did the sketches I gave you) to Hollesley Bay (on the sea) and while he painted on the Shore I got a Boat and had a great splash of sailing."

Later that autumn the two Woodbridgians were staying at the White Lion Hotel in Aldeburgh when an angry sunset broke out in a wild heap of clouds and colours which the painter hastened to catch from out the window giving on to the marsh towards Thorpeness. It "heralded a memorable gale that washed up a poor Woman with a Babe in her arms: and old Mitford had them buried with an inscribed stone in the Old Churchyard peopled with dead Mariners." It would have been a fitting subject for Barton's pen but in his stead the venerable editor of the Gentleman's Magazine composed, beyond their epitaph, "lines suggested by the fatal Shipwreck near Aldborough, 3. Nov. 1855."

In his legal practice too there seemed little interruption in his proceedings. In court he had no rival and remained the most sought after litigant in the east of the county. In the troubled weeks leading up to the auction of his life policy he had won a triumph, obtaining a free pardon for two of his clients wrongfully convicted of rape some months earlier. Whenever in the course of 1855 the newspapers report the solicitor acting, it is he, successful in cases great and small: from defending Dallenger's boy charged with assault, to prosecuting for the Board of Inland Revenue over an illicit still. As with the earlier crises of his marriage and his change of profession he took no steps to remove himself from the sight of those upon whose respect he depended.

Early in 1856 he secured the conviction of a gang who burgled the house of Robert Reeve, attorney, Thoroughfare and of a mob that assaulted Sir Philip Broke's keepers; in March successfully defending a coachman accused by a rival of obstructing his passage. "The case took a considerable time, there being a great conflict of evidence". The style had not changed.

Near the end of April he was urgently called to Ipswich to prosecute Dr Rigaud for a severe and allegedly undeserved flogging of one of his pupils aged fourteen. "No event occuring in the town for many years has created such excitement" the newspapers reported. The twenty to twenty-five strokes on various parts of the body, was for "blackguardly behaviour" in the Arboretum just across the road from the school — running down a grassy bank, jumping over the flower beds, throwing stones at a notice board. There was some doubt as to whether the boy was one of those who had misbehaved on the day in question. He had certainly done such things previously, and the master explained that knowing this he had punished him as being the oldest boy present; adding that he had in mind that at an earlier time he was seen throwing snowballs there. "As long ago as last winter, no less"! Churchyard scornfully commented. Why had the boy not tried to exonerate himself? "Because Dr Rigaud hits you harder if you make excuses". His lawyer left no future in the town for the Head, who the following year departed to a colonial bishopric in the West Indies.

Any suspension of Churchyard's picture buying did not last long. Perhaps the sale of his two great Gainsboroughs put him back into funds. In London on 22 March 1856 he paid "twenty-four pounds ten shillings for upright Land^{pe} Crome". The receipt is signed by Henry Smart, the first English dealer to make an offer to Constable to buy one of his paintings. In due course the family returned to Woodbridge, renting the substantial Hamblin House a hundred yards further down Cumberland Street on the opposite side to Marsden House. For the daughters there had come brighter news, telling of the fortunes of their Hailes cousins. After thirty-two years in India their Uncle John had retired as a Major in 1841, a widower of fifty with three girls to bring up. He returned to Ipswich where his old mother still lived, and in the next year travelled up to Wharton in the Lake District and married the daughter of a wealthy pluralist parson. She was thirty-eight-year-old Mary Green who thenceforward presided over his family at 15 Pittville Lawn, Cheltenham. From their house three years later John's brother Augustus, the half-pay Lieutenant of Marines, himself also a widower, married Mary Green's considerably older sister Elizabeth and came to live nearby at 3 Pittville Terrace.

When Henry Hailes the planter retired, his family settled at Boddington, not five miles from Cheltenham, so the Churchyard girls had three uncles living within walking distance of one another. Not that walking was necessary: the major, made up to Honorary Lieutenant Colonel in 1854, kept his phaeton. His genteel and comfortable establishment ran to three female and two male servants; a pleasant place to visit, for Uncle John in addition owned 28 Clarence Square and 8 Priory Street, while on Sundays there was the distinction of being seen sitting in the pew he owned in Trinity Church.

By these mid 'fifties his two sons had been for nearly ten years in India: John in the Artillery, Charles in the Madras Infantry. Late in 1855 news came of the splendid wedding that had taken place of the gunner at Kurrachee. Now twenty-nine he had married Barbara, seventeen-year-old daughter of Surgeon Major Grierson, Staff Surgeon of the headquarters there. At Woodbridge the Churchyard sisters, two of them already ten yers older than Barbara, all still remained single.

XIX

Young Tom

THERE HAS been a mystery as to what happened to Young Tom. He had sailed away for America according to some people; for New Zealand said others. "The eldest son died early: lost at sea we think," was what the Redstones had been led to believe. His sisters would never mention him to them.

Having no wish to follow his father in a learned profession and wanting to be a farmer he had been sent by 1841 as a boarder to an unusual school at Wickham Market. Its proprietor Mr Downes called it a Classical Academy — but took pride upon its new scientific approach to education. He advertised, beyond the usual curriculum, the facilities of "A Farm, a Laboratory, a collection of Philosophical Apparatus, a Geological Collection and a Library." All this he claimed enabled the boys' studies to be directed "especially with regard to Agriculture."

Among Tom's fellow pupils was his kinsman young Henry Waspe, sent there to prepare him for taking a part in running the close on four hundred acres of Gusford Hall. For Tom the immediate prospect was less extensive, but he could expect Blocks Barn that had been his grandmother's, and look forward to the marshes at Ramsholt and the farms in Clopton and Burgh owned by his great-uncles with no sons to follow them. Perhaps he might also take on, in the third generation, the tenancy of Byng Hall.

In 1851, he was, at twenty-six, farming on forty acres at Ufford. Early next year he decided to see the world. On Friday 27th, February 1852 in a letter to Crabbe's son, FitzGerald wrote "I met Tom (*young Tom*) Churchyard in Woodbridge who tells me he is going to America on Monday! He makes less fuss about it than I do about going to Shropshire." His transatlantic stay was of no more than half a dozen years, for on getting news of the death of Old Isaac of Byng Hall in 1858 he returned and took over the cultivation of Brooks and Lynns Farms.

Great-aunt Hannah, eighty-one, had died at the end of January that year, and her will, as had Ann's and James's, made Isaac the remainderman. First, however, came a number of bequests to relatives and friends including £250 to Young Tom, 19 guineas to each of his sisters and to Charley. The poor of Pettistree were to have £10 for coals at the Christmas following her decease.

Isaac was indeed the centripetal point to which the family fortune had gravitated, coming as it did from Old Jonathan, Charles, Ann, James and now from Hannah. In addition to granting him general remainder she had left him specifically the admirable Hill House, Ufford, let at that time to John Beaumont, gentleman. Isaac survived his sister four months only. He left no will and Thomas Churchyard of Woodbridge, Attorney, Nephew, Next of Kin, was granted Letters of Administration.

This last entry would have closed the ledger on the Byng Hall account were it not for a letter in the United States coming to light in 1972 that disclosed some unexpected debits and credits. It was dated 27th March 1859. Lucy Churchyard, widow of Isaac of Market Hill, having given up the lodging house in Thoroughfare and removed to Ipswich, was writing to Henry, that "one infant son" for whom twenty-five years earlier her husband had been "desirous of making, out of my little property, some provision for his support." In 1850 he had qualified under Moulton as a land surveyor and as soon as he was out of his indentures had emigrated to Wisconsin, secured a farm at West Rosendale and six years later married Delene Monette, a fifteen-year-old Canadian girl who could speak no English while he could speak no French. His mother was now giving him the up-to-date news about the cousinry of his native town.

There was a budget of financial doubt and disaster concerning some Churchyard kinsmen, together with one sentence that opened up a new area of speculation. "Young Thom^s, as we call him, married the Serveant that lived at Binghall." The bare statement was suggestive of a local scandal but when followed up disclosed something altogether different. On October 18th, 1858 in Clopton church in the presence of Thomas and Harriet Goldsmith, Thomas Churchyard of full age, Bachelor, Farmer, son of Thomas Churchyard, Solicitor, had wed Elizabeth Bardwell, of full age, from Grundisburgh; he in fact 33 and she ten years younger. In Elizabeth's case *Father's Name* and *Father's Rank or Profession* were left blank in her marriage lines.

Such omissions pointed to the bride's entry into the world as having been an unfortunate one. The Census Return of 1861 gives Elizabeth's place of birth as Pettistree, but there is no baptismal entry for her there. A couple of miles away at Melton however the register records that a Leah Bardwell returned home with her illegitimate baby and had her christened Elizabeth in December 1834. Leah had then just reached her nineteenth birthday, daughter of one of the labourers at Blocks Barn who had secured for his girl a place at his employer's at the home farm, Byng Hall.

The Reverend Christopher George Watson, Rector of Melton, must have heard the accepted view as to the child's paternity and decided to write it down for the benefit of posterity. The column in the baptismal register for *Father's Quality, Trade or Profession* was, in the case of an illegitimate birth, sometimes used to designate the mother's standing. In this case, and it is the only bastardy at Melton to be so spelt out, it was very fully filled in. "Maid-Servant late in the employ of Mr Isaac Churchyard, Pettistree." The bachelor farmer was just approaching fifty.

The child was brought up in the village by the wife of Joseph Potter agricultural labourer and no doubt Isaac paid for the girl's nurture. At 17 Elizabeth had gone as a House Servant to John Woods at the celebrated Woodbridge Nursery, three hundred yards further out of town than Hamblin House. She was later taken into the Byng household, and Lucy Churchyard's supposition that it was as a servant was the way things appeared to those not in the know. In fact she was Young Tom's illegitimate first cousin once removed.

A few months before the wedding the true state of Isaac's accounts had come to light, his will unsigned and his affairs in sad confusion, with mortgages and debts out in several directions. Elizabeth Bardwell was without a home and if the old farmer had intended to make provision for her she was not now going to get it.

People in Woodbridge hearing of the solicitor's son marrying a servant girl from his great uncle's farm, may have thought it a shabby affair. Contrary to their suppositions, Tom's hurrying back from America, taking over Brooks and Lynns Farms on Old Michaelmas Day and a week later wedding the cousin whose secret history he had known since she was a young girl, giving her a home and the legal right at last to the name of Churchyard, contained all the ingredients for a contemporary romantic novel. Mrs Henry Wood could hardly have found a better plot, a more capital hero or a more tragic conclusion when she came to write, instead, *East Lynne* two years later.

The romantic aspect of the marriage seems to have gone unappreciated by the family in Cumberland Street. None of them apparently drove over to Clopton to help make up the congregation. There are no signatures of witnesses on the groom's side. His sisters could not help seeing the match contrasted with that of his cousin John Clements Hailes of the Bombay Artillery. Letters had described his splendid wedding that had been celebrated at Karachi in full regimentals, with important persons clustering round to attest as witnesses to the ceremony. On the bride's side, several members of her military family. In honour of the bridegroom the register was signed* by the officer commanding John's father's old regiment, while another of the distinguished guests who added his name was the Chief Commissioner of Sind, H. B. F. Frere, a few years later to become, as Sir Bartle Frere, Governor of Bombay. At Clopton there were only the cottagers of Elizabeth's kin present to give her their support. When Leah was nearly twenty-seven she had married Thomas Goldsmith brickmaker, of Melton, himself the illegitimate son of a servant. He was now come to give his step-daughter away and with his own fourteen-year-old girl to put his signature on her marriage lines. Leah was illiterate.

The wedding was not the only surprising piece of news about the Churchyards that Henry's mother had sent him. Lucy was no great scholar but her letters, with their straightforward country talk and the sound of the Suffolk vernacular, bring to life the happenings in a downright way. They give the clearest picture that there is of lawyer Thomas under the strain of the pressing events of his later years. "Now I have to tell you that Isaac Churchyard Binghall died last September." (She had mixed the date with that of young Tom's re-appearance.) "He made a will, but he did not sign it, so Thomas Churchyard administer to his effects as his Heir. I understand he died very poor, just siffichent to pay his debts. The Clopton farm was morgiged for £1,000, also the Ufford House that was his sister's. So poor Thom^s will not git much."

Churchyards had always stood together, coming to one another's help down to second cousins and beyond. Thirty years earlier Isaac of Byng Hall had lent Isaac of Market Hill the £50 towards binding his son Isaac apprentice as chemist and druggist. The debt, that could not be repaid, had had to be charged on the ill-starred butcher's shop. As to what had happened about it Lucy was not clear. Not only had she failed there but its owner, her stepson Isaac, had also come to grief in his chemist's business at Regents Park. "He paid a Dividend, Mr I Churchyard sent in a clame. Whether it was due or not that I must leave. But this I know is correct", and going on she shows that later the boot was on the other foot. For "Isaac Churchyard was due your (half) Brother Isaac £300 when your Brother faild in Busness in London. Mr I Churchyard give your brother 2 i.o.u.'s, first £100, second £200. When he hear^d of his Death he wrote to Thom^s Churchyard. He would not answer his letter."

If the lawyer had looked to the Churchyard farms, lands, houses and government stock coming to him to cure his financial troubles, that was the blow that put an end to his hopes. His uncle aged 73 was found

---

* India Office Library, Church registers.

dead at Pettistree on 30 May, 1858, the inquest verdict "Natural death by the Visitation of God. Disease of the Heart and infusion on the Brain." Byng Hall continued to be farmed within the kindred. The lease was taken over by Jonathan Orford Waspe, eldest of the sons at Gusford. Young Tom in America had missed his chance.

The behaviour of the lawyer under the stress of his disappointment was much as it had been four years earlier over the *Calderon* copy. He could not bring himself to meet face to face those who felt disappointed in him. As he did not answer the chemist's letter "Isaac came to Woodbridge from Brighton", Lucy continued, "ware he and his Wife and Family of 7 Children are living. Now Thomas C. have placed all Isaac C. bussness in Ben Moulton's Hands and he would not see Brother Isaac." Administrator of his uncle's estate but finding there was little to administer but trouble, he had turned the whole thing over to his friend the auctioneer.

A little earlier there had been other mischances cutting Churchyard off from circles of friends and acquaintances. In September 1857 Crabbe died at Bredfield. As a memorial FitzGerald wrote one of those small felicitous things at which he was so adept. In public he told readers of the Gentleman's Magazine that Crabbe "not long before his death left a short paper to be read by his children immediately after it, affirming up to the last period of reasonable thought, that he was satisfied with the convictions he had so carefully come to." In private E.F.G. told Edward Byles Cowell of "the brave old Fellow! he was quite content to depart and had his Daughter up to give her his Keys, and tell her where the different wines were laid."

The month preceding had seen the final separation of FitzGerald and Lucy Barton. Their disastrous marriage had lasted less than a year. The death of his mother having restored him to affluence, matrimony had been his impractical solution of how to provide for Lucy's financial future without giving matter for the tongues of the scandalmongers. In the event he provided ampler grounds for local disapproval. That after the break-up he should have returned to Woodbridge, where sympathies were all on the side of their Poet's daughter marked him off, in the eyes of many, as an unfeeling wretch.

The humiliations of 1855 and 1858, bearing heavily on the Churchyard daughters drove them to become even more a family apart. Their father an only child, and his paternal uncles and aunts with no offspring, they had grown up as the only Churchyard family with no Churchyard relatives in their own generation: no one nearer than a third cousin. Young Tom's strange marriage added to the estrangement. On their mother's side relationships were closer. From the day in 1837 when, as children, most of them had met the two Hailes cousins at the Melton wedding they had kept alive the feelings of kinship. The standing of the officer gentlemen accorded with their father's calling in contrast to that of more distant Churchyard relatives around Woodbridge engaged as farriers, farmers, a farm bailiff, a wheelwright, labourers at Dennington. On the other side of the land, in Gloucestershire, there was the settlement of Hailes manifestly different from all these.

At Woodbridge there was now one fundamental change in their father's law business. The *Farm Labourer* declares that Churchyard so often cleared his client by exposing some technical flaw in a charge of poaching that it "annoyed the game preservers and was gall and wormwood to the head keepers, and in consequence the Marquis of Hertford . . . was induced, through his agent to offer Mr Churchyard a permanent retainer as prosecuting solicitor in all game-law cases that came before the Woodbridge magistrates. This offer was too good to be refused, but his acceptance of it was a sad blow to the poachers, for there was not another lawyer of equal ability in the neighbourhood to take his place."

Glyde, as so often, is right in drift but wrong on his detail. Although the game was still preserved at Sudbourne, the great days of the Marquis's princely shooting parties were, by the time the lawyer changed sides, long past. "Lord Steyne" died in 1842 and Orford Church had been put into mourning for many a year, with black strokes painted down the pillars and along the dado of the walls. His son, living an Epicurean existence in Paris, never visited England. It was Lord Rendlesham who made the tempting offer that was too good to be refused.

Churchyard, as always, immersed himself so wholly in his client's cause that in a bad case he was as dangerous prosecuting the poachers as he had been when defending them. In a game law action for his Lordship he showed himself prepared to do as badly as he had been done by in the shepherd boy's case. A labourer was employed to catch rats and rabbits on his master's land, over which Lord Rendlesham had the sporting rights. He had set a trap in the mouth of a rabbit hole and a partridge wandering too near had got itself caught. The man thought nothing of it and taking out the bird gave it to his ferrets. If it had been his intention to take a rabbit, said Mr Churchyard, he would have set the trap *down* the hole. Placing it in the mouth where it could and did catch a partridge can only be construed as an intention to take game. The gentlemen on the bench were all too willing to accept the attorney's argument. Fine 5/- and 12/6 costs or seven days' imprisonment. The disappearance of any Byng Hall fortune brought Churchyard to look with greater realism on the fact that the preservers paid better than the poachers.

XX

Laughter In and Out of Court

FOR MORE than thirty years Churchyard had been seen as the bright enigmatic figure able to sail confidently through any difficulties that beset him. From this time onwards he was shown in Woodbridge to be someone who could be laughed over as well as be envied. Dallenger, who had previously reported him with all proper deference, henceforward presumed to publish for the amusement of his readers such stories as that of the spaniel and the sausage rolls. The pert penny-a-liner did not delay to write up under the heading *Stop the Train*, an account of the contretemps that befell the lawyer at Woodbridge Station soon after its opening.

The extreme dilatoriness of the Eastern Counties Railway that had advertised its intention in 1834 of bringing forthwith to Woodbridge the benefits of speedy locomotion, had been a never-failing matter to arouse local ire. At long last the Company announced at the end of May 1859 that the first train would run the following week, its Secretary calling attention to the immense manual labour that had to be carried out to overcome almost insurmountable difficulties from landslips and other causes.

The delighted public soon found itself to have some legitimate complaints. It had been promised up-to-date rolling stock, but the second class carriages were "the old latticed things that should have been burnt up: females in them hold up parasols to keep out not the sun but the wind." One evening that August a driver pulling into Woodbridge gave occasion for Dallenger to write his half column on a comedy in which Churchyard was the chief actor at the station's platform.

"A legal gentleman residing in this town, no less celebrated for his forensic abilities than his artistic skill with the pencil, must needs travel from Ipswich to Woodbridge last Wednesday. It was a long train, and our legal friend and his daughter were seated in one of the hind

136

carriages. On arriving at Woodbridge, the line of carriages extending beyond the platform, he thought for the convenience of alighting those would move up higher and so did not get out. Presently the guard blew his whistle, the train was in motion, and from the window of the carriage out popped the head of our traveller shouting "Stop, stop," but it was like whistling against the thunder; a friend on the platform in raillery exclaimed, "so you are off, then." The next station was Melton; here the two got out, but extra fare was demanded. Our friend expostulated, but to no purpose: he was told if he did not pay the Board would be written to, and he would be summoned before the Bench in that court in which he so prominently shines as an advocate. This would not do at all, therefore, he grumblingly paid, and both had to walk back to Woodbridge, a distance of one and a half miles, in the pouring rain without an umbrella." The first class fare between Woodbridge and Melton was three farthings. Second class, should they have decided to put up with the old latticed things, was a halfpenny.

That winter the devil was particularly active in the little country town, pushing along a load of trouble upon which a biting comment by Harriet Churchyard finds its place. In addition to her facility in portraying village children and country folk, she had already in her early twenties acquired great powers as a caricaturist. Later in life she came to regard caricature as a not wholly respectable art and destroyed most of her work. Only one really unkind example from her earlier years seems to have been preserved but it was sufficiently regarded in the family for its survival to have run to two copies.

From the previous May the Churchyards had watched with interest the revival of the Volunteer movement of which their friend Daniel Hart was an early supporter. Dallenger averred that it was himself who had "first projected and unceasingly used every effort to establish a corps in the town" and waxed indignant when Ufford's Captain Capper Brooke of the Guards began taking the chair at meetings on the bland assumption that he was the inevitable choice for commander. Magistrate and game preserver he was as heartily disliked by the scribbler as by the attorney. The newspaperman quickly went into action. "A member of the Wilford Volunteer Rifles connected with the press" persuaded some of the original recruits to memorialise the Lord Lieutenant for permission to nominate their officers for his approval, rather than have them "crammed down the throats of the Volunteers, *nolens volens*". For this he was "unceremoniously shelved" and advised "to send in his resignation and withdraw at once". He announced his intention "to appeal to Caesar" and "protested against some irregularities by writing the War office".

Official dilatoriness in investigating the complaint held up the embodying of the Wilford contingent long after others had become active elsewhere throughout the country. Dallenger filled the interval with a stream of slighting and sarcastic news of the Corps which was "fast becoming a corpse and would soon be bro(o)ken h(e)arted." He published a solemnly facetious warning that their parades, while not yet officially recognised, constituted them, under an Act of 60 Geo III, cap 1, as being an "association of persons for the purpose of being trained in the use of arms and practising military exercises, thereby rendering themselves subject to transportation for seven years."

When at last official approval came through, healths were drunk and cheers given for the Queen, Captain Brooke, and Eliza, his recently-married young second wife who had accompanied her husband at the parades. Shortly thereafter, a grand review was staged at which the police had Captain Brooke's orders that Mr Dallenger was not to be admitted to the meadow. At the next sitting of the Bench he rose to protest that it was a scandalous interference with the freedom of the press that he should be excluded, whereas numerous Woodbridge women of loose morals had been readily admitted. He told them he had, however, scored by returning home for his telescope which had enabled him to make a partial report of the proceedings for the benefit of the public. The magistrates heard him out in silence.

On a subsequent Thursday the Captain revived the Woodbridge Theatre's flagging fortunes with a "bespeak" to be attended by the new military. A "respectable" house turned up to a performance of *All that glitters is not gold* and the succeeding farce *Lend me five shillings*. The Churchyard family attended and enjoyed the spectacle of Mrs Brooke in her glory. They had the satisfaction of knowing that their father, now the scourge of the poachers, had that morning pointedly acted on behalf of one of them accused of setting a trap at Eyke for the purpose of taking Captain Brooke's game, and had secured his acquittal. But even his triumph over the retired guardsman who kept himself young by dyeing his whiskers black, was not so complete as Harriet's demolition of both him and Eliza.

The caricature shows her, fan in hand, rising with gleaming shoulders out of her low cut gown of shining tulle, decked with a grand matching set of ear-rings, necklet and bracelets. Contrasted dramatically against her black hair is an artificial rose and red plume, whirling like some Catherine Wheel above her left ear. Harriet has caught her fixed in a moment of slight uncertainty, in the middle of her triumph. The drawing is "Dedicated to the Members of the Wilford Rifle Corps: Stage Box Woodbridge Theatre: March 8th 1860", and the story behind the intrigue to secure the command is summed up in the words that follow: "The Captain's Captain."

A few days earlier the family had heard of the birth at Clopton of Very Young Tom. Next month the lawyer was in London at Foster's sale of Leslie's collection. He bought Constable's *Willy Lott's House* of 1816; less than eight inches by ten, it is one of the now greatly-admired oil sketches.

That autumn Churchyard was concerned in a scene more fraught with danger than had been any action in the war of the Volunteers. His devotion to field sports had taken him onto the stubbles within a day of the opening of the partridge season and in the next issue of the *Chronicle* Dallenger told of the happening that ensued. Under the heading *Narrow Escape*, people read in the section devoted to Woodbridge news: "Mr Thomas Churchyard, solicitor, of this town, whilst shooting at Campsey Ash on Monday, was overtaken by a thunderstorm, and sought shelter at a farm house, in the occupation of Mr Henry Tillett. Whilst he was at Luncheon, it appears the storm settled directly over the house, the electric fluid striking a chimney, knocking down many bricks, and breaking the slates of the roof. The lightning ran along the floor of the room, struck Mr Churchyard's gun (which was loaded, and standing within a yard of him) at the butt end of the stock, and took a piece out of it. The shock was so violent as to drive Mr Churchyard from one end of the room to the other, also his boy who was in attendance. Mr Churchyard can only compare the shock to a barrel of gunpowder exploding under his feet." The sportsman in his vividly imaginative way.

Earlier that year the daughters had been able to renew acquaintance with the younger generation of the Hailes. Capt. John's young wife Barbara having lost her first boy as a baby had come home from India to await the birth of a child at the grandfather's house in Cheltenham. Some of the Woodbridge family, it seems, journeyed down in the autumn or early the next year to meet her. It may be the time that their father extended the visit into a more general tour of the West Country. There are watercolours by him of Weston-super-Mare and several thought to be in Devon.

Next March Barbara sent to Hamblin House some forty lines of gentle verse addressed "To Ellen", regretting that in the role of poet she was so far behind her cousin in her calling as artist; wishing she had the skill necessary for "painting Nature as she is".

> Oh how I envy you your lot,
> In quite country nook,
> Your shady glade, your rippling streams,
> Your brush and sketching book —
> Your meadows green, your rivers wide,
> Where fancy can roam wild,
> A treat which Nature, Mother kind,
> Has spread out for her child.

Barbara had been well-educated by the Churchyards as to what Natural Painting was about. The Deben at full tide and the low meadows at Ufford she had seen portrayed in Ellen's, Laura's, Anna's and Uncle Churchyard's watercolour drawings. At some time she would have been given one of the family albums; almost certainly the one that carried the "Thos. Churchyard 1820" and which years later had lain disregarded in a Gloucestershire attic.

Although increasing anxieties may have induced a sense of urgency about Churchyard's painting, they left his other abiding interests untouched. FitzGerald, come to lodgings over Berry the gunsmith on Market Hill, was now only a few minutes stroll down Turn Lane from Hamblin House. The earlier enthusiasms of the two friends continued as the lawyer brought back from London fresh discoveries, while older loves were parted with. Almost all the pictures in the inventory of 1854 had gone by 1865, their places taken by a greater number in the connoisseur's last few years.

On one of these visits to Town, Churchyard spent an evening at the Royal Princess Theatre where M. Fechter was appearing in Hamlet. He admitted to FitzGerald that he had gone in "with a strong Prejudice against any Foreigner doing it", for in his young days he had seen the part taken by Charles Kemble and by Macready. But he "came out quite Enchanted, as with a new and true thing." *The Times* said that Fechter's conception was "perfectly original and wholly independent of all traditions of the stage" — a sure attraction to Churchyard with his hope of every day's producing something new.

Something unexpected was for ever presenting itself to delight him in the course of his practice. In no place was he happier than in the County Courts, "the most popular and best appreciated places of public entertainment in Suffolk. Far distant be the day when the hard-working and tax-paying people of this county shall be deprived of this source of innocent enjoyment". So wrote the *Suffolk Mercury*'s reporter, opening a character sketch of His Honour John Worlledge, Fellow of Trinity, Barrister-at-Law and County Court Judge. Equally with Churchyard he had "a remarkable appreciation and enjoyment of the oddities of human nature" so that the galleries could look forward to "many a merry case coming on". For the benefit of those unable to attend and listen, Dallenger reported them *verbatim*.

A typical case involved the bringing of a complaint for assault at second hand, Churchyard's client having been kicked by a horse he was driving, consequent upon the beast's having been struck by the defendant. But as His Honour smilingly pointed out, what was here being alleged was not an assault upon a man but an assault upon a horse: the animal was incapable of appearing as plaintiff. Churchyard promptly elected to be non-suited, saying he would bring the action in another form at the next sitting.

Seeing that there might be some difficulties in law over the question of the kick, he quietly dropped that particular and founded the action on a more secure base. With relish he devised a form of words that produced a copper-bottomed plea without a flaw. "The action is brought by James Friend and Emma Friend against Benjamin Broome, for that the defendant on the 31th of December 1862 at Alderton unlawfully beat and otherwise illused a certain pony then and there drawing a gig in which the said plaintiffs were then and there riding, and caused the said pony to kick, rear and plunge and break the shafts of the said gig, by reason whereof the said plaintiffs had to walk home and the plaintiff Emma Friend, who was then in bad health, became alarmed and has suffered injury to her health."

James Friend was a service pensioner with a wooden leg, one of the keepers of the Martello Towers at Bawdsey. As he and his wife were ambling home from Woodbridge in a hired conveyance, Benjamin Broome, butcher and alehouse keeper of Alderton, poked the horse in the flank and said "Mr Friend, I wou'nt ride behind sich a thing as that, it's wuss than a donkey." (Laughter). As this did not noticibly hurry the beast, the butcher then struck it across its back. "For God's sake Mr Broome, leave the pooney alone" cried Mrs Friend now thoroughly alarmed, "it goo quite fast enough for us; I can't abide the jolt of the gig." "Well," said Churchyard, drawing out his client, "I say now, did the pony endure this with the patience of a jackass? or what?". (Laughter). Very much to the contrary, for there followed the evidence of the pony's kicking, rearing, plunging and breaking the shafts.

Mr Pollard, Thomas's regular opponent from Ipswich, rose to cross-examine.

"What happened to your wife?"

"She half fell out of the gig."

"You, having a wooden leg, were more active?"

"No; unfortunately it was off; I had only one leg to stand on" (Much laughter) "We was a mile and a half from hoom."

His Honour: "And you hadn't your wooden leg on?"

"I put it on as I got out, else I cou'nt ha walked hoom, less I'd ha walked on me hid" (Laughter).

Mr Pollard suggested that Friend had previously been using the spare limb himself to poke the slow-going beast.

"No."

"You didn't use it at all, nor your wife?"

"No."

"Do you mean to say you didn't use your leg at all on the way home?"

141

"Yes I did, for I walked hoom" (Laughter)

"It lay very quietly in the gig?" (Laughter)

"Yes. I must rest that sometimes as well as the other one." (Loud laughter). Emma Friend followed testifying that she was, at the time, being treated by the doctor for debility and had been getting on well till this set-back, since which she had not been able to lift a dish off the table.

Broome produced the gig shafts to prove they were so little damaged that the plaintiffs could quite well have continued their drive. He added the colourful detail that when he saw Friend descending with the leg in his hand he thought he was coming at him with a gun.

£5 had been the damages Churchyard claimed. His Honour awarded £1.

Dumb animals that had to leave it to their masters to speak to their soundness and their value, figure largely in the cases so much enjoyed by Judge Worlledge and Mr Churchyard. Thomas had no great difficulty in winning against a piece of prevarication by William Alexander, shoemaker, who had sold an old pony to Robert Smith in the yard of the Angel, in Theatre Street. After looking her over Smith had said:

"What do you want?"

Alexander took the opportunity of misunderstanding him and replied:

"I'll have some beer and gin, as I've got the backache" (Laughter) When the drink had been downed and price of the pony named, Smith asked about her wind.

"It's as sound as mine."

The Judge sensing something might be wrong here intervened.

"Have you got very good lungs, Alexander?"

"No, your Honour, I'm a *piper*."

Churchyard, shortly thereafter, was not above relying on just such a quibble on behalf of a client who had sold an eighteen-year-old cow that had been taken ill on the way home and was *in extremis* a few days later.

"Is she a cougher?" the purchaser had asked.

"No more a coughter than you or me."

Since anyone, Churchyard pointed out, might suffer from a tissic and be none the worse for it, this statement could not reasonably be regarded as a general warranty of fitness. Judgment given against him.

On an occasion that ended in confusion he appeared for a complainant who had bought a horse for 12/6 but was satisfied he could sell it for £5 if it could be shown that it might be ridden to hounds. Not being a hunting man himself he got the defendant to take it to the meet for him: "a veterinary I think he call hisself: horse farrier they used to call 'em when I was a boy." The animal lasted the day, but hacking back to the

Haugh Lane, Woodbridge. Watercolour, 20.4 x 29.3cm. The Rev
E. C. Charlesworth

Spring Morning, Woodbridge. Watercolour, 20.5 x 29cm

The Down. Watercolour, 20.2 x 30cm.

road the rider put him at what was alleged to be an entirely unnecessary great jump, and they came to grief, with injuries to the beast
that necessitated expensive treatment by the vet. There was much
contradictory hard swearing as to what was the arrangement over the
ride, or as to what happened at the unlucky jump, which the plaintiff
averred he had seen distinctly, since although not mounted, he had followed the hunt "on footback". Contradictory swearing too as to what
was agreed about veterinary treatment. The hearing continued, highly
protracted, till at length the attorney addressed the Judge: "Your
Honour, I do not think it is my duty to struggle with this case any
longer. I quite feel it, and hope I am not neglecting my duty." "I don't
think you are, Mr Churchyard; and it is a great satisfaction to me when
I have gentlemen practising before me who will not keep up a hopeless
case and waste my time and that of the public."

XXI

To Run Away From One's Work

THE ANXIETIES that had gathered around the family since the middle fifties increased as the years moved on. All the girls remained unmarried: four had already reached thirty: none had been brought up to anything other than sketching and domestic deportment. Charley, also at home past his twentieth birthday at the time of the 1861 Census, was therein described as "Student": reading for the law but making slow progress. Young Tom with Elizabeth continued on the Clopton farms. Their second son was baptised Charles in Clopton Church on 23rd June 1861.

It had taken a full three years for the affairs of Isaac of Byng Hall to be unravelled — nominally by Thomas the Administrator, but in fact by Ben Moulton. That Midsummer it was apparent that all the uncle's holdings must be sold to meet his debts. The Clopton farms were advertised to be auctioned on Wednesday 17 July at 4 pm for 5 o'clock. The 72 acres of Brooks and Lynns with "Farm House, convenient outbuildings, excellent Arable and Pasture Lands with Labourer's Cottage" were shown as being leased to Young Tom for 12 years from Michaelmas 1858. Middle Farm (Floreys) was occupied on a similar lease by Mr Thomas Moulton, likely a nephew of Ben. Four o'clock the same afternoon was the time set for the sale of the Butcher's Shop and Business Premises on Market Hill "formerly occupied by Mrs Churchyard". Lucy's tenure there was still green in Woodbridge memory although thirteen years had passed since she quitted it. The complications of her failure, the failure of its owner her stepson, the charges on the property and the contra accounts between Isaac the butcher, Isaac the farmer and Isaac the chemist necessitated their unravelling to be taken back thirty years. Now, Lawyer Churchyard would have nothing to do with it: the tangle had been passed over to Mr Reeve, attorney of Thoroughfare.

The following spring Charles Hailes, now 34 and a Captain in the Madras Staff Corps was home on furlough looking for a wife. He visited his cousins at Woodbridge where Harriet drew his likeness before he went far off and wed one of the daughters of Henry Clarke, Secretary to the North Shields Waterworks Company. He and his wife were both from Ipswich and with them now lived his father, Dr William Barnard Clarke* whose painting of Stoke Bridge in the Suffolk Association show of 1850 had been ''all yellow soap''. It is likely that the family were related to the other Clarkes of Ipswich whose Henry had wed Mrs Churchyard's sister at Melton twenty-five years earlier. Doubling the strands of kinship was a notable trait among the Hailes. Emma Caroline, eighteen, married the Madras Captain in Tynemouth Parish Church that May of 1852 and sailed away with him to India.

In July a third baby was born to Tom's wife at Clopton and christened Laura. With Brooks, Lynns and Floreys sold away out of Churchyard hands, Tom's work of cultivating their fields and meadows as a tenant must have carried a continuing sense of deep disappointment. Not so long ago there had been every expectation that within a few seasons they would have been his own property, together with all the other lands, Hill House Ufford, the plate and furniture, the thousands in the 3½% Annuities and the Four Per Cents. It was now all gone and his father had, moreover, had to sell Blocks Barn and the grandparents' home at Melton. From such scenes he decided to get away and emigrate to Canada.

Next Lady Day he quitted the closely folded farms for the wider spaces he had looked upon ten years earlier. His four year stay on the seventy acres at Clopton, has not gone unremembered. Maybe he was the sort of man to be talked about in the *Crown* long after he had left. From then on, people in the village no longer referred to his land by its ancient names, to them it has, ever since, been Churchyard's Farm.

In the days before Easter 1863 Tom put together what would be needed for starting their new life in the colonies. On April 16th he and Elizabeth, with the children, embarked at Liverpool as steerage passengers aboard the crack Mail Steamship *Anglo-Saxon* of the Allan Line, bound for Quebec. She was speedy and popular and had been doing the transatlantic run for the past seven years: one of the last steamships to continue the outdated fashion of carrying sail as well. On this voyage in addition to the crew of 86, there were 48 cabin passengers and 312 steerage, the last named almost all emigrants setting out for the Canadian West. The fare for Tom and Elizabeth was eight guineas each, their children half price: bedding, cooking utensils and food they furnished for themselves.

---

* He was the first Curator of Ipswich Museum.

145

At the end of the ocean crossing, their ship was to rendezvous with the Associated Press Newsboat off the dismal and forbidding Cape Race at the south-eastern point of Newfoundland to hand over mails and despatches. But on the morning of the 27th, more than three miles out in their reckoning, at 11.10 in a dense fog the *Anglo-Saxon* ran aground, her bows firmly wedged in a fissure between two great twin rocks at Clam Cove. She swung slightly to port on the impact and damaged her stern which crashed sideways onto a submerged rock. Then the long waves rolling in, swung her to starboard till she lay right along the face of the low cliffs.

She carried six boats, sufficient to take off 192 only of the 446 on board, and of these two of the three on the starboard side could not be launched because of the lie of the ship. But no imminent danger was apparent: some of the crew had dropped from the jib-boom that was overhanging the rocks, fixed a hawser and rigged a basket in which, in a brief quarter of an hour, 130 of the passengers were carried ashore. But the ship had all the while been rolling and pounding in the huge ocean swell and undertow, and the vibration eventually shook the great masts out of their steps so that suddenly they crashed down together with all the rigging, yards and booms on to the people on deck, taking a fearful toll.

By this time the middle starboard boat had been safely launched, loaded, under the Captain's direction, with women and children, so Elizabeth and her brood would be in it. As the crew were pulling away for the cove the boat was hit by the falling rigging of the *Anglo-Saxon*, upset and all were lost. It now became apparent that the ship was taking in water through her damaged stern for she was riding lower and the decks had started to become swept from side to side by the great icy Atlantic swells. No further rescue work was possible. For another terrible three-quarters of an hour the hundred and eighty still on deck clung to such railings and stanchions as they could, while the gear and the deck houses now broken loose washed back and forth killing some and knocking others overboard. None of those swept away, nor any who in desperation jumped into the sea, reached safety ashore. A little past noon the decks broke open, the weight of the water in the aft portion of the ship pulled her out of the cleft and she slid over, going down into fourteen fathoms.

As she went, a few more fortunate than the rest found themselves floating on parts of the forward and after saloon decks. On one such were two of the crew, an unnamed steerage passenger and a youth: the passenger may have been young Tom. The lad died of exposure during the night and it was not till next morning that the three boats and the ten still alive on their adventitious rafts were picked up by the paddle-wheeler *Dauntless*.

Fourteen of the crew, fifteen of the cabin passengers and two hundred and eight from the steerage were lost. All survivors were taken by the ice-breaker *Bloodhound* to Quebec, thence by train to Montreal where a relief fund had already been raised for their assistance. Some families had perished entirely; few escaped without some bereavement. Tom's loss was mentioned as being among the most grievous. But along with the rest of the survivors he continued his bitter journey, for apart from two orphaned children given a home in Montreal, every immigrant went on towards the Canadian West in a train chartered for them by the Allan Line. Of those drowned, the fishermen recovered more than a hundred bodies and buried them on the bank of Clam Cove, setting a rough stone at the head and foot of each.

A brief paragraph referring to the shipwreck and the loss of Elizabeth and her children appeared without details in the Suffolk papers. It must have been a subject for speculation in the town. Whatever had been the feelings at Hamblin House over Tom's departure, this was the chilling news that was never talked of to others.

"If his heart had been in his profession . . ." a phrase in the Journal's obituary is the fountain of all the subsequent ideas that distaste for the law made Churchyard only too willing to neglect it. He himself knew it was something more complex. For him it was the same as it had been in the few lines that Constable wrote to Young Pulham in Christmas week 1825, and which he had begged off the East India House clerk after he had retired and returned to Woodbridge. "I go to Brighton tomorrow and John in Suffolk — it is a sad thing thus to run away from one's work." Constable, the most uxorious of husbands and the most doting of fathers, was not, Churchyard knew, sad at going to spend Christmas with wife and children at their seaside lodgings. It was the dilemma of equally valid but irreconcilable claims. Any neglect by Churchyard of his practice no more argues a distaste for the law, than leaving his family totally unprovided for disqualifies him from being seen as a devoted husband and father.

It was thirty years after Churchyard's death that E. V. Lucas wrote up his enquiries and Glyde put out the Labourer's "recollections", both drawn substantially from Loder. It is memories of these, made hazy by the passage of a further forty years, that have become the so-called "traditions still current in Woodbridge". Subsequent writers, so far from unravelling the complications of Thomas's conflicting loves have, one after another, over-simplified his position and drawn him as merely the reluctant lawyer who wanted to be a painter. With every retelling the black has become blacker, at the hands of those who have never read a single case that he fought, or known of the retreat from art to law in 1833. Each has sharpened the language found in his preceding source — "if his heart had been in his profession, he would have grasped its highest honours'' (1865) — ''a lawyer with too little love for his profession ever to attain eminence in it'' (1893) — ''his impatience with his proper profession'' (1914) — ''enthusiasm for painting was nicely adjusted to an indifference to law'' (1947) — ''an enthusiastic amateur painter and a good but unenthusiastic country lawyer'' (1976). The more recent the guesses, the less they resemble the attorney who found himself engrossed by the law as an intellectual and so often humorous exercise.

Lucas, who knew how things were at the end, tactfully emphasized ''his un-professional industry'' as ''amazing . . . the best part of every day on which he did not ramble was spent in his studio.'' Glyde was less considerate to the daughters' feelings. After referring to Churchyard's stoutness and lack of imposing appearance he went on to record the lawyer's fondness for dog and gun, for painting, copying and collecting. ''These loves of his often caused him to be careless, not to say neglectful of his professional duties, and in the latter part of his time it was not uncommon for him to forget to attend the Court, although he had been engaged for special cases . . . When owing to his absence injury was likely to befall his client, the Magistrates consented to defer the case in order that Mr Churchyard might be sent for, and on such occasions it was amusing to see him come rushing into Court, Act of Parliament in hand, which he would hastily scan whilst waiting his turn.'' Glyde's saying that this happened often is likely to be the sort of exaggeration to be found throughout the *Autobiography* when its incidents are compared with the original reports of thirty years earlier. Dallenger related no such occurrences.

Ellen told Lucas that her father never returned from a country walk without one or two new sketches in his pocket book. Recent versions of the amount of time spent *en pleine aire* have considerably extended it. The favourite one, that he would go out painting and shut up his office for days at a time, overlooks the fact that his law clerk Allen was there till eight o'clock every evening. A considerably more abrupt rejection of legal work is now talked of. Its pedigree goes no further back than to a paragraph in the Hon Andrew Shirley's careless and overcoloured, *The Rainbow — A Portrait of John Constable*, 1949. Shirley's account was that ''if he had company or was painting when a client called, Churchyard would advise him to go to hell, where he would find plenty of lawyers to do his business; gently but firmly the door would close on him''.

Jests over the number of lawyers the devil has secured as his own are as much a part of folk humour as are the tales of the quick-witted attorney and the sly seeker after free advice. This one is wholly out of keeping with descriptions of Churchyard by those who knew him — ''He never failed to exhibit great courtesy'' — ''refined and dignified . . .

his manner was polished and gentlemanly in the extreme'' — ''a man of the highest refinement.''

There is no little dapper memoir by FitzGerald from which to savour the last course in their association. Both, by then, had suffered a diminution in the number of their friends in the neighbourhood. Such a company of E.F.G.'s close acquaintances in this corner of Suffolk had died by the end of the 'fifties that he could write ''all the Country round is become a cemetery to me''. After his loss of Churchyard he described Woodbridge as being for him ''as Pomeii — in respect of having any life''. The void was the more palpable from the two having been in the final years even closer neighbours than before.

While the two last of the Wits remained there were, besides the set pieces of conversation, the casual exchanges in which the immensely stored mind of the one was drawn out by that of the other, whose varied information ''made him at all times amusing and delightful''; evanescent talk that was enjoyed and lost to history. Fortunately the diary of Frederick Spalding survives to give an echo of the gossip FitzGerald spun for the lighter entertainment of his legal companion.

Frederick was the son of Thomas Moore Spalding, farmer and ornithologist, of Red House Westleton. In 1859, at twenty-five, he had come to Melton as a clerk to a maltster. His enquiring mind led to his interest in natural history and antiquities to which he gave more time, and in pictures over which he spent more money, than he could properly afford. Like some other cheerful and aspiring young men he saw in Churchyard one who, despite the solid achievement of his longer years, remained adventurous and young in mind: still ''the most sanguine of men''.

The diary does not begin until 1866 and so has no record of meetings with Churchyard. They must, however, early have become well-acquainted — for Spalding was one of the ''few well chosen friends'' who helped make up the party of only a dozen who followed the lawyer to his grave. He was one of the five persons who bought a Churchyard oil at the posthumous sale. Discussion of paintings had been their early meeting point and Frederick was early introduced to the pleasures of being a collector.

FitzGerald when tired of his love of solitude had of necessity to have some tried acquaintance with whom to converse. Spalding found himself, to his surprise taking Churchyard's place after 1865 and noted down many of the conversations he had particularly enjoyed. They must be some of the anecdotes and the comments that used to season E.G.F.'s talk with his painter friend.

Spalding driving FitzGerald past Ipswich gaol, his passenger told him of a remark an acquaintance had overheard in the crowd there at the execution of a young man for having murdered his middle-aged housekeeper. "What a damned shame to hang a fine young fellow like that for killing an old woman that didn't weigh above seven stone." When Spalding greeted his friend with "Many Happy Returns of the Day" he was corrected. He should wish people as many birthdays as will be good for them. He was taken into the older man's confidence as to how the engagement with Lucy came about; had been told how in earlier times E.F.G. had thought himself to be in love with Elizabeth Charlesworth. The tale was passed on about old Lord Leicester late in life, between 70 and 80, marrying Lady Anne Keppel. Enquiries being made next day as to the health of the Earl and Countess, it was said that she was just the same as yesterday and he was as well as could be expected. It could not be that FitzGerald was always wholly accurate, for the Earl, 69 at the time, begat by this second marriage five sons and a daughter. But a good story should not be spoilt.

When E.F.G. journeyed to Shropshire as Young Tom was just off to America for the first time, his friend Archdeacon Allan had told him that his predecessor in the living, when giving out the church notices on Sunday used to include the meets of the foxhounds for the coming week. Tales such as these must have delighted Churchyard with his relish for the oddities in human character; with his "conversation full of wit and anecdote to overflow" he must have enjoyed capping them with his own.

But the fascination of FitzGerald's conversation and the sympathy of his deep friendships could be fraught with danger for the recipients. His impracticability in everyday affairs and a blindness to the true interests of those whom he wanted to go his way, could lead to miserable out-turns — his own marriage; the foolish herring-lugger partnership with Posh Fletcher; his strenuous endeavours to prevent Cowell from going up to Oxford so that he might continue reading Æschulus with him in Suffolk, but thwarted by Elizabeth Charlesworth, now the young scholar's wife, fourteen years his senior.

Frederick Spalding, with his overbrimming enthusiasms that equipped him to become later in life Curator of Colchester Museum, was the last person who should have gone into trade on his own account. Yet FitzGerald enabled him to set up as a corn merchant with a loan of £500 and further compounded his easy-going attitude to business by burning the bond after accepting a few payments of interest: then foregoing anything further with the remark that £7.10/- half yearly would make no difference to him "but might to me in my little business and with my children."

Spalding was many times distracted from his work by being asked by FitzGerald to drive him into Ipswich; to go with him to Sudbury; to sail down the Deben; to go out together buying pictures; to spend a few days at his lodgings in Lowestoft. It is easy to image that Churchyard was sometimes subjected to the same pressures from this Old Man of the Sea, who could not be shaken off when desire for some particular enterprise or conversation took him. It was dangerous company for one like Churchyard, who was himself liable to detain for the rest of the evening a caller due elsewhere in a quarter of an hour: one who might delay seven years before touching up a friend's picture that had been left with him for that purpose.

A month after the cancelling of Frederick's financial obligation, Fitz-Gerald invited him to Lowestoft for a couple of days' stay. At the conclusion of the visit ''I was to leave by the first train leaving at 5.50 to meet my Wife and Edmund and Mrs Garrett for a day ramble at Westleton but awoke late. I missed the first train after breakfast, at 8 o'clock or a little past; sat talking on marriage etc. for two hours in the pleasant room at 12 Marine Terrace overlooking the sea. He saw me to the station and I left by the 11.10 train.'' Actively encouraged by his friend in such casual attention to duties, it is not surprising that a few years later Frederick failed in his wide ranging business of ''corn, coal, coke, lime, cement and brick, pipe and tile merchant.'' The Spalding family put a good share of the blame on FitzGerald. Posh said ''The Guv'nor spoilt me''. The Churchyard daughters disliked him for what they thought had been his bad influence on their father.

XXII

This Is Worth It All

AMONG THE handful of papers still in Harriet's possession in 1927 were two telling of the financial troubles that pursued her father in his last years. Both deal with transactions with friends: raising cash to stave off less accommodating creditors. The first was with the good companion of nearly forty years standing

```
Memorandum — June 26th 1864
Sold to Mr B. Moulton a Picture by Old Crome     £
   Back of New Mills Norwich_____   63
Recd. in payment as under_____ £
   Picture by Constable             20
   Do. by T. Churchyard              8
   Do. by Old Crome
      Norwich Cathedral             20
   Cash to Balance                  15____£63
```

This was the sort of deal that Loder hinted at discreetly when he wrote of Churchyard's delight at "welcoming an old acquaintance . . . back to his collection like a lost sheep returning to the fold." The unspecified Constable, the Norwich Cathedral and his own painting had no doubt been deposited as security for earlier loans.

The second paper detailed a straightforward transaction with Robert Hillen retired from Ferry Farm and now living at Quayside in the town, gentleman.

June 20th 1865
Mem.
   This day deposited with Mr Robt. Hillen two pictures by Crome (that is to say) one of *Boatbuilders Yard Norwich* the

other an upright picture of buildings at Norwich to secure
the sum of £80 and interest at £8 per cent — to be redeemed
at any time on payment of principal money and interest.
Thos. Churchyard.

Like most of his close acquaintances Hillen had been educated into
becoming a picture fancier. He had, in addition to these, several other
paintings that had formerly been the lawyer's, including a notable self-
portrait by Morland working in his studio. There was no upright
Crome in the Churchyard dispersal sale, no *Boatbuilder's Yard*. The
principal money and interest had not been able to be repaid in the few
weeks left to him.

Such stringency did not deter him from searching to the end for
paintings of the English Landscape School worthy of admiration. Early
in 1863 he had acquired a Crome secured for him by the dealer White-
house at Christies big sale of pictures owned by the shadowy Mr
Rainger: "The celebrated *Moonlight Picture, with a View of Bruges in the
Distance*". At fifty guineas it was a great bargain and fetched more than
three times that sum after his death. Short of money, Churchyard the
dealer might have sold it himself at a handsome profit but Churchyard
the connoisseur preferred, man of contradictions, the pleasure of seeing
it hanging at Hamblin House.

As to his law practice in the final months, he is still invariably found
as the attorney engaged in every case of importance in the neighbourhood: clients in all walks of life entrusted him with every kind of plea.
Everywhere he was listened to with the same rapt attention. Lord
Rendlesham briefed him in a dispute with the lord of the manor of
Sutton as to which of them owned the sporting rights over Sutton
Heath. For five hours Churchyard took the Bench through every sale,
partition, transfer, exchange and inheritance concerning it for a century past; called numerous oldest inhabitants to say how the
customary rights had been exacted. It was all to no effect. The opposing barrister briefly recited a judgment delivered in The Great
Swinfen Case that cut the ground from the whole of the attorney's
argument. The magistrates made no complaint of the fruitless expense
of time; on the contrary the Chairman said "We cannot regret that
the case has gone as far as it has done, for we have obtained a good
deal of information which we should not have had if it had been stopped earlier." Others felt the same, for the press reported that "the
case was watched with great interest by a large number of persons
congregated in the Hall."

It was at this time, too, that he enjoyed himself with the complex-
ities of the Tuddenham Maltings case. The Malt Tax Laws were even
more complicated than the Game Laws themselves, with more than a

hundred regulations over the neglect of which the astute gentlemen of the Revenue might catch out an erring maltster.

In March 1865 he had kept Judge Worlledge sitting till 8 o'clock as he strenuously argued two small claims of £3. and of £6. Though unsuccessful he was gratified to hear His Honour say that he never had to complain of the way in which Mr Churchyard conducted a case. He wished he could say the same of all others. That last spring he was briefed at Yoxford to prosecute for the making of a riot at Theberton *White Horse*. The cases "excited much interest in the town and the Court was crowded during the enquiry, the business not concluding till a late hour." People were still prepared to give up a day to attend a performance by the much talked of Mr Churchyard from Woodbridge.

The comic and the pathetic cases invariably still found their way to him. He appeared against the landlord of Kirton Greyhound for damages for assaulting the landlord of the Falkenham Dog in his own pub. It was an accident, the defendant claimed; it was not intended for the plaintiff at all but had been "aimed at the other b---" with whom he was arguing. That same day a poor woman recently widowed, with two small children and another on the way, was being sued by her father-in-law for the return of furniture in her cottage which he said was his and not his late son's. "The judge, as well as many others was visibly affected and enquired who would be taking up the matter for the poor woman. Mr Churchyard said he had great pleasure in acting gratuitously for her".

Nowhere in all this are there to be found grounds for the imagined "impatience with his proper profession"; for "an indifference to law"; or that he was "an unenthusiastic country lawyer". On the contrary it is seen to be with him as it was with old Parson Crabbe — "much of the noble and Cervantic humourist in him", and with "a boy's heart throbbing and trembling" despite the cares of being sixty-seven.

July 1864 there died Mrs Churchyard's brother John, the Lieutenant-Colonel at Pitville Lawn. Late in the year came the news that Captain Charles Metcalfe's young wife from North Shields had died in Madras. She was just twenty-one and left her husband with a small boy of a year and a half.

To the 1865 Book Club auction Churchyard sent in the only bid (apart from his annually securing the issues of Punch) that he made since becoming an honorary member ten years earlier. It was for *Lispings from Low Latitudes, or Extracts from the Journal of the Hon. Impulsia Gushington*; an acount of a trip up the Nile by Lady Dufferin, lately become, by a death-bed marriage, Countess of Gifford: she had refused the Earl when in health. She was, Churchyard would have known, Helen Selina, grand-daughter of Sheridan; with her sisters one of "The Three Beauties", reckoned in Tom's young days the finest women in England.

That July there was held in the Woodbridge Lecture Hall for the first time a five day Industrial Exhibition. Scarcely an appropriate title the Chronicle's reporter rightly said; Fine Arts, he thought, would have been nearer the mark, for it consisted in all sorts of needle-work together with paintings, photographs, models, examples of penmanship, curios and antiquities. The Journal recorded that "the works of art include some oil paintings by Mr T. Churchyard, a gentleman who is well known in the neighbourhood as an enthusiastic lover of the fine arts." His large landscape of *Martlesham Creek* was, in both newspapers, fastened on to as being the outstanding piece in the Exhibition. The Journal noted also his *Cherrytree Inn, Woodbridge*: the Chronicle praised his "pretty little sketch of *A Wood Scene at Nacton* and other paintings of local scenes".

It was thirteen years since Churchyard had shown his work in public but as with the Ipswich exhibition it was something he could not but support. It was in strange company that he did so, for the whole atmosphere was decidedly maiden-ladylike. The exhibits could, if so desired, be entered in their various classes in competition to be assessed by local judges. The main prize went to what the Chronicle described as a "model bonnet which no doubt was denominated by many of the fair sex as a *duck* or a *love*". The Journal called it "excruciatingly fashionable".

"Mr F. Spalding had the largest collection of articles in the exhibition, and amongst them was an early sketch *On the Orwell* by Gainsborough; *Dedham from East Bergholt* by Constable; a painting from *Yarmouth Beach* by Old Crome; a view by Morland" — another "small collection" which was being built up by purchases from Churchyard's extensive one.

By the time of the Exhibition the lawyer had planned in detail what was to happen to his work. He was already in his sixty-eighth year; his father had lived to only fifty-six; his own heart was beginning to trouble him. FitzGerald had noticed the symptoms and thought them similar to Barton's. Most men would have taken these as signs that it was time to make a will. For him there was no point in so doing. It could all have been covered by the words that lawyer White of Halesworth had used fifty years before — "apprehensive from the many debts I may leave behind me it will be of little value." His own paintings would in years yet to come make his daughters their fortunes, but they must have them now, before there was any danger of their going into a sale to satisfy creditors in the winding up of his estate. On nearly four hundred oils he declared whose property each was by painting in verso Ellen, Emma, Laura, Anna, Bessie, Harriet or Kate. For the girls he also made up guard-books each with several score of his finest watercolours and the owner's name shown on the fly leaf. Beyond these, on a great many unmounted pieces he similarly pencilled in the top corner which girl it was to whom it had been given. It became a mania, descending to such trifles as small lithographs of his paintings done by Rowe — some no larger than 3 inches by 4.

During these later years Harriet had drawn numerous likenesses of her father. There are those of the keen sensitive face when he was at the end of his fifties, sketched as he sat drawing or reading at home in the evening. There are the fuller, comfortable ones of him in his blue smoking cap when he had added to his weight a few years on. He is to be seen, too, in her little full length oil, wearing tail coat and stovepipe hat, facing the wind as he strove to record the impression of the gale upon the landscape in the open field. There are watercolours of him similarly dressed, seated on his stool out sketching with his daughters in the calm sunny days.

He maintained to the end close association with his friend George Rowe who had continued till 1860 to send in to the exhibitions in the capital. FitzGerald's scrap book has a few of his Londonscapes that have a pleasant resemblance to the paintings lithographed by his contemporary Thomas Shotter Boys. One of Churchyard's stranger compulsions was to commission him, at some time during the last years, to paint nearly twenty copies of landscapes in the National Gallery for hanging on the walls of Hamblin House crowded already with two hundred and fifty oils, watercolours and engravings. In their last winter it was felt something was needed to warm the cold air in the middle of the house. They decided on a "patent ventilating hall stove", and it was ordered without considering where the money would be coming from to pay for it. The lawyer was now part Scholar Gypsy, "still nursing the unconquerable hope, still clutching the inviolable shade"; part Mr Micawber expecting "something would turn up".

From this time there is to be seen in some of his finest pieces a deep sense of foreboding — the imminence of inescapable fate haunting the quick, stark Norwich Castle *Landscape with Trees and Stream*: seen also in the intensity of a very late, gaunt *Sketch for Self Portrait*. Perhaps it was on one such day that after making a watercolour drawing of his black labrador, he refashioned him as a foul devil, crouched in a corner of the settee, louring over the arm to threaten with an evil presence the very future of life at Hamblin House.

His last picture, drawn a few hours before his death, was said to be the one that Miss Annie Maud Minter had hanging on the wall of her sitting-room in Gladstone Road for many years. Its story rang down the curtain in dramatic fashion. The tale was that her father, proprietor of an ironmonger's business in Woodbridge, had fitted out Young Tom, at his father's expense, with a supply of hardware to establish him in business in New Zealand. More than a couple of years had gone by and the goods were still not paid for. One early evening in August 1865 Richard Minter walking along the bank of the Deben came across the lawyer sketching with his watercolours. ''Mr Churchyard, why are you not in your office earning some money? You owe me enough, in all conscience.'' Up jumped the artist and handed him the drawing just completed. ''This is worth it all. Here, take it.'' With deliberation the ironmonger folded the paper with the reverence due to a banknote, took out his pocket book and inserted it therein; clapped it to, replaced it in his jacket and walked off without a word. Early next morning, with Tom Churchyard distraught by the spectre of ruinous debts, his heart had ceased to beat.

The watercolour, a three-master moored in the Deben, with the line of the fold showing clearly down the middle, was still to be seen hanging framed in the late 1950s. Its story no doubt is true but as the drama had taken place half a dozen years before Miss Minter was born, its details have gone astray.

In 1865 Richard Minter, whose widowed mother carried on the trade of publican at Marlesford Bell, was just thirty; a shopman living in the house of his employer John Webster Issitt, ironmonger in Thoroughfare, and not, for several years yet, taken into partnership. He could not have addressed Churchyard as in the story; it must have been his master who had known the lawyer for many years. The fact that the business had a New Zealand Export Agency, and the knowledge that Young Tom did in fact die in the antipodes, confused South Island with the Canadian West in the story as it had come down the years.

The time in which it is set needs a day's correction also. The *Chronicle* reporting Thomas's death tells that he was engaged in the Woodbridge Court on Thursday 17th August when ''it was remarked by a friend that he looked pale, and he said he felt a shortness of breath from walking up the hill, but beyond that he made no complaint. He had prepared himself for a journey to London on Friday morning; but feeling ill, was obliged to go back to bed and medical assistance was immediately sent for, but he never rallied from the attack, and expired shortly before one on Saturday morning from disease of the heart.'' The *Journal* was more explicit: ''disease of the heart, accelerated by some pressing anxiety''. Like Mary Webb's Deborah he had known the terror and the beauty of life and that intermingled they are something more splendid than the beauty alone.

He was buried beside his father, being on the following Wednesday carried to Old Melton graveyard where ''his remains, followed by a few chosen friends and members of his profession were quietly and unostentatiously interred''. The *Chronicle* details the small band that attended: Rolla Rouse, barrister and his son John William, attorney; Robert Reeve, County Court clerk; George Moor, solicitor; Robert Allen and Reason Goodwin, Law clerks; Ben Moulton, Robert Hillen, John Loder, Frederick Spalding, James Bendall maker of stoves and grates and the egregious Mr Dallenger. FitzGerald away on a cruise to Calais knew nothing of it all. He had been sleeping aboard his little schooner-yacht *Scandal* at the mouth of the Deben the hour of his friend's death and after dawn was off on "really a famous sail from Felixstowe Ferry; getting out of it at 7 a.m. and being off Broadstairs . . . as the clock on shore struck twelve."

Both local papers praised him for bright qualities displayed as lawyer, painter, connoisseur, paterfamilias and boon companion. Loder who knew well of his collecting and disposals commented in the *Journal* on this side of his activities "His devotion to the fine arts was to him the 'breath of life', and it may be questioned whether there is now living a finer judge of the Early English School than he was". Of his painting he wrote: "He himself was an artist of the highest excellence, and his works almost invariably show an affectionate reverence for the great masters we have mentioned" (Crome, Wilson, Gainsborough, Morland) . . . "An ardent lover of nature, his pictures are conspicuous for their fidelity and truthfulness." Loder was blind to the influence of Constable and saw him looking backward rather than forward to newer styles of painting. Dallenger in the *Chronicle*, who had nothing to say of his connoisseurship, was altogether more prophetic. Looking into the future he boldly stated "the productions of his pencil will now become invaluable".

Judge Worlledge at the next sitting of the Woodbridge County Court, referred to the "melancholy loss which this Court and this town have sustained since I was last here. I had the pleasure of knowing the late Mr Churchyard for many years, both privately and in his public capacity. In his private capacity I have ever appreciated his refined mind, his genial spirit, and his courteous manner, but it was chiefly as an advocate in this Court that I valued him: for while on one hand he did his duty fearlessly and ably to his clients, he never tried to mislead me or to overreach his opponents by unworthy arts; and he never wasted the public time by keeping up useless discussions . . . in him I have lost a most valuable aid in the discharge of my duty to the public in the administration of justice."

It was the occasion to forget the days he had been kept sitting till long past dinner time by the length of Churchyard's examinations and cross-examinations; the occasion to accept them as his honest efforts on behalf of his client as long as the case had a leg to stand on; to overlook any such unworthy act as his raising the point of the knocking of a nail into a boat, in the Bawdsey *Star* disability claim.

The Judge expressed "sincere sympathy with his family in their severe affliction, and understanding that his affairs are not left exactly in that position in which it was desirable, I shall be happy according to my means to contribute to the support of his family."

That his affairs were not left exactly in that position in which it was desirable was the most tactful of understatements. So that other well-wishers should be roused to contribute to the support of his family things needed to be spelled out in realistic fashion. A "Provisional Committee" with John Loder its Honorary Secretary came out with the blunt statement that he had left "a Widow and seven daughters totally unprovided for: his two sons not being in a position to give them the smallest assistance."

The Committee most earnestly hoped their appeal would be "so met as to offer to the Widow and Daughters the double solace of respect to his memory, and a provision for those he so dearly loved." The fund would be "for the support of the widow and the advancement in life of the daughters". The eldest was already thirty-nine, the youngest twenty-six. The project is likely to have been set going by FitzGerald, his name heading the list of sums already promised. He and his brother John Purcell each gave one hundred pounds. They were followed by fifty pound donations by Sir FitzRoy Kelly MP, now on the verge of being raised to the Bench as Chief Baron of the Exchequer; and by Sir William Page Wood, one of the Vice-Chancellors shortly to be seated on the Woolsack. Both were well acquainted with Churchyard, the former from his years of fiery elections, petitions and unseatings for Ipswich, for Harwich and for the Eastern Division of Suffolk: the latter had spent his youth in Woodbridge at the home of his grandmother Page.

Apart from the FitzGeralds and Ben Moulton the score of names there printed belonged all to members of the legal profession — barristers and solicitors from Suffolk and Norfolk; Lofty, Potter and Son his London Agents; the great and forgotten Charles Austin Q.C. and his Honour John Worlledge. The five hundred pound mark had been reached by the time the appeal was circulated. A surviving list has manuscript additions bringing in a further £100. One of its names is that of his old crony Mr Dasent, by then Judge of the Bow and Shoreditch County Court. He put himself down for £10 and induced five colleagues in Town to support the cause. Woodbridge tradesmen are entirely absent.

Mrs Churchyard was granted Letters of Administration and it was the next spring before Moulton's sale of her deceased husband's possessions was advertised to take place — "the pictures and books at his late residence on Wednesday the 28th day of March 1866, to be viewed by Catalogue only (one shilling each, to be returned to

Purchasers) to be had of Mr Loder, Bookseller, Woodbridge and of the Auctioneer. The Modern Furniture, China and other Effects to be sold the following Wednesday; to commence at 12 o'clock in both cases.''

The auctioneer, in the preamble to the picture catalogue, had pleasure in calling attention to the Valuable Collection comprised therein. He itemised the number of works by each of the chief artists concerned, ''all the undoubted Works of these great English Landscape Painters. There are also fine specimens of . . . other eminent Painters, all of which have been collected by Mr Churchyard with his well-known taste and judgement, and have been in his possession for many years.'' That all had been in the lawyer's possession for many years was a pardonable misstatement by his friend conveying to the outside world the impression that these were the long held treasures of a gentleman connoisseur, no recent speculations.

A large marquee was put up in the garden and viewers wandered around on Tuesday from eleven o'clock until four and there were others arriving soon after ten on the morning itself. At noon the company drew together before the auctioneer's table where Moulton, determined to say the right things, glanced down at the opening words he had written on his catalogue. ''I don't think it necessary, to take up your time in referring to Mr Churchyard, a man of the highest refinement and most extensive knowledge of the value of landscape paintings. Of him it may be said he was amongst the first who gave value to the pictures of Old Crome. He purchased them 45 years ago when they were selling at a low price, and said one day he will rank among the first of English landscape painters.

''I must draw your attention to the Morlands. There is one of the very highest class, painted at his best time. There is also one by Wilson he purchased at £80 at Mrs Weston's Sale, Norwich. It was considered an extraordinary bargain.

''I dare say this collection ought to have been sold by Christie & Manson London; but if a mistake has been made I alone must take the responsibility. Gentlemen, every lot is the property of the late Mr Churchyard. We have no reserve upon them and not a single bidding will be made on my part, to enhance their value against you. We have no other market to take them to, therefore your price must be ours, let that be whatever it may. Under these liberal circumstances I trust with the large and respectable company I see around me you will give a fair market price.''

Ellen, the practical woman of business, sat throughout the sale recording the buyer of every picture and the price at which it was knocked down. Already she had drawn away from the other sisters and earned their dislike. Her catalogue shows a fair scattering of Woodbridge names, though mostly as purchasers of the engravings and watercolours. Loder and Hillen each bought an oil or two by Wilson and Crome but the most enthusiastic local connoisseur was Edward Packard, the young Ipswich industrialist who spent close on £170 buying a specimen each of Gainsborough, Wilson, Morland, Etty, and two Cromes. He secured also, for £20, the large, often-mentioned Bassano "with its exotic tints and hues". Most of the important paintings were bought by the dealers, for in addition to Roe of Ipswich there were from London, Cox of Pall Mall, Pearce of High Holborn, Lawrence of Wilderness Row, Watson of Piccadilly, and Noseda printseller in the Strand.

In round figures the 23 Crome oils fetched £650, 4 Constables £120, 3 Gainsboroughs £115, 5 Morlands £140 (the best of them making £84), 3 Wilsons £60. Engravings "framed and glazed" aroused little interest — ten shillings to a pound each: while close on two hundred of them, unframed, landscapes and portraits, made less than £7 in total. A Rembrandt etching, "exceptionally fine", went to five guineas. There were few decent prices among the watercolours, Old Cromes ranging between only £1:2s. and £9; Gainsboroughs 13/- to £2:15s. a pair. The Morland pencil drawings did not reach £1 each though the four Cotman watercolours brought in a total of £15. Wilson's *Falls of Tivoli*, considered such a bargain when bought at Norwich for £80, was secured by Lawrence for £30, but against this Crome's *Moonlight Picture with a View of Bruges* more than trebled in price from what it had cost at Christies three years earlier.

There was little interest shown in the "Pictures in the National Gallery copied expressly for the Deceased by Mr George Rowe" and they did not average a pound each. Frederick Spalding secured the "Fine Original Drawing in Coloured Chalk — Head of an Old Man by Titian" for ten shillings. He also bid £7.15/- to secure one of the seven oils by Churchyard himself that had been included in the sale. It was an imposing *Melton Meadows* 19½ inches by 32, but only fetched £4.15/- when it was resold in ten years time. One reporter, apparently from London, came near to the heart of the matter as he praised these paintings for being "without incident or romantic effect, appealing only by the pure love of nature for her own sake".

A week later there followed the dispersal of the modern household furnishings. No catalogue has been found but the newspaper advertisements mention several of the choicer articles that Thomas had brought home subsequent to the Inventory of 1854. There was a "rosewood box elaborately inlaid with ivory; a walnut tree box in fine marquetrie work; a figure of a cherub in marble, fine; pair of foreign Chinese vases, 24 inches high; two fine old violins and bows in mahogany box" — Mr Churchyard on his beam ends but still giving play to his love of elegant things. Mrs Churchyard's more practical choice, the "patent ventilating hall stove (nearly new)", was put into the sale and perhaps Mr James Bendall's bill was able to be met out of the estate. It was he who at the picture sale a week earlier had bought the large oil, so admired at the Industrial Exhibition, *Martlesham Creek*, 35 inches by 48, for which he paid £12.

XXIII

A Family in a Very Small Way

BY THE time of the sales Mamma and the seven girls had moved across Cumberland Street and rented Penrith House, white brick Georgian with its plain flat-looking face. Although they had now to come down to living in a small way, their sense of style prompted them to give to their poverty as lady-like a dimension as might be. Feminine possessions had not been considered as part of their father's estate and so they were able to continue to enjoy their six octave pianette, Canterbury music stand, elegant small work table, inlaid mahogany jewel case, Chippendale mirror in elegant carved frame, tray-top table, antique cane-seated chairs, two elegant ivory fans; Wedgwood, Worcester, Spode and Lowestoft china; a pair of fine, old cut decanters and a spirit decanter. Three hundred of their father's best books, including the seven volume Rowe's Shakespeare 1709/10 were reckoned as having been given to them.

The strangest contrast with the bright home they had had to leave, lay in there being no longer the great Cromes, Gainsboroughs, Morlands, Wilsons and Constables that had glowed on their walls. There were still though, the many paintings by Papa that they could hang here, there and everywhere in the new abode. They had brought also boxes full of his watercolour drawings; albums made up of hundreds of the same; heaps of his oils on canvas, board, paper, cigarbox lids; thenceforward stored away but which would one day be brought out worth more than any money he could ever have hoped to make; releasing them from the straitened way of life they had for the present to embrace.

The gentlemen of the Book Club saw to it that the Churchyard ladies should not be deprived of the pleasures of the polite reading they had enjoyed for so long. By 1865 the number of honorary members had been allowed to rise to six, four of them ladies. It required no precedent therefore for Mrs Churchyard to succeed to her husband's place and so the books continued to arrive at the house for her's and the daughters' entertainment. It was agreed by the members that no subscription be asked for and the guinea against her name was struck out from the accounts. After Mamma's death Ellen was elected into her place and the account was marked "agreed not to be received".

When in December 1866 Mrs Churchyard died of chronic bronchitis, Ellen was granted letters of administration in her stead. Her father's affairs not yet being cleared up, she busied herself about them while the rest of the girls did not bestir themselves in any great concern for the future. They had been trained up to nothing that might have enabled them forthwith to take some decisive action on their own behalf. It was pretty certainly they to whom FitzGerald referred, when he had been talking earlier with one of his Woodbridge acquaintances about "a gentleman in straitened circumstances who had a family of daughters who were allowed to stay at home and amuse themselves in faddling occupations, instead of being forced to go out into the world." He had said "Look at so-and-so! He hasn't a penny yet there are his daughters all at home, kept like white mice." The uncomplimentary simile no doubt got around. When Anna and Bessie and Harriet followed one behind another as they went quietly along on the notoriously narrow pavements, out shopping in the town, brisk young women of a later generation called them "the three little mice — so gentle."

FitzGerald expressed further annoyance about them when he wrote to Marietta Nursey telling her of Mrs Churchyard's death. Although it was nearly a year and a half since their father had died "the daughters go on as before: doing all for their house, but I don't think preparing for other work."

Within a couple more years the hard facts of their position became plain to them. Late in 1869 Emma Whisstock writing to her cousin Henry Churchyard in Wisconsin, told him that "there was a good sum of money collected for the family after the Father's death, and upon the interest of that and the sale of a few drawings the girls are maintained." But it was insufficient and, as she added, "six of the daughters are living in Woodbridge very poorly off".

The reduction in the number of the household to six had been brought about by the departure during 1868 of Ellen; "the eldest is in a situation in Norwich," the letter had gone on. There was news also of the two brothers. "Tom is in America somewhere and Charlie is in a lawyer's office at Ipswich." The latter, approaching twenty-nine, had never qualified and about him FitzGerald had the gravest doubts. In his letter to Marietta he expressed himself with great candour. "The worst is the younger son, Charley, who having been brought up to be idle, is now not only idle but dissipated; and will wring all their money out of them. I don't know what we shall do about him.'' For the time being he had been got out of the immediate way of doing his sisters harm.

With Ellen departed to Norwich, Emma thenceforward became head of the female household. In May 1869 their cousin Charles Hailes, now a major, was granted two years European furlough. His young wife had died two years after arriving in India, leaving him with a small boy to be brought up. That August in Tewkesbury Abbey he made a typically Hailsean second marriage. Again it was within the family, with one of his cousins in Gloucestershire, Elizabeth Mary Andrewetta Hailes, thirty-eight year old daughter of his late uncle Henry the planter.

Of the few spheres in which the Churchyard sisters might find employment, to teach girls of their own class or those from a little below, whose parents wished to see them advanced in a ladylike manner, was the most obvious occupation of all. They had not yet set themselves up as schoolma'ams by the time of the letter to Wisconsin, nevertheless the careful and thoroughgoing Harriet, now past thirty, had felt that she should qualify herself in some formal way before instructing others. Accordingly she made visits to the Ipswich School of Art to equip herself for taking the National Examination of the Science and Art Department of the Committee of Council on Education. Early in April 1868 in the Second Grade Examination her Perspective was passed as *Excellent*; before the end of the month she obtained in Freehand an *Excellent* and in Model Drawing a *Good* She was true to her father's precepts. When one of her pupils later titled a sketch ''Original'' she commented ''Does this mean painted from Nature? I hope so.''

Laura and Harriet in due course went to teach at Brook House, the ladies' Quaker Academy of long standing in Cumberland Street. At Penrith House the sisters at some time had a few pupils themselves. With children they found contact easier than with older persons. The Census Return shows one small boy aged nine a boarder there in 1871; another, all his life remembered being lifted up by Laura to look at a nest of young thrushes in their garden and her finding a hedgehog to show him. Ellen returned from Norwich that year; not rejoining her sisters but living first in New Street, thereafter Thoroughfare, then Castle Street and later going to keep house for the Moultons. It is strange that she did not get on with her sisters; the more so since others have described her as a jolly person; ''Little gay Ellen Churchyard'' E. V. Lucas still remembered her across a gap of 45 years. Perhaps it was her further spoiling of the spoilt boy Charley that caused the split between them — living no more than a few hundred yards apart.

Charley had quickly freed himself from the solicitor's office in Ipswich and returned to Woodbridge to live with Ellen — to live on her, everybody said.

By 1871, the company of the sisters at Penrith House was further reduced by the absence of the not very bright Elizabeth who had gone out into service. That year Young Tom journeyed on again and landed in New Zealand. Nothing is known of his way of life at that time, but in 1880 there is to be found in Nelson, South Island, the only other reference to a Churchyard in the colony, a Thomas describing himself as Artist.

After the many years of sketching with their father, ''the sale of a few drawings'' of their own naturally presented itself to the sisters as a genteel way of eking out the very poor living that Emma Whisstock declared to be their lot. Opportunities for reticent maiden ladies to sell their paintings were few in the extreme. The Woodbridge Industrial Exhibition was not repeated for fifteen years, but from 1875 onwards there were the annual exhibitions of the newly formed Ipswich Fine Art Club. Their friend Mr John Brook Hart, well-to-do maltster, had been one of its founders and is likely to have assisted in their joining. From its third year onwards Laura and Anna sent in their work throughout the rest of their lives. Harriet contributed only twenty-five at twelve different showings and found buyers for but four, at prices from a guinea to two and a half. The titles show the genre pictures she liked to paint — *Fishing, Little Girl Dressing a Doll, First Lessons.* At Woodbridge where she indulged her levity in caricature she brought home thumbnail sketches of faces seen at church.

Laura, in fourteen years sent in to the Ipswich Club just over eighty landscapes, almost all watercolours, and sold seventeen for a total of thirty pounds. In the nineteen years that Anna exhibited close on a hundred and twenty pictures, a third of them oils, all but two were landscapes. Eight only were sold and they brought her in all something less than nineteen guineas.

Ellen took part in three early years only, showing one landscape and seven with titles as *Primroses, Chrysanthemums, Young Thrushes, Thistles and Goldfinches*, flowers being her great interest. None found purchasers, although their painter certainly did not lack ability. ''Yet can thy pencil copy well'' Barton had sung and there has survived a quite splendid copy signed by her of one of Papa's Morlands. At the first two exhibitions in which they had taken part they had essayed something bolder by including (priced three, five and eight guineas) a few of their father's paintings, clean contrary to the rules. The regulations may have been bent for them by the good offices of the Club's prime founder, the Edward Packard who a dozen years before had bought those important works of English Landscape Painting at the Hamblin

House Sale. Later he was to show himself as one of the earliest connoisseurs to appreciate Churchyard.

Woodbridge accepted the criticism of the reporter at the 1865 exhibition and when it was at length revived designated it the Industrial and Art Exhibition. The catalogues of 1880 and of the repeats at three and four year intervals detail the handicrafts by which in addition to their paintings the sisters hoped to earn further small sums. A beaded bag, pair of cloth slippers, photostands, birthday cards, blotting books, painted stools, — all the simple pieces of high Victoriana that could be made by middle aged spinsters brought up to nothing beyond faddling occupations.

More adventurous, was Anna's offering of china plates with "Burnt-in-picture *At Aldeburgh*", 12 and 15 shillings each and a number of terracottas priced from half a crown to five shillings. Several of the sisters offered any number of crewell doilies carrying pen and ink drawings. Most of them are local scenes by Anna, weakly done. Harriet's work, usually Punch jokes, is firm, admirable and amusing. Kate's humour is of a broader kind.

In August 1878 Emma died, just fifty years old. She was buried in Woodbridge Cemetery and her sisters marked the grave with a cross-topped headstone. The next year brought an end to the distasteful decade out teaching. There now came to them the opportunity to leave it and retreat into themselves.

Twenty years earlier the trustees of the great Woodbridge Seckford Charity had found themselves, even after building new almshouses, overwhelmed with the income from their estate in Clerkenwell. Among several new disbursements they had founded in 1861 a Seckford Library and put it into the hands of William Nathan Marsh, hairdresser, of Market Hill as the first librarian at a salary of £20 a year. Upon his death in 1869 his wife Theresa was appointed to succeed him but withdrew after a fortnight. By that date the trustees had virtually refounded the old Grammar School, providing it with new buildings on the outskirts of the town, so that the schoolroom by the Church that had served the boys for two centuries was now free for other uses. It was felt to be an altogether more appropriate setting for a Library than was a barber's shop. The vacancy was advertised for a full time Librarian with residence attached in what had been the headmaster's house. There had been twenty-eight applicants for so attractive a post and Miss Harriet Baxter, dressmaker, from Doric Place, was elected. She served for ten years and then died.

By 1879 it was fourteen years since Lawyer Churchyard had departed leaving his debts behind him. The sting of them was no longer felt and Woodbridge came to look back and remember how colourful a character he had been. The town had long prided itself upon having for its own the universally acknowledged Quaker Poet; his verses had now dropped quite out of sight of everyone. There was really nothing to tell of his life among them except that he had spent it in adding up figures, taking snuff, scribbling without stint, talking unceasingly. Contrariwise there were many pungent tales that could be told of the lawyer-painter's far from ordinary affairs.

Of the children of these two local celebrities, Barton's daughter had removed herself to Brighton and although Woodbridge considered that her husband had treated her shamefully, he had at least ensured that she was comfortably provided for. It was so much the reverse with Mr Churchyard's family of girls who still lived among them in straitened circumstances. The town had neglected to support the appeal and had left it to outsiders to come to the rescue. There was a sense of guilt that needed to be expiated. To give the Churchyard daughters safe harbouring at the Seckford Library could very properly be done to the easing of the Woodbridge conscience. The position of Librarian was offered to Laura and she was free to have her sisters with her. It was an appointment fitting in itself, for she was a great reader.

Of the schoolroom in which since Jacobean times the boys had learnt their Latin, it has been aptly said that "in appearance and atmosphere it resembles a college library rather than one that serves . . . a little town."* *Penrith* suggested starkness and far distance, *Seckford* on the contrary was the great name that since Tudor days had signified the very essence of Woodbridge. The cloistered nature of the place gave the sisters that remoteness they wished for. There was something agreeable in the thought that their Hailes cousins had lived in the old schoolhouse when it was the cynosure of neighbouring eyes, while at the same time "having no associations with the day scholars or allowed to mix with them." The four sisters could in some such way be seen to be important in Woodbridge and yet not of it.

The Headmaster's House No. 3 Seckford Street, provided ample living quarters. It was entertaining to call the larger of the two keeping rooms *Yorkshire*, and the smaller *Rutland*. Upstairs along a dark passage one came at last to *Land's End*. It gave occasion for family joking. There survives a greeting which most likely Kate had executed on behalf of the others: a little coloured drawing of one of the crinolined sisters enthroned there.

> "This Lady's delight is to sit in the Place;
> She cares for nothing but to fill up the Space.
> Giving her compeers no fair play,
> Let's wish her a Happy Birthday."

* *John Constable's Correspondence*, ed. R. B. Beckett (Suffolk Records Society, Ipswich 1962) I, 13.

Sixty years after these times people in Woodbridge recalled how as schoolchildren or young persons they had gone to the Library in the evening to borrow a book or return it to Laura. With her were Anna, Harriet and Kate, one on each of the other three sides of the table. From under lace caps corkscrew curls framed each face as the ladies sat seriously intent upon their work of stitchery or drawing, or relaxing at a game of patience. The occasion seemed to demand from the visitors that conversation should be restrained and in low key. The atmosphere of the ancient schoolroom-turned-library was the nearest thing to being in church. There was, though, a feeling of ease about a visit different from the days of Miss Baxter who had been a bad-tempered woman. Good temper was, by contrast, the feeling sensed in the company of the Misses Churchyard — ''so gentle''.

Conventual though the atmosphere of the library sessions might be, yet, after the hour of closing there was animated conversation and much laughter over the shrewd observations that all of them were adept at making upon the events of the evening just past. Kate, ''the wag'', ''the funny little thing'', exercised her talent of mimicry in recalling the peculiarities of one and another of the borrowers. There were other occasions for diversion among themselves, Christmas and Birthdays above all; but there was no margin for special expenditure to demonstrate their gladness. They chose instead to mark them with some gift made for the occasion — a decorated card, a comic drawing, a verse expressly composed, a painting. There is a brightly coloured miniature sketch showing one of them being kissed under the mistletoe by a bearded gentleman who appears several times among Harriet's likenesses. The inscription ''Wishing you a Merry Christmas and a Happy New Year'', ends with two exclamation marks. This was the world in which their life was entirely their own. They admitted to it only the very few whom they allowed to know them. ''They never went out to call, but the doctors, parsons, Seckford Trustees and the Harts called on them''.

When they emerged from their haven to transact the necessary business of living they came out more as strangers than as natives. The course of life with their father had taken them outside the things that composed the ordinary existence of people in the town. When they had perforce to enter it for brief spells they cloaked themselves with an air of remoteness that bustling Woodbridge did not understand. ''They acted slow as though tomorrow would do, their voices only just above a whisper. They looked as though they wouldn't say anything but came out with quaint sayings.''

By contrast there was the one day every summer when they emerged very much mistresses of the situation. It was when they drove down by carriage to stay at Aldeburgh for a summer holiday; hiring horses from

Garnham at the Royal Oak and taking with them their dog "Lassie", the cat and a bullfinch in his cage. It had been their favourite seaside place since the days when they were small children, and their father had painted a little sketch for them of the donkeys standing patiently on the beach waiting to be hired to set off along Crag Path towards Thorpeness or, contrariwise, down to Slaughden. He had inscribed it *Fourpence an Hour.*

Four years after they had entered upon the tenure of the Library they inherited small bequests under the Will of Edward FitzGerald. Out of an estate of £37,000 (and no dependants) they could not be considered as being generous: £100 to be divided between "Laura, Anna, Harriet and Kate". Emma was already dead by the time E.F.G. made his will; Ellen and Elizabeth were, he knew, earning some money for themselves. The gifts were in striking contrast to the £1,000 left to be shared by the daughters of Frederick Tennyson; or the £1,000 to Caroline Crabbe; £500 to the elder daughter of "Thack", or the annuity of £30 to Marietta Nursey which she had the good fortune to enjoy till 1902 when she died at the age of 95. It is likely that E.F.G. sensed the coldness felt towards him by the ladies of the library. Despite his long friendship with their father he was not welcomed as a caller at No 3 Seckford Street.

Four months after the death of FitzGerald, Ben Moulton likewise departed; having directed his executors to purchase for Ellen "a clear annuity of £30 per annum free of legacy duty." She was thus enabled to continue to enjoy her own establishment in a small house at the bottom of New Street for the succeeding twenty-five years.

Charley was not behindhand in sharing her slender good fortune. Twelve months earlier he had made the journey to Gloucestershire to renew acquaintance with his only distinguished relatives, the military cousins at Cheltenham. John Clements Hailes retired as a Major-General on the last day of 1878 and settled at Southam House, Leckhampton. In October 1881 his brother Charles did likewise in the same rank and took up his abode at Badgeworth, three miles away. Charley went and stayed as a guest with him and with Elizabeth Mary Andrewetta, doubly his cousin. He brought back to Woodbridge a gentle watercolour he had drawn of their house "Sironcha, The Reddings, Cheltenham" — a typical newish Victorian residence with bay windows thrust forward into a garden bright with autumn blossoms; a few young trees growing up; a conservatory; two urns of flowers flanking the steps down to the lawn. How successfully Charley managed during his stay to convey to his cousins the impression of his being a gentleman of leisure well into his forties, is not to be known. The Cheltenham families certainly realised that his sisters were badly off and helped them with presents of money from time to time.

In 1888 Bessie, now fifty-five, returned from service and rejoined her sisters at Seckford Street. The next year there was published a three volume edition of FitzGerald's writings, which Woodbridge of all libraries must have taken in. The fashionable "Omar Cult" meant that the work would be greeted by a wide readership in literary circles throughout the kingdom and in America too. The ladies found in the letters their father's name in a dozen or more references to him some mildly humorous. A great number of people would now come across it for the first time. Strangers would be wondering how he had come to be numbered among such famous friends as Tennyson, Carlyle, Thackeray, Crabbe or Borrow, but the girls could not have thought that E.F.G. had done anything towards advancing *le petit Churchyard* to his proper stature.

Kate's death that November revealed a further facet of the relationship within the sisterhood. Bound together by long custom, through many years completely conformable to one another as the outside world saw them, nonetheless they allowed to each of their number her own inviolability. To have gone through Kate's things after she had left them would have been an unwarrantable intrusion. Mrs Redstone, wife of the history master at the School, was asked to open the box under Kate's bed, to sort out their father's pictures of which the survivors were to continue as the guardians, to put together her clothes and any other personal possessions, pack them in a trunk and have it taken up to the attic never to be looked at.

The pictures that had been given to her by her father were shared out and the new owner's name added below the "Kate" that Thomas had written. Harriet's appears under hers on the flysheet of one of the great album's their father had made up for each of them — the quintessence of what he stood by as the final word in his claim to be a serious painter in the English Landscape School. Among Kate's things was the money that came to her through FitzGerald's bequest six years before. She had so much disliked him that she would not touch it.

In October 1891 Laura died aged sixty-one. A second trunk was packed by the schoolmaster's wife and put away for ever out of sight in the attic. The Seckford Trustees passed the Librarianship to Harriet, as great a reader as her sister had been, and so the surviving three continued their life together without disturbance. It was the following year that the young E. V. Lucas came to Woodbridge to gather information about Bernard Barton's friends for the "Life" of him upon which he was engaged. At last their father's work as a painter would perhaps find serious mention in a book to be put out by a London publisher.

Lucas went to Ellen for tales about his friendship with the Quaker and she showed him the paintings. He recalled that "her house at the bottom of New Street was full of his oils." She brought out also the letters that the Quaker had written her at Mrs Jay's and his manuscript of the verses sent up as a dainty dish to set before the Queen. For twenty-five years Ellen had been robbed of the distinction of being known to be the *Very Young Housewife*. Glyde, reprinting the poem in his *New Suffolk Garland*, 1866, had in his self-assured way not only taken upon himself to alter the author's punctuation, but had declared the original to be Emma Knight, assistant and later successor to her mother in running the school at Brook House. Having gleaned sufficient information for his purpose Lucas returned to London, having first given a standing order to Davy Crowe the grocer in Church Street, to keep Miss Churchyard supplied with tea for the rest of her life.

As to any extensive recognition their father might have gained from the publication, "Bernard Barton and his Friends", the daughters suffered disappointment. Lucas found Thomas "remarkable" but thought of him as one who "had he only had the right training might have achieved a fame hardly less than . . . Constable." Ellen had certainly been old enough in 1832 to know of her father's time in London but had given him no hint of it. Ignorant of his professionalism, he consigned him to a merely local fame: "To a patriotic Suffolk man an album of his water-colour drawings would be of inestimable value."

In the spring of 1897 the death of Anna, just sixty-five, called again for Mrs Redstone to come and perform the singular last offices. A fourth headstone to match those of her sisters was erected in the Cemetery while a third casket was added to the strange family vault in the attic.

Some time a little before or after Anna's departure the news may have reached Woodbridge of Young Tom's death in New Zealand. Wright in his *Life of FitzGerald*, 1904, did not know the date to within a couple of years. In fact Tom died 1st July 1896 at Ashburton Hospital, a shepherd on the Canterbury Plains, aged seventy-one. He had told people that he was born at Woodbridge in Suffolk; he was recorded as having been twenty-five years resident in the colony but he had kept silent on family details. "Parent's name unknown . . . Unmarried." He had, it seems, never been able to talk of the terrible overturning of the lifeboat as he had watched it pulling away to safety from the *Anglo-Saxon* so many years ago. "A poor woman with a babe in her arms."

XXIV

The Old Ladies

WITH THE death of Anna there were left two Churchyard establishments similarly small but dissimilar in all else. The one was where Harriet cared for her artless sister, the other where Ellen was fondly content to be imposed upon by her wily brother. Except for the subject of Charley, time had already rubbed away any differences between Ellen and her remaining sisters. For the 1892 birthday of "Dear Anna" she sent over to Seckford Street, "with Ellen's kind love and best wishes" a watercolour drawing by her father titled *At Aldbro*, showing a schoolboy sitting on the beach facing the painter, Charley most likely.

Four years earlier, those at the Library had sent for her own anniversary of the second of September their kind wishes dressed up as condolences and composed by Anna:

> "This Lady was Born in the Season of Game
> But she seldom has any, O what a Shame;
> All other things she will have in their Season
> Or she will know well what is the reason:
> A Glass of good Cheer she keeps in the Sly
> Although a cruel *Heart* has stopped the Supply."

Their friend Mr John Brook Hart had failed to send the customary bottle. There was ample time in their daily life for communications to be written, back and forth, in rhyme. Ellen, wanting her birdcage repainted sent across to the Library the lines:

> "In your dear bright eyes
> Love untold lies —
> 'Neath the lashes they peep

> So loving — so deep —
> The colour is blue
> Of a lovely hue,
> So please paint my cage
> To match your sweet eyes,
> And my bird will then fancy
> She soars in the skies"

Harriet put the paper into their store of family trivia having first written on it "Ellen's favourite way of making a request".

When E. V. Lucas visited Ellen she had shown him E.F.G.'s fleeting publications that he had given to her father. Eight years later, with a *Bibliography of Edward FitzGerald* about to be published, collectors had become keen to acquire the anonymous and virtually unknown writings of the now so well-recognised author of the *Rubaiyat*, particularly those privately printed for giving to friends; slim works of great scarcity. Lucas bethought him that Ellen might like to turn hers into money and wrote offering to put them for her into a forthcoming London book auction. "But I think you must not think too much about their value. Set a low figure on them in your mind and then if we get a higher one the surprise will be the more". He put a reserve of £5 on her copy of *Polonius* and 30/- each on the fatal *Calderon* and another by the Spanish author.

In the meantime E.F.G.'s preface to the *Polonius* was reprinted without its substance. Lucas wrote anonymously to *The Academy* protesting that the public was being robbed of the good things it contained and gave examples. "The copy from which I am quoting is unique. It was presented by FitzGerald to a friend in Woodbridge and has a number of marginalia in the author's own hand." Loder who subscribed to *The Academy* read the article and thought that the Woodbridge associations made it for him a good buy. He wrote a postcard to the Editor asking if he could be put in touch with the owner. The Editor passed the card to Lucas; Lucas passed it to Ellen: "Perhaps you know Mr Loder and would like to tell him, perhaps you would like the Editor to tell him; perhaps you would rather he did not know." Ellen preferred most decidedly that he did not know.

The sale came on in February 1901 and Sothebys printed a note: "The foregoing, three lots, were presented by FitzGerald to his friend Thomas Churchyard, Lawyer, Woodbridge, and they subsequently passed into the hands of his daughter Ellen, also a friend of Fitz-Gerald." The catalogue told Loder what his postcard had failed to elicit and persistence was rewarded by his securing the *Polonius* for £11.10/-. The two *Calderons* fetched more; one £14, the other £30.10/-and both went to America.

Landscape with trees and stream. Watercolour, 26.8 x 39.5cm. Norwich Castle Museum

Atail Park. Oil. Mth. Oil ... ... 1 1 1 ... 1 ... 2 ... 5 ...

Two years later Ellen was freed of the expense of having Charley living with her. At the age of 62 he was able to retire from a life of idleness when his friend Robert Banyard got him into the Seckford Hospital, "(euphemism for alms-house) . . . These ancient pensioners wore a blue uniform with big silver buttons embossing the arms of old Sir Thomas Seckford . . . three scallop shells . . . The old fellows . . . had a saintly aspect until you heard them talk".*

Lucas's catalogue note very correctly described Ellen as "also a friend of FitzGerald". Elsewhere he told of how he "had the story from her own lips . . . that (she) was continually at FitzGerald's house". It was another instance of her differing from her sisters. She felt able to talk to E.F.G. just as she chose and on one occasion he found himself "severely scolded" by her for failing to notice that his housekeeper was unwell. On another, he turned to her for help after half a dozen of his acquaintances had been confident they could easily get him a root of the Hen and Chicken Daisy to send to Cowell (now dabbling in botany), but had failed. Ellen who was a great one for flowers found what he wanted in a cottager's garden at Hasketon.

A few years before his death FitzGerald had at last achieved something he had long been toying with — an abridgement of his beloved Crabbe's *Tales of the Hall*, "edited by means of Scissors and Paste, with a few words of plain Prose to bridge over whole tracts of bad Verse". Ellen was given a copy and had not parted with it when she sold FitzGerald's earlier gifts. In March 1908 something arose in connection with the work that caused Harriet, sending her sister a gift of tongue, to ask in the accompanying note whether she had ever had a copy of the then much sought after *Readings in Crabbe*. "Yes dear I have a little book in its paper cover† of some of *Crabbe's* poems abridged and described by E.F.G.: there were only a few copies published and distributed among friends. I was one of the lucky friends to have one given to me by himself". Her distrust of John Loder from several years before, comes into the light. "J. Loder wanted to borrow it some time, but I declined lending it to him — a *printer*. I don't know anything about E. V. Lucas now — I never get a message or a card — although the tea still comes from Crowe's."

Ellen, well into her eighty-second year, enjoyed her independent establishment at New Street with the soft light of her old fashioned oil lamps. The letter from Harriet, with the enquiry about the *Readings in Crabbe*, had told how, one evening a few days before, the mirror had fallen from the wall at 3, Seckford Street. "*What* an *unfortunate* accident to have happened to that nice mirror" Ellen wrote in reply. "But if it had fallen *in the night* it would have frightened you both dreadfully. I

---

* Christopher Morley, *Thorofare* (London 1943), 25.
† A very early state being bound in its red cloth boards.

suppose gas is the sole cause of it — What a nasty thing it must be to breathe such air.''

In her forthright way she felt that her powers were failing — and said so. ''I was very *dizzy* and sadly at 8 o'clock this morning when I would have got up but was afraid of falling so got into bed again for some while. I had been restless and slept I suppose too heavily in the morning. I *stood* and did *too much* yesterday so could do *nothing* today! Truth is, I am *good for nothing.*'' The boy who was to take this to Seckford Street would arrive in a minute — ''he made me forget to put my letter in the parcel last night by worrying outside.''

Three days into 1909 she died. In the Spring of 1913 Bessie followed, aged 78, and was buried beside her. Now that Mrs Redstone was dead it fell to Elsie, the second daughter, to go through her possessions. There was a discovery that surprised the few who were close to life at the Library: Bessie had made a Will. Drawn up nearly twenty-five years earlier, it left everything ''in equal shares to my sisters who shall survive me.'' There was with it, untouched through the intervening years, £155 that she had saved during her time in service.

Harriet, left as last of the sisters, came to her own special stature as the embodiment of the Churchyard name. There was a particular fitness in that the fates should have chosen her for the role of torch-bearer. The least reclusive of those at the Library, she was the quickest to make rapport with outside people. In her young days, the witty mischief of her caricatures spoke of her penetration into the oddities of human nature. Later there were the perceptive likenesses of her family, friends and neighbours; often, though, given an ironic twist by their being portrayed in imaginary situations that would have surprised them had they known the scenes into which she had brought them: Dr ''Betty'' Jones in especial. The titles of her submissions to the Art Club suggest her sympathy with others: *Tired Out*; *Lost*; *The Day's Work Done*; *Castles in the Air*; *Gleaners Resting*.

Through the thirty-five years since she had succeeded Laura* ''she was ever ready to supply the wants of all readers who frequented the Library; her knowledge of the books distributed and their authors was complete.'' A great reader herself she knew ''thereby what books to recommend for the use of general readers.'' To the more particular she was able to give more abundantly. ''The appearance of Miss Harriet Churchyard as she sat at her library table was stately yet homely, striking and pleasing . . . she would unbend to converse jocularly and wittily with those whom she knew as her frequent visitors and esteemed to be her friends. To the young folk she was especially attractive.'' Pleasing stateliness, jocularity and wit, attractive to the young, it recalls her

---

* V. B. Redstone, *Woodbridge Reporter and Wickham Market Gazette*, 20 January 1928.

father in his public life and in association with his friends, particularly those his junior.

Beyond the role of Seckford Librarian there now fell upon Harriet the responsibility of being sole trustee of her father's claim to distinction as an artist. The sisters had never weakened in their long held determination that when their father came to be "discovered", the work by which he would be acclaimed should be at hand virtually in its entirety. With one or two exceptional favourings to particular friends, they took care that the collection was not diminished.

As against this there went, for the first quarter of the new century, yet another of the Great Contradictions never for long absent from the Churchyard scene. Charley going from the Hospital into the town along Seckford Street went by No. 3 "with head well up". From time to time he passed the Library with one of his father's oils under his arm, for he had managed to get his hands on to some of Ellen's store when he left New Street. He was on his way to Banyard's the butcher in Church Street to exchange the picture for a bottle of port. Major Hart living at the Melton end of Thoroughfare once asked him, "Why don't you let me buy some? I'd give you much more than you get from Banyard". "Can't be bothered. It's too far to bring 'em". So in his charity garb, but with his silver-headed cane he continued to stroll in distinguished fashion to one after another of these shabby transactions. "He always walked like a gentleman."* In this way a number of Churchyard paintings became dispersed around a wide variety of households in the town; lightly regarded, seeing that a bottle of Ruby could be bought for two shillings before the Great War.

The grand exception to keeping their father's *oeuvre* intact was in the sisters' allowing Mr John Wrinch to have eighty splendid watercolours. Brother-in-law and partner of their great friend John Hart, he painted in "an advanced style" himself and had joined the Ipswich Club in 1884 together with Laura, Anna and Harriet, a full twenty years their junior. He grew up an Admirable Crichton. "In anything he took up seriously he excelled and had a wonderful acumen in recognising those likely to make a mark in any game or art with which he was acquainted." He prophesied a great future for Hayward at the Oval "long before he attained his present eminence" and it was the same with the lawyer-painter as with the cricketer. Both, he said, would achieve national fame. At a Woodbridge Exhibition of 1887 he had suggested for the lawyer's paintings a higher worth than the four guineas at which the sisters occasionally parted with an oil. He asked twenty-five for *"At Major Morris's Farm* by Old Churchyard."

Wrinch died young in 1906. Seven years later Alderman Edward

---

* Mr Harry Cole.

Packard persuaded Ipswich Borough to buy from his friend's widow the eighty Churchyard watercolours for £200. Every one was a prime example. A small room was set aside for them upstairs in Christchurch Mansion, its walls crowded with his coloured patches of landscape in so many different moods — *Thunder About, Melton*; *Midsummer Heat at Earl Soham*. There is a curious note attached to *Carting Hay, Tye's Meadow, Melton*: "Rain came on and the Artist would never finish the drawing". Thomas desisted because he saw that he had perfectly achieved the representation of rain coming on.

The collection on view at Ipswich was not the universal revelation so long awaited and the War intervened to delay any further attempts. By 1920 Lilian, youngest of the Redstone sisters was in London as a researcher at the Public Record Office. Time was pressing if Churchyard's work was to be discovered while Harriet was still alive. In the May of 1921 Lilian wrote H. M. Cundall for advice "as to bringing his paintings to light. They, I feel sure, will interest you as they resemble in many points the Norwich School in which you have taken an interest. Outside his native district of Melton and Woodbridge he is little known as his daughter and her sisters were until recently loath to part with his paintings."

Out of this approach there arose an ambitious attempt the next year to get entry to the Tate itself. Nearly a hundred and fifty pieces were put out for a selection to be made by two professional painters living locally — Stephen Batchelder the elderly "Artist of Broadland" and Colijn Thomson, an exhibitor at the Academy and the New English Art Club. They chose seven oils and thirteen watercolours that Lilian and Mabel took to Millbank having secured an interview with the Director, Mr Charles Aitken. He kept two oils and four watercolours to show the Board. Lilian wrote home saying that "he thought the pictures very clever and pleasant, amusing and facile, though there was nothing very outstanding in them . . . I told him Miss Churchyard would be ready to give if they did not purchase, but that she was really not in a position to do so."

An unfavourable reply came the day after the Board's meeting. In acknowledging this, and again when collecting the examples, Lilian pressed her offer of a gift. Mr Aitken declined, saying that the Board considered them very clever amateurs, more suitable for the walls of a private house than a national gallery, that should confine itself to those who had worked professionally. Lilian was not to be turned from her purpose. The same day she took the paintings to the Walker Galleries in New Bond Street. "Mr Walker seemed to think quite favourably . . . I told him Miss Churchyard was anxious they should be sold under her father's name, and that therefore she was offering him the chance of 'discovering him'. He said he must see them all first and if he purchased he would take the lot, provided Harriet did not want too high a price. The only figure he mentioned was £100. I said I thought she expected rather more than that, although she knew that in selling *en bloc* she could not expect the £4 apiece she had for the few selected ones she had sold already. If he would offer a fair price this seems to me to be the best way of making sure that Churchyard should receive his own dues. Now how are we to get the pictures here soon?''

With Mabel's help all were ready for inspection at Lilian's rooms in Alderney Street where ''On 29th May Mr. Augustus Walker called . . . he would not make an offer at all. They were, he said, not good enough to exhibit among the work of his minor masters; there was too much of the amateur's work about them. He was very courteous and apologised about having given so much trouble''. The slighting ''Amateur'' had to be endured. The events of 1832 and 1833 had long been lost to the general memory; no one now but Harriet had the story and she would not divulge it.

Within a year or two of these abortive endeavours it seemed that once again, after an interval of more than thirty years, Thomas was to find serious mention in a book to be brought out by a London publisher. Colonel Maurice Harold Grant was collecting information for his comprehensive work on *The Old English Landscape Painters in Oils*. His enquiries about Churchyard he addressed to Harriet, the ''venerable lady well known and highly respected in Woodbridge''. She told him, among other things, of ''the fine English pictures which passed into his hands as a collector and out of them as a dealer'' and of how he often made copies before parting with them. The voodoo that bedevilled every effort at the emergence of Churchyard was still potent. Grant misread his notes when he came to write them up, for in addition to referring to Harriet as Thomas's sister he stated that Churchyard's ''own works are few compared with his copies'' and that ''for the last thirty years of his life he seems to have abandoned art.'' A disastrous misstatement conveying to any collector the idea that Churchyard lost faith in his work. The Colonel had been misled by Thomas's not exhibiting in London after 1833.

Into 1926 Harriet continued monarch of the Library: still ready to supply the wants of all readers, still with her quill pen entering up the borrowings and the returns, though no longer carrying all the work, for she now had Elsie Redstone as her assistant. At last when she had reached her ninetieth birthday, the Seckford Trustees obtained the sanction of the Charity Commissioners to grant her a pension and the right to remain in the old headmaster's house. There, attended by her ancient little Irish maid, she lived for the best part of a further year, happily conversing with her former assistant, now appointed Librarian, who came to the schoolroom each morning. In her hooded wicker garden chair she sat to enjoy the summer days, the trees, the birds and the sight of the great flinty tower of St Mary's standing serenely. The New Year of 1927 found her still well. When Elsie called on Sunday afternoon January 16th, Harriet's retainer mentioned that Miss Churchyard had been very drowsy all day. The visitor went in to her and it seemed that after taking tea she had just dozed off in her armchair by the fire; but she had gone beyond awakening.

Charley was not behindhand in coming over from the Hospital to ask "Where's the money?" He was convinced that his father's gold watch was hidden in the chimney-breast and wanted them to take out some bricks and open it up. Everything that had survived from the singular household of the Churchyards was now his. The pictures and furniture would fetch money but all else that had no cash value — papers, family jottings, sentimental trivia — he was certain to throw onto the fire. These were the handful that cousin Annie, wholly without authority, spirited away before Charley came upon them. It was a small sheaf but precious to the historian — the Constable papers, the Inventory, some of the lawyer's receipts and I.O.U.s, newspaper cuttings, sketches in court, letters from E. V. Lucas and letters between the sisters, Barton's screeds to Ellen. With them was a small, gentle Rowlandson watercolour drawing of a village ford, with on the reverse a desperate and brilliant pen and ink sketch of a lewd drunken debauch by men and women around a punch table.

In a couple of months the sale was advertised of "the very numerous OIL PAINTINGS, Water Colours, Albums and Portfolios, Old Books relating to Art, Old China, Glass and Earthenware and Antique Furniture of Miss Harriet Churchyard deceased." A well-wisher suggested to Charley that he would get the best price for his parents' portraits by offering them forthwith for hanging in the Churchyard Room at Christchurch and negotiated their sale on his behalf for £10. The old man lived on till 3rd December 1929, by which time the £600 he had received from the sale had been reduced to £225. In April of his last year, Almsman of No. 24 Seckford Hospital, he appointed William Brinkley, collector of taxes, as his executor and left him £5 for his trouble. £10 was to go "to Nurse Anne Burch for her kind attention and care to me, the rest to my friend Robert James Banyard of Woodbridge."

XXV

Always a Different Day

W.M.M.   "Although one can pretty nearly always iden-
tify the local scene in a picture by Churchyard,
I feel he was really painting the day rather than
the place."

Edgar Dowsing. "Yes; and always a different day"

Woodbridge
1946

THE SALE of 11 April 1927 could not have brought Churchyard's work
into public view in a way less suited to win for it the fame that his
daughters had so long awaited. Many a collector had only first heard of
his name when reading through Grant a few months earlier; scarcely
any had seen his work. Now it was being poured out, a bewildering collection of four or five thousand paintings and drawings, together with a
profusion of smaller sketches. The auctioneers offered nine hundred
and eighty oils, a quarter of them already framed, lotted in pairs, fours
or sixes. Four hundred watercolours unframed but mostly mounted
were sold in lots of from six to a dozen. Vastly more came pasted into
albums or loose, as the contents of portfolios and boxes.

The catalogue warned that not all were by the artist himself.
"Nearly all the undermentioned pictures are by members of the family
of Churchyard, and many are by the late THOMAS CHURCH-
YARD. The initials T.C. where stated indicates that the picture is
believed to be by him, but no guarantee is given." The auctioneers
were safe in marking some three hundred and fifty of the oils in this
way, for they were those that had been initialled by Thomas when giving them to his daughters and attaching one or another's name. No
such distinction was attempted in the catalogue in the case of the watercolour and other drawings.

Charley wanted his sisters' paintings to be turned into money as well as his father's. Far from an effort being made to separate the sheep from the goats, the opposite was the case. Major Hart was called in to help in preparing the pictures for the sale and to ensure disposal of the more pedestrian of the girls' work he lotted them up, many times adding in one of their father's with nine or ten of theirs. Thus was confusion worse confounded.

No certainty was attempted over the thirty two guard-books — Large, Folio, Large Quarto, Quarto and Small, that were greatly diverse one from another. Some were entirely of treasures of Churchyard's own hand that he had assembled, two or three volumes for each of the girls to make her fortune. Others were the family scrapbooks pasted up by the sisters, their own efforts, juvenile and mature, and with sometimes a few of Papa's included.

A few smaller albums were of Comic Sketches, the work of Kate, seemingly from a time when she made on-the-spot drawings of London life, perhaps during a stay with Uncle Augustus or an Obbard cousin. They had the streak of mild vulgarity that prompted the birthday rhyme upon the occupant of the closet.

In twenty-one portfolios there were "many charming Water Colour Paintings and sketches in good condition, and many of local interest." There were also "Six Picture Boxes containing sketches." Mixed in were pieces by the hands of friends and fellow painters with whom Thomas had consorted and casual things picked up over the years. "Thack's room at Larkbeare" must have come from the 1820s, finding its way into the Churchyard household years later via FitzGerald: a drawing perhaps by him, perhaps by the novelist himself. Watercolours initialled *E.F.* were by his friend Edward, who was not without skill in this field. There were George Rowes painted while he was still in Woodbridge. There were exercises by Harriet's pupils. There were many other pieces from this accumulation of two lifetimes.

Purchasers, furthermore, could have found in their lot something that had the look of a Crome or Gainsborough, Morland, Wilson or Constable. They were not to know that these were often mementos of treasures that had passed out of Churchyard's hands. Some were full scale copies, some mere miniature versions. They varied in quality between those done by the daughters as young girls up to executions by Rowe or their father himself.

Among those who had come to bid at the sale, were a few able to espy the true Thomases that were there for the winning. From around Woodbridge there were acquaintances who had seen enough of Churchyard's work to be able to recognise his hand. From Ipswich came those who had concerned themselves with the acquring of the Wrinch collection, likewise a keen Mr Clarke (probably a relation by the Hailes marriage) and Tibbenham the picture dealer. To such fell most of the prime guard-books stuffed with the finest watercolours. "Bidding continued brisk to the end of the long catalogue of 475 lots . . . much interest attached to a number of portfolios of dainty watercolour Sketches which sold up to five guineas."

Many of the pictures went to bidders inexperienced in the realm of art: people of the neighbourhood who bought them for their "local interest". Such pictures framed up and displayed at home as Churchyards, or offered for resale, included a large number that were in fact by the daughters. Their currency as the supposed work of the painter himself made collectors and dealers shy of committing themselves to someone so uneven in performance that sometimes a work taken to be his could only be described as "Churchyard at his worst".

Six years later Miss Annie White presented to the V. and A. six splendid examples, selected for her, it is likely, by Major Van Someren then living in Woodbridge, a friend of the Redstones. The sifting out continued as dealers began to handle the true Churchyards that reached London from Tibbenham. Unfortunately some of the most outstanding paintings became, en route, attributed to Constable before they eventually reached private hands. There was but little yet to hinder such a transposition, both the name of the Woodbridge artist and his ways being known to so few. At a London auction as late as the 1950s an oil of the River Orwell marked with his sloping T.C., was catalogued as a Constable with the innocent note "in verso *J.C.* and *Harriet*". And so there arose yet a further impediment to the hope "that Churchyard should receive his own dues". Loaded with the inferior work of others, he was at the same time being robbed of his own best, that became attributed to his "great exemplar".

Scholarly collectors, however, began to recognise his achievement. Sydney Kitson, the biographer of John Sell Cotman, bought an arresting *Landscape with Trees and Stream*, something that would have seemed decidedly *avant-garde* to the later Norwich School. In 1939 it passed by his will to the Castle Museum. In 1937 and 1938 there were presented to the Ashmolean three oils, the gifts of collectors of taste who cast their nets wide: Mrs W. F. R. Weldon, a great benefactress to the Museum; Mr Victor Reinaecker at one time on its staff, and Sir Karl Parker the Keeper. In these same years the British Museum had secured for the Print Room four of his larger watercolours, 12" by 18", full coloured and powerful.

By 1939 the Hon Andrew Shirley had assembled twenty-eight small oils with which to mount at the Nicholson Gallery, St James's Place, a first London exhibition. The voodoo continued powerful. By the date fixed for the opening, 28 February 1940, the ordinary peacetime life of the capital had given way to the dislocations of the Phoney War, the

Blackout and the carrying of Gas Masks. Churchyard himself could hardly have exercised his propensity for bad timing to worse effect.

Shirley had been put into touch with the Redstones for some information about the painter. ''I can't say how much I was helped by your kindness and your sister's without which I should have got nowhere in my researches.'' It was his own optimistic imagination that led him to proclaim headlong that Old Crome and Constable were ''his personal friends; he used to go sketching with them . . . and bought several Constables at his posthumous sale.'' Such was not case.

He praised Churchyard for being one of those who were ''the best of amateurs in the sense that he painted conscientiously for the love of art and without any intention of making a living by it.'' The Great Contradiction that lay beneath the apparently uncomplicated proceedings of the lawyer-artist was hidden from Shirley. In other respects he saw clearly into his position: ''never a painting or study of his that was not prompted by a genuine emotional reaction . . . the element of spontaneous delight.'' He wrote of his ''rare and attentive eye for the effect of clouds, for the sun filtering through foliage;'' of his refreshingly bold colouring ''well in advance of his time'' and that ''although all his scenes come from the district, the variety of his skies prevent any accusation of sameness.'' Shirley saw that with him the light was always the light of a different day. The prices put on the paintings ranged from four to fifteen guineas, adding up to a total of £182 for the twenty-six that were for sale. The next year a Mr E. Amey brought twenty similar oils to the Ipswich Museum Authorities and parted with them for £5 the lot.

For the second time a Great War had interposed to cause an hiatus in the emergence of the painter's work. More than a decade passed before the second Churchyard Exhibition came to be mounted. It was organised by the Hon Robert Gathorne-Hardy for the 1951 Aldeburgh Festival: forty paintings, half oils, half watercolours. From his own collection was the Kingston-on-Thames watercolour that had been submitted unsuccessfully to the Tate. The catalogue spoke of the painter as ''to the end of his life seeing Constable in the landscapes of East Suffolk and painting them lyrically and in miniature.'' Some critics had set this down as imitation but Gathorne-Hardy judged perceptively that ''although the vision and often the idiom'' were those of the master, in the ultimate analysis Churchyard bears much the same relation to Constable as Samuel Palmer does to Blake.

The next year Colonel Grant in his *Dictionary of British Landscape Painters*, 1952, went beyond his salute of a quarter of a century earlier. At that time he had commended Churchyard's ''bright, swift painting, his skill with sunlight on meadow country and his painter-like management of a loaded palette.'' In the interval he had seen a good number more of the works — "not a poor but many fine among them." In his heightened admiration he stumbled over the very threshold of the truth in now saying of him that "presumably an amateur . . . he became a professional painter in all but name, and certainly in skill."

From this time onward the separation of Thomas's work from the best of Laura's and Ellen's became understood while similarly the touches that distinguish him from Constable had become recognised. In consequence his own standing began to be established. *The Pond* in the 1955 Arts Council Exhibition of watercolours from the Gilbert Davis Collection showed those who saw it in St James's Square the quality of Churchyards that other collectors would henceforward have to aim for if they wished to have examples of his best. "On occasion [he] came very close to the master" Mr Davis himself wrote, comparing him with Constable in his Introduction to the catalogue.

The following year a particular opportunity arose for the acquiring of just such paintings. The Wrinch Collection had for years been caught by the westering sun that poured into the little room at Christchurch Mansion and some were beginning to fade. All needed to be taken from the walls. There was a misapprehension as to how many Churchyard watercolours the Borough in fact possessed. In 1938 there had been bought an album of sixty-four of his "water-colour drawings of various places in Suffolk, including Woodbridge, Melton, Aldeburgh, etc." It was felt that these together made a greater number than would ever be properly shown and so some fine pieces from the Wrinch Collection were auctioned among other paintings surplus to their needs.

In fact the 1938 album was a selection nearly all of Laura's that had been put together and given to Bessie. It now leaves no doubt as to which of the many "Churchyards" are by this most apt and dashing of his pupils. There are to be seen here, her putting down the brush too many times in rendering leafy trees and thick hedges; details such as gates, walls and roofs that are sometimes not in their proper plane and, most characteristic of all, foregrounds left clumsily open. Gathorne-Hardy's "if he couldn't properly manage part of a picture, he would fill up the gap with an unpretentious blob which fitted in with its composition" applied in fact to Laura.

The centenary of Churchyard's death gave an obvious spur to the still growing interest in his achievement. As 1965 drew near galleries made comprehensive showings of his work. The Aldeburgh festival of that year staged another Churchyard Exhibition, but the seven that were lent by Christchurch were all Laura's that had been removed from Bessie's album and mounted and framed for the occasion. Visitors were, even thus late in the story, led to feel how insipid he could sometimes be when painting carefully and how boldly he could

185

go astray when his drawing was at its worst.

Mr Denis Thomas in his *Thomas Churchyard of Woodbridge*, 1966, became the first to write a book devoted specifically to his work. The book and the exhibitions, setting the painter in his proper place, multiplied the number of those who felt they must have him in their collection. Five years later the way was opened for such connoisseurs to make acquisitions from some splendid offerings of the watercolours and other drawings. Two of the notable guard-books that had stayed in the vicinity of Woodbridge since the time of their making up, were taken apart, and over the greater part of two years sold at a number of auctions in the town of their origin. They were the contents of that which her father had given to Kate, and of the birthday one that the sisters put together for Anna in 1880, a hundred and fifty drawings in all. They fetched a total of £5,000.

In the course of the sales the Seckford Trustees put into the auction of 26 July 1972, an oil 8¼ × 11¾ in. that had been presented to the Library some years before — a gloriously bright *Barge at Melton Dock.** It was bought for £650 and resold to the Tate. In 1922 Harriet's gift had been declined as unsuitable for the walls of a national gallery. It had taken a further fifty years for the whirligig of time to bring in its revenges; but the long course of Churchyard's slow emergence "to receive his own dues" at last had reached its goal.

In his years of painting he had always, as Shirley saw, been moved by an emotional reaction to the scenes around him and the spontaneous delight of recreating them as a work of art. Though he had believed that the future would bring him fame, what had been paramount in his present was to be painting for his own satisfaction. In the days before he began garnering his works for his daughters he would sometimes treat even an assured achievement as a throwaway. A fine, larger than usual oil, *Landscape, Storm Approaching* had originally a portrait on the back. *April Day, Old Melton* one of his best small millboards has, in verso, a startling *Cistus Cyprius*, as brilliant a flower piece as he ever made.

There have come to light a few paintings by Churchyard as far flung as scenes in the Lake District, in Southern England, of the Dorset downs and the cliffs of Devon. Nothing is known of these journeyings; contrariwise it is of his coming and going around Woodbridge that so great a number of memorials remain. It was natural for him to put on to paper a kaleidoscope of scenes that presented themselves to his delighted sight: neat figures of people composing an event or illustrating a joke; quayside clutter: ships riding at anchor; the discomfort of travelling outside on the coach in driving rain; a few confident-

---

* Now titled "View on the Deben".

looking portraits*. Too many things slighter than these that others would have thrown away, trifling exercises of half a dozen square inches his daughters preserved, pasted them up framed round by narrow strips of fancy paper. Better, they saved many of the pencil sketches that Ellen said he brought home from any walk — compositions that had suggested themselves to him; single features or effects of light he would wish to remember. Too little has survived of his pen and ink drawing, dashing and adept.

Beyond all this was landscape painting that was his being; the landscape of the Woodbridge country that sustained him. Though its every scene was completely familiar, he would find something that surprised him there in the light of each changing day. To chronicle his own changes no help is given after the sight of the early influences on him of Crome and Constable. The many years that he painted with no one to view, remain closed to us.

There is one development in his last years that can be guessed at. Examples among his assured work give a strong hint of his feeling his way towards abstraction. Clearly these were not the "pretty little sketches" he showed at the Woodbridge exhibition a few weeks before he died. He knew that the paintings he was leaving his daughters would have to wait for years before they would be understood.

The final statements in this advanced, unheralded and unknown genre are now to be seen in watercolours with the shorthand of *The Gate to the Low Meadows*, the *Woodland Stream* in the Fitzwilliam, *River Landscape with Kilns at Woodbridge*, or the doom-laden Kitson gift of *Landscape with Trees* in Norwich Castle Museum. Prospecting by himself into new modes of handling light, he achieved landscapes with the minimum of drawing but to which form is given by the building up of blocks of one colour laid against another in varying densities. His *Waning Light, Melton* in the Wrinch Collection at Christchurch could fit in happily with Ipswich's Wilson Steers. *Spring Morning, Woodbridge* in a dozen tones of green might well be thought to have been inspired by Steer's *Common 1926*, achieved sixty years after Churchyard's days.

The fates that at first sight seem always to have been adverse were, in the ultimate, kinder to him than might have been supposed. That his most forward-looking work should have been kept clean out of sight for more than sixty years, till it should be better appreciated when looked at through eyes accustomed to Impressionism is a considerable gift. That the many drawings he stood by, put all fresh into the guardbooks, should have emerged a hundred years later with their pristine colours undimmed, is a fortune not given to every painter. Accordingly

---

* In P. de Polnay *Into an old Room*, (London 1950) a painting entitled "Fitzgerald in Old Age, painted by Churchyard" is shown. This dotard cannot be by Churchyard, as FitzGerald was only 56 when Churchyard died.

it is now possible to see them as the visitors saw some in the Wood-bridge exhibition of 1865 and to say of them as the unknown newspaper man said (and his apparently contradictory words cannot be bettered): "Mr Churchyard has caught the aspect of the quiet Suffolk countryside and rendered it with great spirit and boldness."

For Epitaph

"Ah! but if a man is part of and rooted in one steadfast piece of earth, which has nourished him and given him his being, and if he can on his side lend it glory and do it service (I thought), it will be a friend to him for ever, and he has outflanked Death in a way."

Hilaire Belloc
The Four Men

189

Appendix

Dear Lucas,

I send a list which may possibly be a final arrangement — as it looks well — you will see I have put the *Glebe Farm*, and the *Red Hill* to match in the 4th No. for reason that they are the same size, and will want no alteration on the plate or very little.

Will you send or bring another *Head of the Lock* — and when the White Horse is ready I shall be glad of any sort of proof — as I am now getting them together.

You can have the Salisbury for I know of nothing better — & Old and New Sarum will suit each other.

I think you will like the enclosed arrag^t — The Title & Vignette come in well.

Take all the care you can of yourself — & do not flurry yourself about anything — and for myself I wish you to be perfectly at ease

     May 17 1831   Yours try J. Constable

Bibliography

Anon, in the Three Banks Review, *Curries & Co.*, 1964

Barton, Bernard, *Metrical Effusions*, 1812

Barton, Bernard, *Household Verses*, 1845

Barton, Bernard, *Selection from Poems and Letters*, edited by his daughter, 1849

Bonser. K. G., *The Drovers*, 1970

Browne, John, *History of Congregationalism in Suffolk*, 1877

Churchyard, James Nohl, *The Churchyard Family, USA*, 1967

Clifford, Derek and Timothy, *John Crome*, 1968

Constable, Freda, *John Constable*, 1975

Constable, John, *Correspondence*, edited by R. B. Beckett, 1962 – 1968

Constable, John, *Discourses*, edited by R. B. Beckett, 1970

Constable, John, *Paintings, Watercolours & Drawings*, Bicentenary Exhibition, Tate Gallery, 1976

Constable, John, *Further Documents and Correspondence*, edited by Leslie Parris, Conal Shields and Ian Fleming-Williams, 1975

Cowell, George, *Life and Letters of Edward Byles Cowell*, 1904

Cunningham, Allan, *Life of Sir David Wilkie*, 1843

Day, Harold, *East Anglian Painters*, 1967

FitzGerald, Edward, *Works*, edited by Aldis Wright, 1902

FitzGerald, Edward, *Some New Letters*, edited by F. R. Barton, 1923

Fleming-Williams, Ian and Parris, Leslie, *The Discovery of Constable*, 1984

Glyde, John, *Autobiography of a Suffolk Farm Labourer*, 1894

Grant, Col. M. H., *Old English Landscape Painters in Oil*, 1926

Grant, Col. M. H., *Dictionary of British Landscape Painters*, 1952

Hocking, C., *Dictionary of Disasters at Sea during the Age of Steam*, 1969

Holmes, C. J., *Constable and his Influence on Landscape Painting*, 1902

Ipswich Art Club, *Exhibition Catalogues*, 1884 – 1895

Johnson, A., *The tragic loss of the Anglo-Saxon on Clam Rocks near Cape Race* c. 1960

Johnson, Catherine B., *R illiam Bodham Donne and his friends*, 1905

Leslie, C. R., *Memoirs of John Constable Esq. RA*, 1843

Lucas, E. V., *Bernard Barton and his friends*, 1902

de Polnay, Peter, *Into an Old Room*, 1950

Prideaux, Col. W. F., *Notes for a Bibliography of Edward FitzGerald*, 1901

Redgrave, Samuel, *A Dictionary of Artists of the English School*, 1874

Ross, J. B., Chronicles of Ipswich during his Mayoralty, 1848 – 1850. MS. S.R.O.

Shepherd, Thomas H., *Metropolitan Improvements*, 1827

Sutcliffe, Shirley, *Martello Towers*, 1972

Terhune, Alfred K., *The Life of Edward FitzGerald*, 1947

Thirsk, Joan and Imray, Jean, *Suffolk Farming in the Nineteenth Century*, 1958

Thomas, Denis, *Thomas Churchyard of Woodbridge*, 1966

Trench, C. C., *The Poacher and the Squire*, 1967

White, William, *Directories of Suffolk*, 1844 and 1855

Wright, Thomas, *The Life of Edward FitzGerald*, 1904

Young, Arthur, *General View of the Agriculture of Suffolk*, 1797

Index

194

20, 21, 25, 37, 157

Churchyard, Kate (Catherine), 25, 68, 92, 104, 121, 122, 155, 168, 169, 170, 171

Churchyard, Laura, 25, 38, 92, 122, 155, 165, 166, 168, 169, 170, 171

Churchyard, Laura, infant at Clopton, 145, 146

Churchyard, Lucy (née Smith), 53, 104, 131, 133, 134, 144

Churchyard, Margaret (née Moore), 16

Churchyard, Mary (née Turner), 9

Churchyard, Sarah (née Smith), 52

Churchyard, Susan, 52, 53

Churchyard, Susan (m. Robert Minter), 23, 24

Churchyard, Susan Harriet, 24

CHURCHYARD, THOMAS, Ancestry, 8; grandfather and father Smithfield cattle dealers, 10; Napoleonic Invasion scares, 8; grandfather farms at Byng Hall, Pettistree, 16; goes to Dedham Grammar School, 13; articled to solicitor at Halesworth, 20; flower painting, 23; collects Old Crome landscapes, 23; possible instructors in own painting, 23; in London for last year of articles, 25; takes up practice in Woodbridge, 27; two months before birth of son, marries daughter of local naval officer, 34; paints with young artist friend and may have been influenced personally by Constable, 42; hung at Academy, 46; left handsome bequests, 47; decides to throw up law and become professional painter in London, 45; sale of his household furniture and fine collection of works of landscape painters, 48; paints in Wiltshire and Dorset, 48; sets up at Upper Stamford Street, London, 50; fails to make his mark and after year and a half returns to Woodbridge, 52; resumes legal practice, living at Melton, 54; highly successful lawyer, 56; John Charles Constable calls and describes his father's death, 57; association with Bernard Barton, 62; makes acquaintance of Edward FitzGerald, 75; much activity as amateur picture dealer, buying masterpieces of English Landscape School, 76-85; spends evenings with fellow "Wits of Woodbridge", 86-90; time of financial prosperity, 90; prepares defence for arsonists at assizes during the "Hungry Forties", 95-98; joins in first exhibition of Suffolk Fine Arts Association at Ipswich, 102; catastrophic recommendation of Fitz-Gerald's *Calderon* dramas to Book Club leads to his resignation, 111; in trouble with his bankers who make him insolvent, 127; goes to Melton but within year returns to Woodbridge and full activity in the law, in painting and in picture dealing, 127; uncle's

death at Byng Hall reveals loss of the family fortune, 131; son marries great-uncle's illegitimate daughter, 132; trouble on the Lowestoft train, 136; struck by lightning, 139; mistaken ideas as to indifference to his legal practice, 147, 154; in deep financial trouble, 152; still buys masterpieces, 153; still briefed in every important case in the locality, 154; joins in first Woodbridge Exhibition, 155; transfers own paintings to daughters telling them they will one day make their fortunes, 155; death, 157

A bad correspondent, 76, 78, 81; careless of public opinion, 34, 52, 127; courteous, 64, 148, 149; dilatory, 87; a genial conversationalist, 1, 6, 89, 149, 150, 158; sanguine, 76, 87, 156

Public appeal for family left destitute, 159; sales of his collection of pictures and fine furniture, 160; daughters remove to Penrith House, 163; resolve to keep his *oeuvre* intact, 164; do little practical for themselves, 164; later do some teaching, 165; exhibit at Ipswich Fine Art Club, 166; are given Seckford Librarianship, 167; their straitened way of life, 168, small bequests from FitzGerald, 170; E.V. Lucas visits Ellen, 171, their deaths, 167, 171, 172, 176, 180; failure to make father's work known in London, 179; Charley has his sisters' work mixed with his father's when auctioned, 181; Col. Grant's encomiums, 179, 184; gradual recognition of his true worth, 183-86; final achievements and move towards abstraction, 187

Bequests inherited by Thomas, 26, 37, 47, 54, 90; cases in court, comic, 67, 119, 140, 141, 143; lengthy, 67, 68, 114, 128, 153; poaching, 29, 64, 114, 116, 117, 135; weighty, 66, 94, 95, 96, 119, 128, 153; his library, 48, 109; picture buying trips, 68, 75, 76, 78-82, 138, 140; style in court, 64, 95, 114-20, 143, 148, 154, 158

Pictures by celebrated artists that he owned, Adrianen, 124; Bassano, 79; Bright, 82; Constable, 62, 73, 80, 81, 82, 100, 124, 125, 126, 152, 161; Cotman, 75, 79, 83, 100, 161; Crome, 36, 48, 62, 63, 64, 78, 79, 80, 81, 82, 83, 84, 107, 128, 152, 153, 161; Dunthorne, 125; Dutchmen, 83, 126; Etty, 81, 82, 99, 125, 161; French School, 125; Frost, 62, 124; Gainsborough, 48, 124, 161; Heaphy, 176; Linnell, 76; Morland, 48, 62, 63, 82, 152, 161; Northcote, 125; Nursey, 126; Read, 126; Rembrandt, 161; Romney, 80; Rowe, 125; Rowlandson, 180; Rubens, 125; Stothard, 125; Strange, 125; Titian, 161; Violet, 45; Wilson, 62, 79, 80, 125, 161

195

and association with Frederick Spalding, 149; his talk, 150; disliked by Churchyard's daughters except Ellen, 151; sails to Calais, 158; death and will, 170; his abridgement of Crabbe's Tales of the Hall, 175; other private publications, 174

FitzGerald, John, 100; J Purcell, 159

Flatford Mill, 82

Flatt, John, 67

Flora Londinensis, by Samuel Curtis, 22

Floreys Farm, Clopton, 11, 26, 47, 54, 144

Flower Painting, three books, 33

Fludger, Sir Samuel, 72

Framlingham, 9; Congregationalists' meeting place, 9; peace celebrations, 19

Frere, Sir Bartle, 133

Friend, Emma and James of Bawdsey, 141

Friend, James of Tunstall, 96, 97

Frost, George, 24

Fulcher's Sudbury Pocket Books, 55, 80

Fulham Workhouse, 61

Gainsborough's Lane, 93

Gall, Benjamin, 111

Game Laws, 53; Preservation, 54

Garnham, William, Nacton, 117

Garnham, William, Woodbridge, 170

Garrett, Newsome, 118; Mrs, 151

Gathorne-Hardy, Hon. Robert, 184

George IV, King, 19

Gentleman's Magazine, 73, 134

Gibbs family, 14

Gifford, Countess of, 154

Giles, Thomas, 47, 107

Gillingham, Dorset, 48

Girling, William, 16, 18

Glasgow University, 24

Glebe Farm, 81

Glyde, John, 20, 29, 65, 147, 148

Goblet, sculptor, 41

Goldsmith, Leah and Thomas, 131

Golty, Parson, 9

Goodwin, Reason, 158

Gorham, Dr Richard, 122

Goult, Charles, 114

Gowing, Frederick, 66

Grant, Col. Maurice H., 42, 179, 184

Graves, Rear-Admiral Thomas, 31

Great Exhibition, 86

"Great Swinfen Case", 153

Grierson, Barbara, 129; Surgeon-Major, 129

Grimwood, Rev. Dr Letchmere Thomas, 14; Rev. Thomas, 13, 14, 15

Groom, John and William, 67

Gurneys, bankers, 22

Gusford Hall, 10, 130, 134

Hadleigh, Suffolk, 35

Haggit, Rev D'Arcy, 35; Rev. John, 15; his

son, John, 15

HAILES FAMILY:

George, Lt. R.N., his naval career, 31-34; marries Susan Harris, 32; at Henley, Suffolk, with children George, Susan, Sophia, John, Augustus, Henry, James, Harriet and Mary Elizabeth, 33; lives at Melton apart from wife, 34; dies there, 38; her Will, 96

George, grocer at Bury St Edmunds, 34; dies, 35

Susan, wife of Charles Obbard of London, 34; Harriet marries from her home, 34

John, attends Ipswich Grammar School and enters Honourable East India Company service, 35; fights in Nepal and Mahratta Wars, 35; retires as Lt. Colonel to Cheltenham and marries second wife, Mary Green, 128; dies, 154; sons Charles Metcalfe and John Clements follow him in H.E.I.C. Service, 55, 56

Augustus, second Lt. Royal Marines, 35; marries second wife, Elizabeth sister of Mary Green and settles at Cheltenham, 129

Henry, planter, 35; retires to near Cheltenham, 129

Harriet, marries Thomas Churchyard in London, 34; *passim*

Mary Elizabeth, marries Henry Clarke of Ipswich, from the Beeches, Melton, 56

John Clements, marries Barbara Grierson, Karachi, 129, 132; retires as Major General to Leckhampton, 170; wife meets Churchyard in England, 139

Charles Metcalfe, on furlough visits Woodbridge, 145; marries Emma Caroline Clarke of North Shields, 145; she dies in Madras, 154; marries second wife his cousin Elizabeth, daughter of Henry, planter, 165; retires as Major General to Badgeworth, 170; visited by Charley Churchyard, 170

Halesworth, 20, 21, 24, 29; Brewery House, 22; Attorneys' unmarried daughters, 31

Hamilton, Sir William and Lady, 8

Hamlet, 140

Hampstead, 58

Harris, John, 31; Susan, 32

Hart, Daniel, 137; John Brook, 166, 173; Major, 182

Harwich Harbour, 32

Hawkesworth, engraver, 55

Heard, Thomas, 107

Henley, Suffolk, 33

Herald and Genealogical Magazine, 28

Hertford, Marquis of, 30, 49, 135

Higham, Suffolk, 80, 82

Hill House, Ufford, 54, 131